HOW SHOULD WE THEN LIVE?

Other books by Francis A. Schaeffer

The God Who Is There
Escape from Reason
He Is There and He Is Not Silent
Death in the City
Pollution and the Death of Man
The Church at the End of the 20th Century
The Mark of the Christian
The Church Before the Watching World
True Spirituality
Basic Bible Studies
Genesis in Space and Time
The New Super-Spirituality
Back to Freedom and Dignity
Art and the Bible
No Little People
Two Contents, Two Realities
Joshua and the Flow of Biblical History
No Final Conflict
Whatever Happened to the Human Race?
(with *C. Everett Koop*)
A Christian Manifesto
The Great Evangelical Disaster
The Complete Works of Francis Schaeffer
(including all the above titles in five volumes)
Everybody Can Know
(with *Edith Schaeffer*)
Letters of Francis A. Schaeffer
(edited with introductions by *Lane T. Dennis*)

THE RISE AND DECLINE OF

WESTERN THOUGHT AND CULTURE

HOW SHOULD WE THEN LIVE?

Francis A. Schaeffer

CROSSWAY BOOKS
WHEATON, ILLINOIS

Copyright © 1976 by Francis A. Schaeffer

Originally published by Fleming H. Revell, 1979

First trade paperback edition, Crossway Books, 1983

50th L'Abri Anniversary Edition, 2005

Publisher's Foreword copyright © 2005 by Crossway Books

Published by Crossway Books
> a publishing ministry of Good News Publishers
> 1300 Crescent Street
> Wheaton, Illinois 60187

Printed in the United States of America

Excerpts from the Francis Crick article "Why I Study Biology," which appeared in the Spring 1971 issue of *Washington University Magazine*, are used by permission.

The Hans Arp poem "Für Theo Van Doesburg" is used by permission of Madame Marguerite Arp.

Excerpt from "The Waste Land" by T. S. Eliot is used by permission of the publishers, Harcourt Brace Jovanovich, Inc.

Front cover photos: *Raising of the Cross* by Rembrandt.
> *Nude Descending a Staircase* by Marcel Duchamp.

Original conception, overall book design, and coordination of research by Franky A. Schaeffer V.

Cover design: Josh Dennis

Twenty-ninth printing, 2005

Printed in the United States of America

Library of Congress Catalog Card Number 83-70956

ISBN 13: 978-1-58134-536-0

ISBN 10: 1-58134-536-4

LB		19	18	17	16	15	14	13	12	11	10	09	08
19	18	17	16	15	14	13	12	11	10	9	8	7	6

To my son,
FRANKY SCHAEFFER

Who had the original vision for this project,
both the book and the film, and who had much to do
with every aspect of the hard work and heavy practical realities of
carrying it to completion. This included his being the
producer of the film and the overall coordinator
of the production of the book. My only regret is
that it has cost him two years away from his studio as a painter.

Contents

Publisher's Foreword

by Lane T. Dennis

Few Christians have had greater impact during the last half of the twentieth century than Dr. Francis A. Schaeffer. A man with a remarkable breadth of cultural interest and with penetrating insight into post-Christian, postmodern life, Schaeffer was also a man who cared deeply about people and their search for truth, meaning, and beauty in life. If there is one central theme throughout Schaeffer's twenty-four published books (all of which are still in print), it is that "true truth" exists as revealed in the Bible by "the God who is there," and that what we do with this truth has decisive consequences in every area of life and culture.

This book, *How Should We Then Live?* was Schaeffer's nineteenth book and clearly among his most important. It grows out of Schaeffer's life-long study of Western thought and culture in light of biblical truth and the Christian worldview. It was written at a time—in the mid-1970s—when Christian and non-Christian leaders were trying to understand the cultural upheaval of the 1960s generation and to assess the implications of this for the future of the church and Western culture. Schaeffer's thesis was that if we are to understand (as stated in the title) "how we should live" today, then we must understand the cultural and intellectual forces that brought us to this day. Schaeffer thus begins his penetrating analysis with the fall of Rome, followed by the Middle Ages, the Renaissance, the Reformation, and the Enlightenment, while focusing in the twentieth century primarily on the influence of art, music, literature, and film.

Though written nearly three decades ago, Schaeffer's basic analysis of Western culture has deeply influenced a generation of Christian leaders and is as relevant today as it was thirty years ago. Many of Schaeffer's insights carry the prophetic ring of truth concerning the moral, spiritual, and intellectual upheaval of our day. Thus Schaeffer noted the devastating impact of the post-Christian consensus on "art, music, drama, theology and the

9

mass media," lamenting the tragic result that "values died." Consequently, Schaeffer noted, people are left with no basis for meaning or truth, or hope in life, and instead have adopted the two impoverished values of "personal peace and affluence . . . regardless of what the result will be in the lifetimes of [our] children and grandchildren."

Similarly, Schaeffer foresaw the postmodern breakdown of any basis for moral absolutes. One result is what Schaeffer called "arbitrary absolutes" imposed on the culture by a professional elite (e.g., abortion "rights" supported by the legal and medical professions). Another result is abolition of any basis for sexual ethics, with implications that are now being played out in the legal battle over "gay marriage." Again, though written nearly three decades ago, the timeliness and significance of Schaeffer's insights are remarkable—as is evident, for example, in Schaeffer's critique of Alfred Kinsey in light of the recent Hollywood adulation of Kinsey as the liberator of sexual freedom, in the Academy Award-nominated movie *Kinsey*.

What place does *How Should We Then Live?* have among Schaeffer's published works? For the person who has never read Schaeffer, this book provides an overview of his best insights into biblical truth and its relationship to all of culture—and as such *How Should We Then Live?* provides an ideal introduction to Schaeffer's thought and work. Beyond this, however, a number of Schaeffer's other books continue to make a significant contribution. Especially noteworthy are: *The Francis Schaeffer Trilogy* (Crossway Books), which includes Schaeffer's three foundational books *The God Who Is There, Escape from Reason,* and *He Is There and He Is Not Silent.* Likewise, *True Spirituality* (available from Tyndale House) provides in-depth insight into what it means to live out the Christian life in truth and reality. In addition to these volumes, twenty-two of Schaeffer's books are available in a five-volume set of *The Complete Works of Francis A. Schaeffer* (Crossway Books).

Lastly, we should mention that this new edition of *How Should We Then Live?* is published on the occasion of the fiftieth anniversary of the founding of L'Abri Fellowship—the worldwide work founded by Francis and Edith Schaeffer in Huémoz, Switzerland, in 1955. The remarkable story of L'Abri in its early years is told in the classic book *L'Abri* (Crossway Books) written by Edith Schaeffer. Today L'Abri has ten branches located around the world in Switzerland, England, the Netherlands, Sweden, Australia, Germany, Korea, and Canada, including two branches in the United States. For more information about L'Abri we would encourage you to visit the L'Abri website at www.labri.org. The new cover on this fiftieth anniversary edition is also noteworthy in its design and the selection of the two paintings it features, both of which were central to Schaeffer's message. Thus the rise of Western thought and culture is depicted on the upper left corner of the cover with Rembrandt's painting of the "Raising of the Cross," and the decline is depicted by Marcel Duchamp's painting of "Nude Descending a Staircase," epitomizing the fragmentation of modern life and culture.

Schaeffer's question to each of us—"How should we then live?"—is especially urgent in our own day as we see the growing disintegration and decline of truth and morality throughout our world. What then is the answer that Schaeffer offers in response? It is a commitment to God's Word as truth. It is a compassion for a culture that is lost and dying without the gospel. It is a commitment to the costly practice of truth in the midst of the intellectual, moral, and philosophical battles of our day. It is living in the power and reality of the God who is there, bearing the witness of His truth across the full spectrum of life and culture. As stated by Schaeffer in his closing words: "This book is written in the hope that this generation may turn from . . . the paths of death and may live." Few have articulated this message more clearly and demonstrated this message more consistently than Francis Schaeffer. And because of this, few will come to the end of this book without a new vision for how, indeed, we should live.

Lane T. Dennis, Ph.D.
President and Publisher
Crossway Books
February 2005

Acknowledgments

In July 1974 my son, Franky, came to me with a suggestion. The suggestion was that, given time, finances, and hard work by himself and others and by me, a major cultural and historical documentary film series and book could perhaps be produced. Using my study, over the past forty years, of Western thought and culture as a base, we could attempt to present the flow and development which have led to twentieth-century thinking, and by so doing hope to show the essential answers. After much thought, I agreed that we had the responsiblity to try.

First of all, let me thank Billy Zeoli for his immediate recognition of the potential of this project and for his steadfast backing and support which made this project possible.

To begin with, I wrote the basic text as a foundation for both the film script and the book manuscript. This basic text was then divided into two separate projects: first, a film script, and second, an expanded version, this book. The book, of course, could utilize the full basic text and thus gives more substantiating material than was possible within the time limits of even a lengthy film series.

For both book and film espisodes to succeed, however, careful research was necessary, and I am therefore especially grateful to Dr. Jeremy Jackson, who was our chief historical researcher, for the hundreds of hours of research that he did on the basic text and on the indexes and bibliography of this book. His help and timely suggestions were a constant source of inspiration.

Doctor H. R. Rookmaaker, my longtime associate in the work of L'Abri Fellowship and professor of art history at the Free University in Amsterdam, was our chief art researcher. His expert knowledge of art history and his consistent concern for the project were invaluable to both the book and the film.

It was a privilege to have Jane Stuart Smith as a staunch friend and supporter to whom to appeal on all aspects of the text related to music. Jane was our chief music researcher, and her knowledge on the subject was invaluable.

There was much research needed in areas not easily categorized, so it is with appreciation that I thank John and Sandra Bazlinton for the research they did as our general cultrual researchers. Their suggestions often provided a source of clarification on many subjects.

Beyond these basic researchers there were a host of those who were involved in detailed areas of research, in typing and checking the succeeding versions of the text, in the thousands of details involved in the film, and in many other ways too numerous to be able to mention. Their time and effort were invaluable to the project, and I want to say "thank you" to them all.

As ever, James W. Sire was a great help on the editorial work of the book text; many thanks to him.

It was a pleasure working with all those at Fleming H. Revell Company; especially enjoyable were the friendship and support of Bill Barbour and Richard Baltzell. Richard Baltzell gave the final editorial touches to the book. He was also a great help in the final critical reading of the book manuscript, as were Udo Middelmann, Jeremy Jackson, and Franky Schaeffer.

I wish to express my gratitude to my co-workers at L'Abri Fellowship, whose work was increased during the two years I was working on this project, for the very practical help they often provided in addition to their moral support.

Acknowledgments would be totally incomplete without saying "thank you" to Edith, my wife. She was patient beyond words through my tense periods, both while writing and filming. Without her constant encouragement, I simply would not have made it through this project.

I trust that the work and the vision of the people named or mentioned above will be rewarded in their being able to see a tangible change for the better brought about in our day and age by this book and its film counterpart.

Francis A. Schaeffer

Author's Note

In no way does this book make a pretense of being a complete chrono-
logical history of Western culture. It is questionable if such a book could
even be written. This book is, however, an analysis of the key moments in
history which have formed out present culture, and the thinking of the people who brought those moments to pass. This study is made in the hope
that light may be shed upon the major characteristics of our age and that
solutions may be found to the myriad of problems which face us as we look
toward the end of the twentieth century.

List of Illustrations

1 Ancient Rome

There is a flow to history and culture. This flow is rooted and has its wellspring in the thoughts of people. People are unique in the inner life of the mind—what they are in their thought world determines how they act. This is true of their value systems and it is true of their creativity. It is true of their corporate actions, such as political decisions, and it is true of their personal lives. The results of their thought world flow through their fingers or from their tongues into the external world. This is true of Michelangelo's chisel, and it is true of a dictator's sword.

People have presuppositions, and they will live more consistently on the basis of these presuppositions than even they themselves may realize. By *presuppositions* we mean the basic way an individual looks at life, his basic world view, the grid through which he sees the world. Presuppositions rest upon that which a person considers to be the truth of what exists. People's presuppositions lay a grid for all they bring forth into the external world. Their presuppositions also provide the basis for their values and therefore the basis for their decisions.

"As a man thinketh, so is he," is really most profound. An individual is not just the product of the forces around him. He has a mind, an inner world. Then, having thought, a person can bring forth actions into the external world and thus influence it. People are apt to look at the outer theater of action, forgetting the actor who "lives in the mind" and who therefore is the true actor in the external world. The inner thought world determines the outward action.

Most people catch their presuppositions from their family and surrounding society the way a child catches measles. But people with more understanding realize that their presuppositions should be chosen after a careful consideration of what world view is true. When all is done, when all the alternatives have been explored, "not many men are in the room"—that is, although world views have many variations, there are not many basic world views or basic presuppositions. These basic options will become obvious as we look at the flow of the past.

To understand where we are in today's world—in our intellectual ideas and in our cultural and political lives—we must trace three lines in history, namely, the philosophic, the scientific, and the religious. The philosophic seeks intellectual answers to the basic questions of life. The scientific has two parts: first, the makeup of the physical universe and then the practical application of what it discovers in technology. The direction in which science will move is set by the philosophic world view of the scientists. People's religious views also determine the direction of their individual lives and of their society.

As we try to learn lessons about the primary dilemmas which we now face, by looking at the past and considering its flow, we could begin with the Greeks, or even before the Greeks. We could go back to the three great ancient river cultures: the Euphrates, the Indus, and the Nile. However, we will begin with the Romans (and with the Greek influence behind them), because Roman civilization is the direct ancestor of the modern Western world. From the first conquests of the Roman Republic down to our own day, Roman law and political ideas have had a strong influence on the European scene and the entire Western world. Wherever Western civilization has gone, it has been marked by the Romans.

In many ways Rome was great, but it had no real answers to the basic problems that all humanity faces. Much of Roman thought and culture was shaped by Greek thinking, especially after Greece came under Roman rule in 146 B.C. The Greeks tried first to build their society upon the city-state, that is, the *polis*. The city-state, both in theory and fact, was comprised of all those who were accepted as citizens. All values had meaning in reference to the *polis*. Thus, when Socrates (469?–399 B.C.) had to choose between death and exile from that which gave him meaning, he chose death. But the *polis* failed since it proved to be an insufficient base upon which to build a society.

The Greeks and later the Romans also tried to build society upon their gods. But these gods were not big enough because they were finite, limited. Even all their gods put together were not infinite. Actually, the gods in Greek and Roman thinking were like men and women larger than life, but not basically different from human men and women. As one example among thousands, we can think of the statue of Hercules, standing inebriated and urinating. Hercules was the patron god of Herculaneum which was destroyed at the same time as Pompeii. The gods were amplified humanity, not divinity. Like the Greeks, the Romans had no infinite god. This being so, they had no sufficient reference point intellectually; that is, they did not have anything big enough or permanent enough to which to relate either their thinking or their living. Consequently, their value system was not strong enough to bear the strains of life, either individual or political. All their gods put together could not give them a sufficient base for life, morals, values, and final decisions. These gods depended on the society which had made them, and when this society collapsed the gods tumbled with it. Thus, the Greek and Roman experiments in social harmony (which rested on an elitist republic) ultimately failed.

In the days of Julius Caesar (100–44 B.C.), Rome turned to an authoritarian system centered in Caesar himself. Before the days of Caesar, the senate could not keep order. Armed gangs terrorized the city of Rome and the normal processes of government were disrupted as rivals fought for power. Self-interest became more significant than social interest, however sophisticated the trappings. Thus, in desperation the people accepted authoritarian government. As Plutarch (A.D. 50?–120) put it in *Lives of the Noble Greeks and Romans,* the Romans made Caesar dictator for life "in the hope that the government of a single person would give them time to breathe after so many civil wars and calamities. This was indeed a tyranny avowed, since his power now was not only absolute, but perpetual, too."

After Caesar's death, Octavian (63 B.C.–A.D. 14), later called Caesar Augustus, grandnephew of Caesar, came to power. He had become Caesar's son by adoption. The great Roman poet Virgil (70–19 B.C.) was a friend of Augustus and he wrote the *Aeneid* with the object of showing that Augustus was a divinely appointed leader and that Rome's mission was to bring peace and civilization to the world. Because Augustus established peace externally and internally and because he kept the outward forms of constitutionality, Romans of every class were ready to allow him total power in order to restore and assure the functioning of the political system, business, and the affairs of daily life. After 12 B.C. he became the head of the state religion, taking the title *Pontifex Maximus* and urging everyone to worship the "spirit of Rome and the genius of the emperor." Later this became obligatory for all the people of the Empire, and later still, the emperors ruled as gods. Augustus tried to legislate morals and family life; subsequent emperors tried impressive legal reforms and welfare programs. But a human god is a poor foundation and Rome fell.

It is important to realize what a difference a people's world view makes in their strength as they are exposed to the pressure of life. That it was the Christians who were able to resist religious mixtures, syncretism, and the effects of the weaknesses of Roman culture speaks of the strength of the Christian world view. This strength rested on God's being an infinite-personal God and his speaking in the Old Testament, in the life and teaching of Jesus Christ, and in the gradually growing New Testament. He had spoken in ways people could understand. Thus the Christians not only had knowledge about the universe and mankind that people cannot find out by themselves, but they had absolute, universal values by which to live and by which to judge the society and the political state in which they lived. And they had grounds for the basic dignity and value of the individual as unique in being made in the image of God.

Perhaps no one has presented more vividly to our generation the inner weakness of imperial Rome than has Fellini (1920–) in his film *Satyricon*. He reminds us that the classical world is not to be romanticized, but that it was both cruel and decadent as it came to the logical conclusion of its world view.

A culture or an individual with a weak base can stand only when the pressure on it is not too great. As an illustration, let us think of a Roman bridge. The Romans built little humpbacked bridges over many of the streams of Europe. People and wagons went over these structures safely for centuries, for two millennia. But if people today drove heavily loaded trucks over these bridges, they would break. It is this way with the lives and value systems of individuals and cultures when they have nothing stronger to build on than their own limitedness, their own finiteness. They can stand when pressures are not too great, but when pressures mount, if *then* they do not have a sufficient base, they crash—just as a Roman bridge would cave in under the weight of a modern six-wheeled truck. Culture and the freedoms of people are fragile. Without a sufficient base, when such pressures come only time is needed— and often not a great deal of time—before there is a collapse.

The Roman Empire was great in size and military strength. It reached out over much of the known world. Its roads led over all of Europe, the Near East, and North Africa. The monument to Caesar Augustus at Turbi (just above modern Monte Carlo) marks the fact that he opened the roads above the Mediterranean and defeated the proud Gauls. In one direction of Roman expansion the Roman legions passed the Roman city Augusta Praetoria in northern Italy which today is called Aosta, crossed the Alps, and came down the Rhone Valley in Switzerland past the peaks of the Dents du Midi to that place which is now Vevey. For a time the Helvetians, who were Celtic and the principal inhabitants of what is now Switzerland, held them in check and made the proud Romans pass under the yoke. The Swiss painter Charles Gleyre (1806–1874), in a painting which now hangs in the art museum in Lausanne, has shown the conquered Roman soldiers, hands tied behind their backs, bending to pass under a low yoke. All this, however, was temporary. Not much could hold back the Roman legions, neither difficult terrain nor enemy armies. After the Romans had passed what is now St. Maurice and the peaks of the Dents du Midi, and as they flowed around Lake Geneva to modern Vevey, they marched over the hills and conquered the ancient Helvetian capitol, Aventicum, today called Avenches.

I love Avenches. It contains some of my favorite Roman ruins north of the Alps. Some have said (although I think it is a high figure) that at one time forty thousand Romans lived there. Today the ruins of Roman walls rise from the blowing wheat in the autumn. One can imagine a Roman legionary who had slogged home from the vastness of the north, mounting the hill and looking down on Avenches—a little Rome, as it were, with its amphitheater and its theater and temple. The opulence of Rome was at Avenches, as one sees by the gold bust of Marcus Aurelius which was found there. Gradually Christianity came to Roman Avenches. We know this by studying the cemetery of that time—the Romans burned their dead, the Christians buried theirs. One can find many monuments and towns similar to Turbi, Aosta, and Avenches all the way from Emperor Hadrian's wall, which the Romans built to contain the Scots (who were too tough to conquer), to the forts of the Rhine and North Africa, the Euphrates River, and the Caspian Sea.

Rome was cruel, and its cruelty can perhaps be best pictured by the events which took place in the arena in Rome itself. People seated above the arena floor watched gladiator contests and Christians thrown to the beasts. Let us not forget why the Christians were killed. They were *not* killed because they worshiped Jesus. Various religions covered the whole Roman world. One such was the cult of Mithras, a popular Persian form of Zoroastrianism which had reached Rome by 67 B.C. Nobody cared who worshiped whom so long as the worshiper did not disrupt the unity of the state, centered in the formal worship of Caesar. The reason the Christians were killed was because they were rebels. This was especially so after their growing rejection by the Jewish synagogues lost for them the immunity granted to the Jews since Julius Caesar's time.

We may express the nature of their rebellion in two ways, both of which are true. First, we can say they worshiped Jesus as God and they worshiped the infinite-personal God only. The Caesars would not tolerate this worshiping of the one God *only*. It was counted as treason. Thus their worship became a special threat to the unity of the state during the third century and during the reign of Diocletian (284–305), when people of the higher classes began

1   *The Gladiator,* Capitoline Museum, Rome. "Rome was cruel . . . ." *Photos by Mustafa Arshad.*

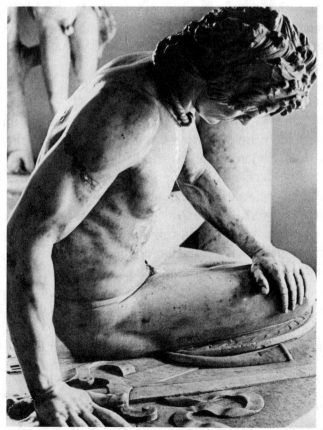

to become Christians in larger numbers. If they had worshiped Jesus *and* Caesar, they would have gone unharmed, but they rejected all forms of syncretism. They worshiped the God who had revealed himself in the Old Testament, through Christ, and in the New Testament which had gradually been written. And they worshiped him as the *only* God. They allowed no mixture: All other Gods were seen as false gods.

We can also express in a second way why the Christians were killed: No totalitarian authority nor authoritarian state can tolerate those who have an absolute by which to judge that state and its actions. The Christians had that absolute in God's revelation. Because the Christians had an absolute, universal standard by which to judge not only personal morals but the state, they were counted as enemies of totalitarian Rome and were thrown to the beasts.

As the Empire ground down, the decadent Romans were given to a thirst for violence and a gratification of the senses. This is especially evident in their rampant sexuality. For example, in Pompeii, a century or so after the Republic had become a thing of the past, the phallus cult was strong. Statues and paintings of exaggerated sexuality adorned the houses of the more affluent. Not all the art in Pompeii was like this, but the sexual representations were unabashedly blatant.

Even though Emperor Constantine ended the persecution of the Christians and Christianity became first (in 313) a legal religion, and then (in 381) the official state religion of the Empire, the majority of the people went on in their old ways. Apathy was the chief mark of the late Empire. One of the ways the apathy showed itself was in a lack of creativity in the arts. One easily observed example of the decadence of officially sponsored art is that the fourth-century work on the Arch of Constantine in Rome stands in poor contrast to its second-century sculptures which were borrowed from monuments from the period of Emperor Trajan. The elite abandoned their intellectual pursuits for social life. Officially sponsored art was decadent, and music was increasingly bombastic. Even the portraits on the coins became of poor quality. All of life was marked by the predominant apathy.

As the Roman economy slumped lower and lower, burdened with

Next two pages: 2   Detail, Arch of Constantine, Rome. "In poor contrast to its second-century sculptures . . . ." *Photo by Mustafa Arshad.*   3   Ruins at Pompeii, Italy. "And Rome gradually became a ruin." *Photo by Mustafa Arshad.*

an aggravated inflation and a costly government, authoritarianism increased to counter the apathy. Since work was no longer done voluntarily, it was brought increasingly under the authority of the state, and freedoms were lost. For example, laws were passed binding small farmers to their land. So, because of the general apathy and its results, and because of oppressive control, few thought the old civilization worth saving.

Rome did not fall because of external forces such as the invasion by the barbarians. Rome had no sufficient inward base; the barbarians only completed the breakdown—and Rome gradually became a ruin.

2 The Middle Ages

With the breakdown of Roman order and the invasions came a time of social, political, and intellectual turmoil. The artists of the Middle Ages forgot many technical things, such as the use of that type of perspective which the Romans employed in their paintings and mosaics. Roman painting had been full of life. In the early days Christian art was also full of life. One can think of the catacombs where the figures on the walls were realistically though simply portrayed. For all the limitations of the visual means, the people were real people in a very real world.

A parallel can be drawn between the "living" quality of this early Christian art and the living Christianity of the early church. Leaders like Ambrose of Milan (339–397) and Augustine (354–430) strongly emphasized a true biblical Christianity. Later in the church there was an increasing distortion away from the biblical teaching, and there also came a change in art. Interesting examples of a carry-over of the earlier, more living Christian art are the mosaics in the Arian Church of St. Lorenzo in Milan. These mosaics are probably from the mid-fifth century. The Christians portrayed in these mosaics were not symbols but real people.

Michael Gough in *The Origins of Christian Art* (1973) writes of the change from "the acceptance of an element of naturalistic realism to a preference for the fantastic and unreal." He also points out that by the mid-sixth century "the last vestiges of realism were

abandoned." The Byzantine art became characterized by formalized, stylized, symbolic mosaics and icons. In one way there was
something good here—in that the artists made their mosaics and
icons as a witness to the observer. Many of those who made these
did so with devotion, and they were looking for more spiritual
values. These were pluses. The minuses were that in the portrayal
of their concept of spirituality they set aside nature and the importance of the humanity of people.

Since A.D. 395 the Roman Empire had been divided into eastern
and western portions. The Byzantine style developed in the east
and gradually spread to the west. This art had a real beauty, but
increasingly only religious themes were given importance, and people were depicted not as real people but as symbols. This came to
its climax in the ninth, tenth, and eleventh centuries. The portrayal
of nature was largely abandoned, and even more unhappily, the
living, human element was removed. This, we should stress once
more, was in contrast to the early Christian catacomb paintings
in which, though simply portrayed, real people lived in a real world
which God had made.

Ravenna was a center of the Byzantine mosaics in the west, a
center brought to its greatness by the eastern Emperor Justinian,
though he never visited it. Justinian, who ruled from 527 to 565,
built many churches in the east, the most famous being Hagia
Sophia in Constantinople, which was consecrated in 537. These
new churches of the east stressed the interior, placing an emphasis
on light and color.

During this time there was a decline in learning in the west,
though the growing monastic orders, gradually organized around
the rule of Benedict (480?–547?), provided a depository for many
of the things of the past. Benedict himself had built a monastery
on Monte Cassino near the main road from Naples to Rome. In
the monasteries the old manuscripts were copied and recopied.
Thanks to the monks, the Bible was preserved—along with sections
of Greek and Latin classics. The old music, too, was sometimes
kept alive by constant repetition. Some of the music came from
Ambrose, who had been bishop of Milan from 374 to 397 and
who had introduced to his people antiphonal psalmody and the
singing of hymns.

Nevertheless, the pristine Christianity set forth in the New Testament gradually became distorted. A humanistic element was added: Increasingly, the authority of the church took precedence over the teaching of the Bible. And there was an ever-growing emphasis on salvation as resting on man's meriting the merit of Christ, instead of on Christ's work alone. While such humanistic elements were somewhat different in content from the humanistic elements of the Renaissance, the concept was essentially the same in that it was man taking to himself that which belonged to God. Much of Christianity up until the sixteenth century was either reaction against or reaffirmation of these distortions of the original Christian, biblical teaching.

These distortions generated cultural elements which mark a clear alternative to what we could otherwise call a Christian or biblical culture. Part of the fascination of medieval studies is to trace the degree to which different aspects of the complex Western cultural inheritance were emphasized or deemphasized according to the moral and intellectual response of people to the Christian God they claimed to worship. It would be a mistake to suppose that the overall structure of thought and life was not Christian. Yet it would be equally mistaken to deny that into this structure were fitted alien or half-alien features—some of Greek and Roman origin, others of local pagan ancestry—which at times actually obscured the outlines of the Christianity underneath.

This was not and is not a peculiarly medieval problem. From the earliest days of the Christian church, when Christianity was a small minority movement, believers had struggled with their personal and corporate response to Christ's prayer that they be *in* the world but not *of* it. On one level, this challenged Christians in their attitude toward material possessions and style of living. Not only in the time of Peter and Paul but for generations after, believers were noted for openhanded generosity. Even their enemies admitted it.

On another level, this raised the issue of God's law as against the will of the state, especially when the two came into conflict. During the persecutions of the Christians under the Roman emperors, the action of the Roman military commander Maurice is a good example of a possible response. When he received an order

Next two pages: 4 Catacomb frescoes in Rome. ". . . real people in a very real world." *Photos by Mustafa Arshad.* 5 Typical Byzantine mosaics, Rome. "The last vestiges of realism were abandoned." *Photo by Anderson.*

to direct a persecution of Christians, he handed his insignia to his assistant in order to join the Christians and be killed as a fellow believer. This action took place in the Rhone valley in Switzerland about A.D. 286, against a giant cliff just under the peaks of the Dents du Midi. It is for him that the little town of St. Maurice is now named.

Finally, on the intellectual level, Christ's prayer posed the problem of whether or not it was edifying to read or quote the non-Christian classical authors. Tertullian (160–240) and Cyprian (200?–258) decided not, but they proved to be in the minority. It is interesting that in the area of music a strict view did prevail. The reason for the disappearance of the traditions of Roman musical practices in the beginning of the Middle Ages was that the church looked with indignation on the social occasions and pagan religious exercises connected with them. And thus the old Roman musical traditions disappeared.

In the Middle Ages proper, which everyone defines his own way but which we will call the period from about 500 to 1400, we can trace in general terms the continuing response to these same issues. Concerning material possessions, the pendulum swung back and forth between utter disregard of the command to live modestly (caring for the poor, orphaned, and widowed) and a razor-sharp application of these same injunctions (the early monastic ideal to have no money). Thus, at one extreme one could have a papal court popularly rebuked for its material lust. The twelfth-century *Gospel According to the Mark of Silver* pictured the pope egging on his cardinals to fleece litigants at the papal court, using phrases deliberately mimicking Christ's teachings: "For I have given you an example, that ye also should take gifts, as I have taken them," and "Blessed are the rich, for they shall be filled; blessed are they that have, for they shall not go away empty; blessed are the wealthy, for theirs is the Court of Rome." John of Salisbury (1115?–1180), friend of Thomas à Becket and no enemy of the church hierarchy, told a pope to his face that people thought that "the Roman Church, which is the Mother of all Churches, behaves more like a step-mother than a mother. The Scribes and Pharisees sit there placing on men's shoulders burdens too heavy to be borne. They load themselves with fine clothes and their tables with precious plate; a poor man can seldom gain admittance. . . ." In the midst of all this, Saint Francis (1182?–1226), recognizing the corrupting effect of this emphasis on wealth, forbade his followers to receive money at all.

Even if its upper echelon was far from pure, the church did make an effort to control the destructive effects of exorbitant money-lending by first prohibiting it and later trying to limit the interest rate on loans to an accepted market level. With further support of secular rulers, the church also sought to enforce just prices, by which it meant prices which did not exploit human beings through selfish manipulation or through hoarding goods during scarcity. However much one may argue about the success of these attempts at economic control in the name of love for one's neighbor, it would be false to assume no difference between a society which at least makes repeated public efforts to control greed and economic cruelty and a society which tends to glorify the most expert economic manipulators of their fellow citizens.

Even beyond this, the medieval economic teaching was not wholly negative. It exalted the virtue of honest, well-executed work. This is no better illustrated than in the beautiful late-medieval Books of Hours, private prayer books in which typical occupations are depicted as month succeeds month. The most famous of such books belonged to Jean, duc de Berry, and was executed by the Limbourg brothers in 1415. An earlier illustration of the same thing was the series of reliefs from the early fourteenth century on the Campanile in Florence. And if age or infirmity precluded work, the church provided society with an impressive network of hospitals and other charitable institutions. One in Siena is still in working order. The downstairs women's ward, just through the main entrance, has a fifteenth-century display of frescoes illustrating what went on in a medieval hospital. If twentieth-century patients are grateful for modern medical advances, they can at the same time admire the superior artistic taste of the old Sienese interior decorators. Nowadays we expect the state to provide hospitals or deal out charity, and this expectation underlines a vast change in the powers of the modern state as against its medieval counterpart. But the state, strong or weak, has always posed a problem to the

Next two pages: **6–7** Fourteenth-century reliefs taken from the Campanile in Florence. "It exalted the virtue of honest, well-executed work." *Photo courtesy of F. Alinari.*

church, especially when it concerns questions of moral principle. To this area we must now turn.

The medieval situation was at the same time easier and more complex than it had been for the Roman officer Maurice. It was easier insofar as Europe was regarded as Christ's kingdom—Christendom. Thus, Christian baptism was not only spiritually but socially and politically significant: It denoted entrance into society. Only a baptized person was a fully accepted member of European society. A Jew was a non-person in this sense, and for this reason he could engage in occupations (such as moneylending) which were otherwise forbidden. But if the church baptized or consecrated the state, this only made more complex the problem of conscience, because a government which is to all appearances in tune with society can, for that very reason, betray society with the greatest impunity. This, of course, was and is true of the church as an organization, too.

Probably the greatest artistic study of this subject produced in the medieval era is Ambrogio Lorenzetti's (c. 1290–1348) *Allegory of Good and Bad Government,* painted in 1338 and 1339 for the council chamber in the great Palazzo Pubblico (town hall) in Siena. Lorenzetti clearly distinguishes between good and bad government, showing on one side the devil presiding over all those vices which destroy community, and on the other side the Christian virtues from which flow all those activities—including honest toil—which manifest oneness between men under God. Considering our own day, it is interesting that one of the marks which is shown characterizing good government is that it is safe for a woman to walk alone in the streets, while under bad government she is subject to being attacked, raped, or robbed. However, as the painter knew well enough from Siena's own turbulent city politics, if the sources of good and evil were distinct, the effects were humanly mixed together in a more or less jumbled heap of good and bad intentions.

Looking at medieval reality, one observes the same mixed record with respect to state power in financial matters. The church, though often indeed furnishing models of effective economic and political management, was so involved with other medieval institutions that it was frequently difficult for it to be salt to its society. For example, estate management and various types of agricultural pioneering were most notably enterprised by the selfsame monastic orders which, in their infancy, were dedicated not to profit but to poverty. Also, if we are looking for a model of effective centralizing monarchy guided by an efficient bureaucratic apparatus, we need travel no farther than the church court in Rome. The pope—who was called the Servant of Servants—was, by a choice irony, the most effective medieval monarch at the height of papal power between 1100 and 1300.

To leave off the discussion here, however, would be to caricature the church-state situation. For, if the church provided a model for absolute power, it also generated an impressive though eventually thwarted challenge to personal monarchy. Many people are familiar with the parliamentary assemblies in the Middle Ages; most are less aware that the Conciliar Movement in the late-medieval church was another potent force for decentralization. The Conciliar Movement stood for a revival of the idea that real authority in the church is vested not in one bishop, the pope, but in all the bishops together —in a council. Thus the Council of Constance (1414–18) deposed three rival popes, thereby ending a scandalous epoch in church history, while at the same time declaring that the council's authority came directly from Christ and that all men, including the pope, were subject to its authority in questions of faith and church reform. The Conciliar Movement, however, was destined to wither and disappear; the principle of monarchy rather than of representative government would triumph within the Roman church.

Meanwhile, paradoxical as it may seem, the church, through its frequent tussles with secular rulers over the boundary between church power and state power, had encouraged the evolution of a tradition of political theory which emphasized the principle of governmental limitation and responsibility. There was, in other words, a limit—in this case, an ecclesiastical one—on worldly power; and the theme of kingship balanced by priesthood and prophetic office is important in the statuary of Chartres and many of the great Gothic cathedrals.

To complete our analysis we must also consider the relationship between Christian and classical thought in the Middle Ages. The writings of Greek and Roman thinkers who had such an impact upon Renaissance and post-Renaissance culture were in many cases

Next two pages: 8–9 Lorenzetti's *Allegory of Good and Bad Government* and film crew with the author. ". . . on one side the devil . . . on the other side the Christian virtues." *Photos by Mustafa Arshad.*

available to be read because their works had been preserved, read, and discussed by medieval intellectuals. So how did the Middle Ages handle its pagan culture heritage? It is important to assert that although early Christians like Cyprian (d. 258) and Tertullian (d. c. 230) had a strictly negative attitude toward classical Greek and Roman learning, Paul had not been so inhibited. When it was to his purpose, he cited Greek authors just as he at other times employed the subtle rabbinic lines of reasoning which he had mastered as a pupil of the great Rabbi Gamaliel (d. pre-A.D. 70), grandson of the yet greater Rabbi Hillel (70 B.C.?–A.D. 10). Ambrose (339–397), Jerome (347–419) and Augustine (354–430), following Paul rather than Tertullian, learned to appreciate and utilize classical learning. Indeed, they set out thoroughly to domesticate it within the context of a majestic curriculum of Christian education which became the general model followed right up to the Renaissance. But if a robust Christian faith could handle non-Christian learning without compromising, it was all too easy for Greek and Roman thought forms to creep into the cracks and chinks of a faith which was less and less founded on the Bible and more and more resting on the authority of church pronouncements. By the thirteenth century the great Aquinas (1225–1274) had already begun, in deference to Aristotle (384–322 B.C.), to open the door to placing revelation and human reason on an equal footing.

We will consider this in detail later, but first we must conclude this whirlwind tour through the medieval centuries by looking at some of its most outstanding artistic achievements—achievements, in the main, of the church. Remembering that this church was universal in its European context, we should not be surprised that it worked along with society as a whole, particularly the leaders of society, to produce its greatest artistic monuments. This is very well emphasized in one of the founder-figures of the Middle Ages, Charlemagne (742–814), and in Carolingian culture as a whole.

Charlemagne, son of Pippin, became king of the Franks in 768 and was crowned emperor by Pope Leo III in Rome on Christmas Day of 800. He was a formidable man with colossal energy. He was also a great warrior and constantly on campaign. After he gained control over much of the western European territory formerly in the Roman Empire, his coronation by the pope as a Roman-style emperor followed easily. In return he strengthened the church in many ways, giving the pope a strong land base in Italy and also supporting the Anglo-Saxon missionaries in the areas he conquered, especially among the Germanic tribes. Charlemagne made tithing compulsory, and this supplied funds for the establishment of church administration. He also built impressive churches, including the Palatine Chapel, consecrated in 805 at Aachen (located in what is now West Germany), the home of his old age.

Under Charlemagne, the church became a more general cultural force. Church power became coextensive with state power, and culturally the two spheres fed one another. Scholars were encouraged, and though their work was not very original, there was a restirring through sheer industry, enthusiasm, and systematic propagation. Scholars came from all over Europe to Charlemagne's court; for example, Alcuin (735–804) came all the way from York in northern England when he was fifty years old. He became Charlemagne's advisor, head of the palace school at Aachen, and attracted a constellation of scholars to join him there. Charlemagne invited singers from Rome to his court and founded a school of song which he personally supervised. In short, Charlemagne and his scholar-courtiers laid a base for the unity of ideas throughout western Europe. This unity was certainly aided by the invention of the beautiful Carolingian minuscule script, a handwriting which was widely copied. But, note carefully, all of Charlemagne's scholars were clergy. Learning was not general. We still remember those days in our English language—our word *clerk* is related to the word *cleric,* that is, a member of the clergy. It seems that, though Charlemagne himself learned to read, he never learned to write.

With the scholarly revival of the Carolingian Age, there also came an artistic revival. People in later centuries wondered at the costly and exquisite jewels, religious objects, and books. Most of these—like a talisman of Charlemagne which contained a relic, and an ivory bookbinding of the crucifixion—emphasize the religious orientation of the artistic revival of that time.

In considering the culture of the Middle Ages, we must not overlook its music. Pope Gregory I (pope from 590 to 604) brought the music of the western church into a systematic whole.

10 Carolingian carvings in ivory. ". . . costly and exquisite jewels." *Photos by Mustafa Arshad.*

This impersonal, mystical, and other-worldly music is named after him: the Gregorian chant or plainsong, a monophony. From about 1100 to 1300 there were the *troubadours,* a title which means "inventors" or "finders." They were mainly aristocratic poet-musicians of southern France who inaugurated a flowering of secular music. From 1150 to 1300 was the period of a distinct epoch of music called *ars antiqua*—which developed various forms of polyphonic compositions. The instruments of the Middle Ages were psalteries, flutes, shawms (a double-reed wind instrument of the oboe family), trumpets, and drums. The universal folk instrument was the bagpipe. There were also the great organs in the churches, and smaller, portable organs. With the rise of *ars nova* in the fourteenth century in France and Italy, for the first time composers began to be known by name. Guillaume de Machaut (c. 1300–1377), a canon at the cathedral at Rheims, is the outstanding representative of French *ars nova* music. In Italy, Francesco Landini (1325–1397) of Florence was the foremost Italian musician of the fourteenth century.

When we think of the artistic achievements of the Middle Ages, we usually think of architecture. It would be impossible to speak of the gradually awakened cultural thought of the Middle Ages and not consider the developments in architecture in some detail. Let us start with the first great medieval style—the eleventh-century Romanesque, whose essential distinguishing marks are the rounded arch, thick walls, and dim interiors. With the original developments in Romanesque architecture came a leap forward. Because Romanesque, as the name suggests, looked back to Roman styles, it owed a lot to Carolingian churches, such as the Palatine Chapel (ninth century) modeled on San Vitale at Ravenna (sixth century) and such early Christian churches as St. Paul's-Outside-the-Walls in Rome (fourth century). But whereas in Italy architects remained slavishly tied to the old Roman style, as in Romano-Byzantine San Marco in Venice whose plan was from the eleventh century, one can see in French and English churches the creative adaptation which made the style Roman-*esque,* rather than just Roman. In France the abbey churches of Vézelay from the eleventh and twelfth centuries, and Fontevrault from the twelfth century exemplify this.

The crucial moment in England came with the Norman invasion

in 1066. The Chapel of St. John in the White Tower of the Tower of London was built about 1080. Winchester Cathedral was built between 1079 and 1093, and Durham Cathedral was begun in 1093. The latter is one of the primary sources of the rib-vault—as our eyes follow the columns upwards, our gaze is carried to ribs in the ceiling. This prepared the ground for the later Gothic architecture.

Then, in 1140, Abbot Suger supervised the building of the abbey of Saint-Denis. Now surrounded by a rather depressing suburb of Paris, it is one of the places of wonder of the world, for here the Gothic style was born and the awakened cultural patterns of the Middle Ages took another great leap forward. Whoever designed the choir of Saint-Denis invented the Gothic style. Here the Gothic was born, with its pointed arches, the lightness supplied by its many large high windows, and its clerestory (the windows set high in the walls which allow light to stream down from above). Out of the Gothic also came the wonder of the rose window as well as the flying buttress, which, by taking the weight of the outward thrust of the walls caused by the weight of the roof, enabled the walls to be thinner and the windows larger. When we see the Cathedral of Chartres, begun in 1194, we see the Gothic in all its purity: the pointed arch, the flying buttress, and the rib-vault. At Chartres, too, we have fine examples of advance in sculpture, for instance in the west facade. One could date the early or classic Gothic from 1150 to 1250, and the late Gothic (which was more ornate, especially in England) from 1250 to 1500.

Florence showed marks of the Gothic in its art from the thirteenth century onward. Arnolfo (1232–1302), who worked on the old palace beginning at 1266 and began the cathedral in Florence, in 1294, worked in the Gothic style. Although the Florentine Gothic was never a fully developed Gothic, the earlier Gothic of northern Europe did have its influence. Santa Trinita (second half of the thirteenth century), Santa Maria Novella (1278–1360), Santa Croce (commenced 1295) were all built in the Gothic style, and the Loggia (1376–1382) is late Gothic. Although the Baptistry itself is Romanesque, the panels of the bronze South Door (1330–1336)—done by Andrea Pisano (c. 1290–1348), who was a friend of Giotto—are Gothic. In Lorenzo Ghiberti's (1378–1455) North

Door, which he made between 1403 and 1424, Ghiberti still used the Gothic panel frames, though the subject matter within the panels was much more free. By the time Ghiberti reached the wonder of the eastern portal (1425–1452)—called by Michelangelo the Golden Gate of Paradise—the Gothic frames were completely gone and the Renaissance was in bloom. The transition from the Gothic period to the Renaissance period can be seen and felt most clearly at the wonderful doors of the Baptistry.

During the change from the Romanesque to the Gothic, Mariology began to grow in the church. The Romanesque churches were not dedicated to the Virgin, but the Gothic churches of France were overwhelmingly dedicated to her. Here again we see and feel a growing tension: The birth pangs of the Middle Ages were characterized by an awakened cultural and intellectual life and an awakened piety. Yet at the same time the church continued to move away from the teaching of early Christianity as distortions of biblical doctrine increased. Soon European thought would be divided into two lines, both of which have come down and influenced our own day: first, the humanistic elements of the Renaissance, and second, the Bible-based teaching of the Reformation.

When we approach the Renaissance we must not make either of two mistakes. First, as we have seen, we must not think that everything prior to the Renaissance had been completely dark. This false concept grew from the prejudice of the humanists (of the Renaissance and the later Enlightenment) that all good things began with the birth of modern humanism. Rather, the later Middle Ages was a period of slowly developing birth pangs. Second, while the Renaissance was a rich and wonderful period, we must not think that all which it produced was good for man.

In the last half of the eleventh century and into the twelfth century came a surge of activity which laid an economic foundation for the thirteenth-century peak of medieval culture. The population rose; integrated villages appeared, which increased the efficiency of agriculture; towns were planned on a convenient grid pattern. Even the Crusades became vehicles of economic expansion. By 1100 the heavy plow had become common, central to a process which historians regard as a revolution in cultivation. Italian towns became wealthy with Oriental trade, and Flemish towns became

Next two pages: **11**   The Chapel of St. John in the White Tower of London. "The crucial moment in England came with the Norman invasion in 1066."   **12**   Chartres and Saint-Denis Cathedrals, France. "The Middle Ages took another great leap forward." *Photos by Mustafa Arshad.*

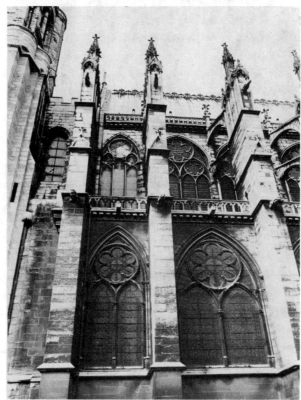

rich through textiles. Gradually, the towns freed themselves from feudal restraints to achieve varying amounts of political freedom, expressed in the proud town halls erected in the fourteenth and fifteenth centuries.

The early universities also began to emerge. By the late thirteenth century there were universities at Paris, Orléans, Toulouse, Montpellier, Cambridge, Oxford, Padua, Bologna, Naples, Salerno, Salamanca, Coimbra, and Lisbon. These universities offered a rival education to one which was purely clerical. The vernacular languages began to be used in written form; for example, portions of the Bible were translated into French. In the tenth and eleventh centuries, the proclamations of "the peace of God" and later "the truce of God," while of doubtful success, were at least attempts to limit the wars between the nobles. And, of course, Romanesque and later Gothic architecture were great breakthroughs in the annals of human thought and achievement.

Having said all that, we must recognize that there eventually came a change which does merit the name *Renaissance.* But we should realize that it was not the rebirth of man; it was the rebirth of an idea about man. There was a change in thinking about man, a change which put man himself in the center of all things, and this change was expressed in the arts. The word *Renaissance,* taken to mean "rebirth," has less obvious meaning if applied at this time to political, economic, or social history, although changes of mentality do have an impact in all areas of life. But even where the word can be used without qualification, it should not be taken to imply that every aspect of the rebirth was a gain for mankind.

The Renaissance is normally dated at the fourteenth, fifteenth, and early sixteenth centuries, but to understand it we must look at events which led up to this, especially its philosophical antecedents during the Middle Ages. And that means considering in a bit more detail the thought of Thomas Aquinas (1225–1274). Aquinas was a Dominican. He studied at the universities of Naples and Paris, and later he taught in Paris. He was the outstanding theologian of his day and his thinking is still dominant in some circles of the Roman Catholic Church. Aquinas's contribution to Western thought is, of course, much richer than we can discuss here, but his view of man demands our attention. Aquinas held that man had revolted against God and thus was fallen, but Aquinas had an incomplete view of the Fall. He thought that the Fall did not affect man as a whole but only in part. In his view the will was fallen or corrupted but the intellect was not affected. Thus people could rely on their own human wisdom, and this meant that people were free to mix the teachings of the Bible with the teachings of the non-Christian philosophers.

This is well illustrated by a fresco painted in 1365 by Andrea da Firenze (?–1377) in the Spanish Chapel in Santa Maria Novella in Florence. Thomas Aquinas sits on a throne in the center of the fresco, and on the lower level of the picture are Aristotle, Cicero (106–43 B.C.), Ptolemy (active A.D. 121–151), Euclid (active around 300 B.C.) and Pythagoras (580?–? B.C.), all placed in the same category as Augustine. As a result of this emphasis, philosophy was gradually separated from revelation—from the Bible—and philosophers began to act in an increasingly independent, autonomous manner.

Among the Greek philosophers, Thomas Aquinas relied especially on one of the greatest, Aristotle (384–322 B.C.). In 1263 Pope Urban IV had forbidden the study of Aristotle in the universities. Aquinas managed to have Aristotle accepted, so the ancient non-Christian philosophy was reenthroned.

To understand what result this had, it is worthwhile to look at Raphael's (1483–1520) painting *The School of Athens* (c. 1510) to comprehend some of the discussions and influences which followed in the Renaissance period. The fresco is in the Vatican. In *The School of Athens* Raphael painted Plato with one finger pointed upward, which means that he pointed toward absolutes or ideals. In contrast, he pictured Aristotle with his fingers spread wide and thrust down toward the earth, which means that he emphasized particulars. By particulars we mean the individual things which are about us; a chair is a particular, as is each molecule which makes up the chair, and so on. The individual person is also a particular and thus you are a particular. Thomas Aquinas brought this Aristotelian emphasis on individual things—the particulars— into the philosophy of the late Middle Ages, and this set the stage for the humanistic elements of the Renaissance and the basic problem they created.

Next two pages: **13**   Thomas Aquinas. "His thinking is still dominant in some circles." *Photo courtesy Radio Times Hutton Picture Library.*   **14**   Raphael's *The School of Athens.* ". . . absolutes or ideals and particulars." *Photo courtesy Organizzazione Milan.*

This problem is often spoken of as the nature-versus-grace problem. Beginning with man alone and only the individual things in the world (the particulars), the problem is how to find any ultimate and adequate meaning for the individual things. The most important individual thing for man is man himself. Without some ultimate meaning for a person (for me, an individual), what is the use of living and what will be the basis for morals, values, and law? If one starts from individual acts rather than with an absolute, what gives any real certainty concerning what is right and what is wrong about an individual action? The nature-and-grace tension or problem can be pictured like this:

> *Grace, the higher: God the Creator;* heaven and heavenly things; the unseen and its influence on the earth; *unity,* or universals or absolutes which give existence and morals meaning.
>
> ---
>
> *Nature, the lower: the created;* earth and earthly things; the visible and what happens normally in the cause-and-effect universe; what man as man does on the earth; *diversity,* or individual things, the particulars, or the individual acts of man.

Beginning from man alone, Renaissance humanism—and humanism ever since—has found no way to arrive at universals or absolutes which give meaning to existence and morals.

Aquinas's teaching had a *positive* side in that before his time there was little emphasis on the normal, day-to-day world, that is, the world and our relationship to it. These things do have importance because God has created the world. By the mid-thirteenth century, certain Gothic sculptors had begun to fashion leaves and flowers and birds, and had given these figures a more natural appearance. Thanks to Thomas Aquinas, the world and man's place in the world was given more prominence than previously. The *negative* result of his teaching was that the individual things, the particulars, tended to be made independent, autonomous, and consequently the meaning of the particulars began to be lost. We can think of it as the individual things, the particulars, gradually and increasingly becoming everything and thus devouring all meaning until meaning disappears.

Two things, then, laid the foundation for what was now to follow: first, the gradually awakened cultural thought and awakened piety of the Middle Ages; and second, an increasing distortion of the teaching of the Bible and the early church. Humanist elements had entered. For example, the authority of the church took precedence over the teaching of the Bible; fallen man was considered able to return to God by meriting the merit of Christ; and there was a mixture of Christian and ancient non-Christian thought (as Aquinas's emphasis on Aristotle). This opened the way for people to think of themselves as autonomous and the center of all things.

The unfortunate side of the Renaissance was the reaffirmation of the distortions. But soon there would be steps in another direction—a reaction against the distortions. There were earlier stirrings in this direction, but an important step came when an Oxford professor named John Wycliffe (c. 1320–1384) taught that the Bible was the supreme authority and produced his English translation of the Bible, raising a voice which had influence throughout Europe. John Huss (1369–1415) was influenced by Wycliffe. He also spoke out, affirming the Bible as the only final authority, emphasizing a return to the teaching of Scripture and the early church, and insisting that man must return to God through the work of Christ only. These teachings of Wycliffe and Huss moved away from the humanism which had gradually but increasingly entered the church. Thus the way was now open for two movements which were to have their influence down into our own day: the humanistic elements of the Renaissance and the scriptural Christianity of the Reformation.

1. What do you think of the churches attitude in the middle ages?
2. Do you think the author is pro-Catholic?

3 The Renaissance

The positive side of Thomas Aquinas's thinking was soon felt in art. Before Giotto (1267?–1337), Florentine painting was merely a less polished form of Byzantine art—flat and without depth. For example, Mary and Christ were not portrayed realistically; they were not so much *pictured,* as represented by symbols. Five hundred years had made no real change in Florentine art.

With Giotto, whose teacher was Cimabue (1240–1302), came a radical change. Giotto gave nature a more proper place, and his people were real people. Giotto's first great work, produced in Padua in 1304, was a picture of the Last Judgment. In this he painted a genuine likeness of Enrico Scrovegni, the man who had commissioned the picture. Giotto's work did, however, have some technical flaws. For one thing, he never mastered the technique of having people's feet fastened on the earth. His figures all seem to stand on tiptoe. And his people are much larger in scale than the world around them—hills, houses, and trees are too small for the size of the people. Nevertheless, Giotto took a huge step toward giving nature its rightful place. That is proper, for, because God made the world, nature is indeed important—and nature was now being portrayed more like it actually is. Giotto also began to show the versatility which was to characterize Renaissance man. At the end of his lifetime he designed the bell tower, the Campanile, next to the cathedral in Florence (1334–1337).

The positive drift toward an art in which nature had more emphasis occurred not only in painting but also in writing. The writers wrote the way the painters painted. Specifically Dante (1265–1321), who may have known Giotto and who refers to him in *The Divine Comedy* (1300–1320), wrote in the way Giotto painted. A native of Florence, exiled in 1302 because of his political activity, Dante was one of the first men to write important works in the vernacular. His writing has a deep and profound beauty and is a work of genius on its highest level. But in the development of the humanistic elements of the Renaissance, Dante followed the unfortunate side of Thomas Aquinas in mixing the Christian and the classical pagan world in allusions throughout his work. To mention two examples from *The Divine Comedy:* First, Dante's guide through hell is the Roman poet Virgil, who was to Dante what Aristotle was to Aquinas; second, the worst sinners in hell are Judas who betrayed Christ and Brutus and Cassius who betrayed Caesar.

It is interesting that the nature-versus-grace problem is clearly reflected in the contrast in Dante's writing between Beatrice and Dante's wife. All his life Dante loved Beatrice (whom he actually only saw a couple of times), and he held up their love as a romantic ideal. For example, in about 1293 he wrote *La Vita Nuova,* celebrating his love for Beatrice: "Seeing her face is so fair to see . . . love sheds such perfect sweetness over me." On the other hand, the wife he married in 1285 never had a place in his poetry. She was only for doing his cooking and rearing his children. Those in this school of thinking saw a strong contrast between two views of love—one totally sensual, the other totally spiritual. They understood that sensual love needs the spiritual to give it any real meaning beyond a physical response at the passing moment, but instead of keeping this as a unity, they allowed it to be separated into a kind of *upper* and *lower story.* The sensual love of the novelists and poets was the lower story; the spiritual, supposedly ideal love of the lyric poets was the upper story. This situation did not produce beauty but ugliness. The wife was a dray horse; the idealized woman, a disembodied phantom.

Other writers followed in Dante's train. Petrarch (1304–1374) is rightly called "the father of the new humanism." He had a deep enthusiasm for the classical Roman writers, such as Cicero, and a

15   Giotto's *Last Judgment*. ". . . Giotto's first great work."

deep love for ancient Rome. Boccaccio (1313–1375), author of *The Decameron,* learned Greek in order to study the classics better. His translation of Homer was one of the foundation stones of the Renaissance, reviving Greek literature after seven hundred years of neglect. From Petrarch came a line of professional humanists. These paid men of letters translated Latin, wrote speeches, and acted as secretaries. They were largely laymen, like the Florentine chancellors Salutati (1331–1406) and Bruni (1370–1444). Their humanism meant, first of all, a veneration for everything ancient and especially the writings of the Greek and Roman age. Although this past age did include the early Christian church, it became increasingly clear that the sort of human autonomy that many of the Renaissance humanists had in mind referred exclusively to the non-Christian Greco-Roman world. Thus Renaissance humanism steadily evolved toward modern humanism—a value system rooted in the belief that man is his own measure, that man is autonomous, totally independent.

The enthusiasm for the Greek and Roman classics was further stimulated by two events. First, a church council in Florence in 1439 discussed relations with the Eastern Orthodox Church and so opened the way for contacts with Greek scholars. Second, the fall of Constantinople in 1453 resulted in an exodus of Greek scholars who brought manuscripts with them to Florence and other northern Italian cities. It was the humanists of that time who, under the enthusiasm for the classics, spoke of what had immediately preceded them as a "Dark Age" and talked of a "rebirth" in their own era. Harkening back to the pre-Christian era, they visualized man as taking a great forward leap. The concept of autonomous man was growing. In other words, humanism in the form it took in the Renaissance (and after the Renaissance) was being born.

There was indeed a positive side to all that was occurring: a new and proper emphasis on nature and the enjoyment of it. About 1340 Petrarch climbed a mountain, Mont Ventoux, in the south of France just to climb it—something brand-new. Though this ascent may seem trivial, it was a parallel in life to Giotto's painting of nature.

A bit later, in the early fifteenth century, architecture was beginning to change dramatically with Brunelleschi (1377–1446). His

16 Dante. ". . . a romantic ideal."

DANTE·

architecture shifted the emphasis from the Gothic back to the classical. His churches in Florence of San Lorenzo (1421–1434) and Santo Spirito (built in 1445–1482 from his designs) show his use of the classical form. In 1421 he began work on the Foundling Hospital, which can be said to be the first Renaissance building. His dome of the cathedral in Florence (1434) was an immense architectural breakthrough: It brought together great artistic triumph with an overwhelming feat of engineering. It was and is one of the wonders of the world in architectural engineering. It was not only an artistic expression, but it showed the high state of his grasp of mathematics. In this dome Brunelleschi went beyond any dome ever built before—including the Pantheon of ancient Rome.

To see the interplay of the arts in the Renaissance period, it is interesting to note that the musician Guillaume Dufay (c. 1400–1474) wrote a motet especially for the consecration of the dome built by Brunelleschi. Later, Michelangelo used Brunelleschi's dome as the model for the dome of St. Peter's. All this is especially impressive when one realizes that Brunelleschi was trained not as an architect but as a goldsmith, which again emphasizes the versatility of the men of the Renaissance. The Renaissance architects emphasized the simple geometrical forms of the square and circle. And Leonardo da Vinci (1452–1519) made drawings that fitted man himself into these simple forms. Brunelleschi worked out perspective, as did Ghiberti and Donatello (1386–1466), while Leone Battista Alberti (1404–1472) wrote the first treatise on its theory and technique. Perspective made possible a new way of depicting space. Brunelleschi, the master of space, also greatly influenced the painters and sculptors of his day by making open space an important factor in their artistic concepts.

But for the men of the Renaissance the new view of perspective was also something more: It placed man in the center of this space, and space became subordinated to mathematical principles spun out of the mind of man. The emphasis on man was coming out in other new ways. For example, we know very little about those who built the cathedrals in the Gothic era or about those who wrote the Gregorian chants. By contrast, Brunelleschi's biography was written in detail by a friend, and Cellini (1500–1571) later wrote about his own life in a swaggering autobiography in which he

Next two pages: **17** Cathedral dome in Florence, Italy, designed by Brunelleschi, and bell tower by Giotto. ". . . an immense architectural breakthrough." *Photo from Mary-Evans Picture Library.* **18** The architect Leone Battista Alberti who "even made self-portraits."

Leo Baptiſta Albertus.

assumed that ordinary morality did not apply to a genius like himself. Now, too, for the first time, portraits became a generally accepted art form. The architect Alberti even made self-portraits.

Now we come to the next big step forward in the flow of the art of the Renaissance. Masaccio (1401–1428), who died as a young man of twenty-seven, has been called the father of Renaissance painting. He knew Brunelleschi and, in turn, his work influenced Ghiberti's work on the North Door of the Baptistry. The best place to see Masaccio's work is in the Brancacci Chapel, Church of the Carmelite Order in Florence. He seemed to have had a special relationship with the Carmelite Order, for he had already worked in one of their churches in Pisa. In the panels of this chapel where Masaccio and his master, Masolino (1383?–1447?), labored together, his work far surpassed his master's in its lifelikeness. When Masaccio left some work unfinished in the chapel, Filippino Lippi (1457–1504) was brought in fifty years later to complete it. Even though Lippi's contribution was so much later, Masaccio's work was still far superior to Lippi's. In Masaccio's work many faces were clearly portraits. He made studies from life and was able to give his work a true-to-life quality. Nature had thus now truly come to its proper place.

Masaccio was the first painter who consistently used central perspective, though Donatello's earlier relief *St. George and the Dragon* also showed some knowledge of this. The Romans never knew central, one-point perspective, though they used a kind of perspective, seen for example in the wall paintings of Pompeii. So in painting (as in Brunelleschi's dome in architecture) the men of the Florentine Renaissance surpassed the ancients. Masaccio also was the first to bring light into his paintings from the naturally correct direction. He painted so that his figures looked "in the round" and in the midst of a realized space. One can feel the atmosphere about Masaccio's figures, this sense of true atmosphere being caused by the combination of perspective plus light. In addition, his work had real composition; there was a balance to the total work in the relationship of the figures and the whole. Vasari (1511–1574), who was also an architect and painter, in *The Lives of the Painters, Sculptors and Architects* (1550), wrote that Masaccio was the first artist who painted people with their feet actually standing on the ground. One can see this by comparing Masolino's and Masaccio's *Adam and Eve* on two walls facing each other in the Carmine chapel. In short, in the painting of Masaccio there were a massive number of breakthroughs and firsts.

In the north of Europe, the same techniques were wrestled with by the Flemish painters, of whom Jan van Eyck was the greatest (c. 1390–1441). Van Eyck in the north worked at the same time as Masaccio in the south in Italy. Van Eyck mastered light and air and placed a strong emphasis on nature. He also used a new technique of oil plus tempera. In this he preceded the painters in Italy. By 1420—earlier than the Italians—the Flemish painter Campin (1378?–1444) had made real portraits, and van Eyck followed. The painting by van Eyck of Rolin in *Madonna with Chancellor Rolin* (about 1436), for example, is a true portrait.

At an earlier period in the north than in the south, painters also were interested in landscapes. Van Eyck, who was doing landscapes as early as 1415–1420, was the first great master of this subject, the first great landscape artist. A number of paintings show this early interest, but let us examine just one: his *Adoration of the Lamb* (1432) in the Cathedral of St. Bavon in Ghent, Belgium. It is an altarpiece containing wonderful pictures of Eve, Adam, and singing angels. But most impressive is the central theme: the rich, the poor—people of all classes and backgrounds—coming to Christ. And who is this Christ? Van Eyck comprehended the biblical understanding of Christ as the Lamb of God who died on the cross to take away the moral guilt of those who accept him as Savior. But this Christ is not now dead. He stands upright and alive on the altar, symbolizing that he died as the substitute, sacrificed, but he now lives! As van Eyck painted this, almost certainly he had Jesus' own words in mind, as Christ speaks in the Apocalypse, the last book in the Bible: "I am the living one that became dead, and behold, I am alive for evermore, Amen; and I have the keys of death and hades."

The background of this painting is marvelous, a real landscape. Soon the Flemish painters' work in natural backgrounds was copied in the south—for example, in the background of Piero della Francesca's (c. 1416–1492) *Duke of Urbino,* now in the Uffizi Gallery in Florence.

19   *Adoration of the Lamb* by van Eyck, Cathedral of Saint Bavon, Ghent, Belgium. ". . . the biblical understanding of Christ as the Lamb of God."

In passing, we should note that the north influenced the south in music as well as in painting. Josquin des Prez (1450–1521) was a Fleming who came to Italy and served in the court of Milan. He excelled in his music as a "tone painter." He was one of the great composers of all time, and had considerable influence on the development of Renaissance music in the south. Music in the Renaissance made both technical and artistic advances. Technically, for example, the first printer of music, Ottaviano Petrucci (1466–1539), worked in Venice and printed music with movable type in 1501. Artistically, perhaps the most significant innovation was the art of orchestration. The main instruments were the lute (the most popular solo instrument), sackbut (like a trombone), shawm, viol, drum, and krumhorn (a curved horn), along with an extraordinary variety of wind instruments, all built in sets so that one uniform timbre was available throughout the entire range from bass to soprano. This was in keeping with the Renaissance ideal of homogeneous sound. Music was important in the Renaissance, and popular interest in music soon led to the rise of opera in Florence.

It is crucial to notice that with Masaccio and the others up to this point, art could still have moved toward either a biblical or a nonbiblical concept of nature and the particulars (that is, the individual things, including the individual man). Up to this time it could have gone either way. It was good that nature was given a proper place. And there could have continued an emphasis on real people in a real world which God had made—with the particulars, the individual things, important because God made the whole world. Masaccio, as we have noted, pictured Adam and Eve as the Bible portrays them—as real people in a real world. Or at this point humanism could take over, with its emphasis on things being autonomous. Immediately after Masaccio, the die was cast and the movement went in this direction. Man made himself increasingly independent and autonomous, and with this came an increasing loss of anything which gave meaning, either to the individual things in the world or to man. With this we begin to see the dilemma of humanism which is still with us today.

This position and its dilemma is strikingly shown in a shift in art. In France, one sees this with Fouquet (c. 1416–1480) in his paint-

Next two pages: **20**   *The Red Virgin* by Fouquet. ". . . the king's mistress."   **21** One of the four statues in a series by Michelangelo, commonly known as *The Captives.* "Man will be victorious." *Photo by Mustafa Arshad.*

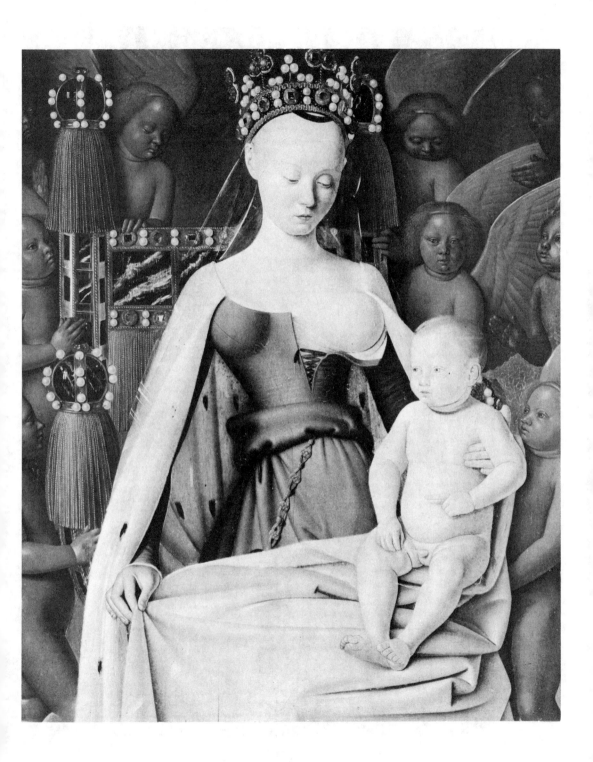

ing *The Red Virgin* (1450?). The word *red* refers to the overall color used in part of the picture. The girl was shown with one breast exposed, and everybody who knew the situation knew that this was a picture of the king's mistress, Agnès Sorel. Was this the Madonna about to feed her baby? No, the painting might be titled *The Red Virgin,* but the girl was the king's mistress; and when one looked at the painting one could see what the king's mistress's breast looked like. Prior to this time, Mary was considered very high and holy. Earlier she was considered so much above normal people that she was painted as a symbol. When in the Renaissance Mary was painted as a real person, this was an advance over the representations of Mary in the earlier age, because the Bible tells us that Mary was a real girl and that the baby Jesus was a real baby. But now not only was the king's mistress painted as Mary with all of the holiness removed, but the meaning, too, was being destroyed. At first it might have seemed that only the religious aspect was threatened. But, as we can see in retrospect, gradually the threat spread to all of knowledge and all of life. All meaning to all individual things or all particulars was removed. Things were being viewed as autonomous, and there was nothing to which to relate them or to give them meaning.

Let us now look at another aspect of art to show that humanism had taken over. In the Academy in Florence is Michelangelo's (1475–1564) great room. Here we see on either side Michelangelo's statues of men "tearing themselves out of the rock." These were sculpted between 1519 and 1536. They make a real humanistic statement: Man will make himself great. Man as Man is tearing himself out of the rock. Man by himself will tear himself out of nature and free himself from it. Man will be victorious.

As the room in the Academy is arranged, it strikingly sets forth humanistic thought. As we go past these men tearing themselves out of the rock, we come finally, at the focal point of the room, to the magnificent statue of *David* (1504). As a work of art it has few equals in the world. Michelangelo took a piece of marble so flawed that no one thought it could be used, and out of it he carved this overwhelming statue. But let us notice that the *David* was not the Jewish David of the Bible. *David* was simply a title. Michelangelo knew his Judaism, and in the statue the figure is not circumcised. We are not to think of this as the biblical David but as the humanistic ideal. Man is great!

The statue was originally planned to stand forty feet above the street on one of the buttresses of the cathedral, but was placed outside the city hall in Florence, where a copy now stands. The Medicis, the great banking family which had dominated Florence since 1434, had run the city by manipulating its republican constitution. A few years before *David* was made, the Medicis had been thrown down by the people and a more genuine republic restored (1494). Thus, as the statue was raised outside the city hall, though Michelangelo himself had been a friend of the Medicis, his *David* was seen by the populace as the slayer of tyrants. Florence was looking with confidence toward a great future.

The *David* was the statement of what the humanistic man saw himself as being tomorrow! In this statue we have man waiting with confidence in his own strength for the future. Even the disproportionate size of the hands says that man is powerful. This statue is idealistic and romantic. There was and is no man like the *David*. If a girl fell in love with the statue and waited until she found such a man, she would never marry. Humanism was standing in its proud self and the *David* stood as a representation of that. But there are signs that by the end of his life Michelangelo saw that humanism was not enough. Michelangelo in his later years was in close touch with Vittoria Colonna (1490–1547), a woman who had been influenced by Reformation thought. Some people feel they see some of that influence in Michelangelo's life and work. However that may be, it is true that his later work did change. Many of his early works show his humanism, as does his *David*. In contrast stand his later *Pietàs* (statues of Mary holding the dead Christ in her arms) in the cathedral in Florence and in the castle in Milan, which was probably his last. In the *Pietà* in the cathedral in Florence, Michelangelo put his own face on Nicodemus (or Joseph of Arimathea—whichever the man is), and in both of these *Pietàs* humanistic pride seems lessened, if not absent.

Another giant of the Renaissance, equal to Michelangelo, is Leonardo da Vinci (1452–1519) who historically stood at a crucial place. He was a chemist, musician, architect, anatomist, botanist, mechanical engineer, and artist. He was the embodiment of the

22   *David* by Michelangelo. "There was and is no man like the David." *Photo by Mustafa Arshad.*

true Renaissance man: he could do almost everything and do it well. The classic work *Leonardo da Vinci,* published in Italy and translated into English in 1963, contained a section by Giovanni Gentile (1875–1944) on Leonardo's thought forms. He spells out the fact that Leonardo really grasped the problem of modern man. Leonardo anticipated where humanism would end.

Leonardo is generally accepted as the first modern mathematician. He not only knew mathematics abstractly but applied it in his *Notebooks* to all manner of engineering problems. He was one of the unique geniuses of history, and in his brilliance he perceived that beginning humanistically with mathematics one *only* had particulars. He understood that man beginning from himself would never be able to come to meaning on the basis of mathematics. And he knew that having only individual things, particulars, one never could come to universals or meaning and thus one only ends with mechanics. In this he saw ahead to where our generation has come: Everything, including man, is the machine. Realizing this, Leonardo thought that perhaps the painter, the sensitive man, could come to meaning, so he tried to paint "the soul"—not the soul as a Christian thinks of it, but rather the universal. He attempted to paint one thing that would include all of that class of things.

As you will remember, Thomas Aquinas emphasized Aristotelian thought. Think back to Raphael's fresco in the Vatican, *The School of Athens.* There Plato pointed upward, Aristotle downward. Aristotelian thought was directed toward the particulars and led through Thomas Aquinas to all the subsequent problems of an emphasis on the particulars at the expense of meaning. But in Florence the emphasis gradually shifted to Plato (427?–347? B.C.). The western interest in Plato accelerated as Greek scholars fled after the fall of Constantinople in 1453 and brought their texts with them. Marsilio Ficino (1433–1499) taught neo-Platonic thinking to Lorenzo the Magnificent (1449–1492), and this thinking became important in Florence. He was an influence on Michelangelo and other artists such as Sandro Botticelli (1444–1510), as well as on Lorenzo and the thinkers surrounding him. As Aristotelian thought emphasized the particulars, neo-Platonic thought emphasized the universals. The early men of the Renaissance had tried to syncretize Christianity and Aristotelian thought, but had failed. Thereafter,

Next three pages: **23–25** Sketches by Leonardo da Vinci. ". . . one of the unique geniuses of history." *Photos courtesy of Anderson-Giraudon.*

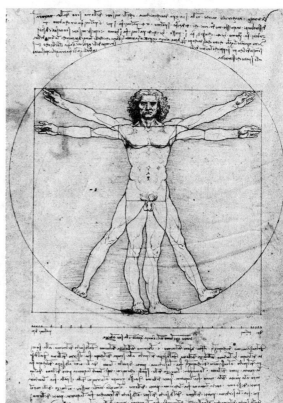

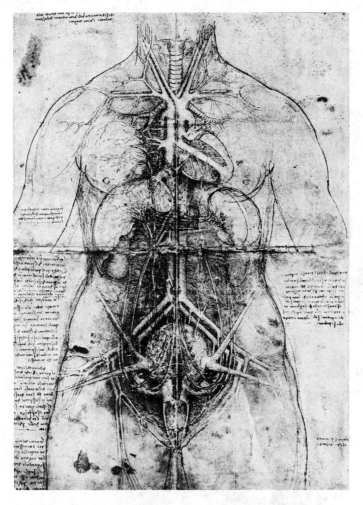

men of the Renaissance tried to syncretize Christianity and Platonism—and likewise failed.

In the midst of these crosscurrents of thought, Leonardo tried to paint the universal, thinking that a painter might be able to achieve what the mathematicians could not. But he never was able to paint the universal on a humanistic basis, any more than the mathematician could provide a mathematical universal on a humanist basis. Leonardo, the humanistic man (beginning only from himself) failed both as the mathematician and also as the artist who tried to paint the universal out of his observation of the particulars. The humanists had been sure that man starting from himself could solve every problem. There was a complete faith in man. Man starting from himself, tearing himself out of the rock, out of nature, could solve all. The humanistic cry was, "I can do what I will; just give me until tomorrow." But Leonardo, in his brilliance, saw at the end of his life humanism's coming defeat.

There was a split between Leonardo's theory and the way it worked out in practice. He could not bring forth the universal or meaning in either mathematics or painting, and when King Francis I of France (1494–1547) brought Leonardo to the French court as an old man, Leonardo was in despondency. *As a man thinketh so is he*—and humanism had already begun to show that pessimism was its natural conclusion. Actually, we could say that we went to Renaissance Florence and found modern man!

4 The Reformation

W hile the men of the Renaissance wrestled with the problem of what could give unity to life and specifically what universal could give meaning to life and to morals, another great movement, the Reformation, was emerging in the north of Europe. This was the reaction we mentioned at the end of our study of the Middle Ages—the reaction against the distortions which had gradually appeared in both a religious and a secular form. The High Renaissance in the south and the Reformation in the north must always be considered side by side. They dealt with the same basic problems, but they gave completely opposite answers and brought forth completely opposite results.

As we have seen, there had been forerunners of the Reformation. John Wycliffe (c. 1320–1384), whose life overlapped Giotto's, Dante's, Petrarch's and Boccaccio's, emphasized the Bible as the supreme authority, and he and his followers produced an English translation which had wide importance throughout Europe. John Huss of Bohemia (the heartland of modern Czechoslovakia) was a professor at the University of Prague (the Charles University). He lived between about 1369 and 1415. Thus his life overlapped Brunelleschi's, Masaccio's and van Eyck's. In contrast to the humanistic elements which had come into the church—and which led to the authority of the church being accepted as equal to, or greater than, the authority of the Bible and which emphasized human

79

work as a basis for meriting the merit of Christ—Huss returned to the teachings of the Bible and of the early church and stressed that the Bible is the only source of final authority and that salvation comes only through Christ and his work. He further developed Wycliffe's views on the priesthood of all believers. Promised safe-conduct to speak at the Council of Constance, he was betrayed and burned at the stake there on July 6, 1415. Wycliffe's and Huss's views were the basic views of the Reformation which came later, and these views continued to exist in parts of the north of Europe even while the Renaissance was giving its humanist answers in the south. The Bohemian Brethren, the antecedents of the Moravian Church, were founded in 1457 by Huss's followers, and, like Luther's doctrines later, their ideas were spread not only by their teaching but by their emphasis on music and use of hymns. Huss himself wrote hymns which are still sung today. Another voice was the Dominican monk, Girolamo Savonarola, who drew large audiences in Florence between 1494 and 1498. He was not as clear as Wycliffe and Huss, but he did see some of the growing problems and spoke out against them until he was hanged and then his body burned in the square before the town hall in Florence.

Martin Luther (1483–1546) nailed his Ninety-five Theses to the church door in Wittenberg on October 31, 1517. To put this into historical perspective, we should remember that Leonardo da Vinci lived from 1452 to 1519. Thus, Luther's Theses were set forth just two years before Leonardo's death. Calvin was born in 1509, ten years before Leonardo's death, and the year Leonardo died Luther had his disputation in Leipzig with Dr. Eck. Francis I, who in 1516 took Leonardo to France (where Leonardo died), is the same Francis I to whom Calvin (1509–1564) addressed his *Institutes of the Christian Religion* in 1536.

One must understand that these two things were happening almost simultaneously: First, in the south, much of the High Renaissance was based on a humanistic ideal of man's being the center of all things, of man's being autonomous; second, in the north of Europe, the Reformation was giving an opposite answer. In other words, the Reformation was exploding with Luther just as the High Renaissance was coming to its close. As we have said, Luther nailed his Theses to the door in Wittenberg in 1517.

Zwingli led Zürich to its break with Rome in 1523. Henry VIII of England broke with Rome in 1534. (This was at first political rather than religious, but it did lead later to a Protestant England.) Then, as we have mentioned, Calvin's *Institutes* were written in 1536.

But while the Reformation and the Renaissance overlapped historically and while they dealt with the same basic questions, they gave completely different answers. You will remember that to Thomas Aquinas the *will* was fallen after man had revolted against God, but the *mind* was not. This eventually resulted in people believing they could think out the answers to all the great questions, beginning only from themselves. The Reformation, in contrast to Aquinas, had a more biblical concept of the Fall. For the people of the Reformation, people could *not* begin only from themselves, and on the basis of human reason alone think out the answers to the great questions which confront mankind.

The men of the Reformation did learn from the new knowledge and attitudes brought forth by the Renaissance. A critical outlook, for example, toward what had previously been accepted without question was helpful. And while the Reformers rejected the scepticism of Lorenzo Valla (c. 1409–1457), they gladly learned from his study of language. But from the critical attitude toward the traditions which had been accepted without question, the Reformers turned not to man as beginning only from himself, but to the original Christianity of the Bible and the early church. Gradually they came to see that the church founded by Christ had since been marred by distortions. However, in contrast to the Renaissance humanists, they refused to accept the autonomy of human reason, which acts as though the human mind is infinite, with all knowledge within its realm. Rather, they took seriously the Bible's own claim for itself—that it is the only final authority. And they took seriously that man needs the answers given by God in the Bible to have adequate answers not only for how to be in an open relationship with God, but also for how to know the present meaning of life and how to have final answers in distinguishing between right and wrong. That is, man needs not only a God who exists, but a God who has spoken in a way that can be understood.

The Reformers accepted the Bible as the Word of God in all that it teaches. Luther translated the Bible into German, and translations of the Bible began to be available for the people in the languages they could understand. To the Reformation thinkers, authority was not divided between the Bible and the church. The church was *under* the teaching of the Bible—not above it and not equal to it. It was *Sola Scriptura,* the Scriptures only. This stood in contrast to the humanism that had infiltrated the church after the first centuries of Christianity. *At its core, therefore, the Reformation was the removing of the humanistic distortions which had entered the church.*

It is worth reiterating the ways in which the infiltration by humanistic thought—growing over the years but fully developed by 1500—showed itself. First, the authority of the church was made equal to the authority of the Bible. Second, a strong element of human work was added to the work of Christ for salvation. Third, after Thomas Aquinas there had come an increasing synthesis between biblical teaching and pagan thought. This synthesis was not just a borrowing of words but actually of content. It is apparent in many places and could be illustrated in many ways. For example, Raphael in one of his rooms in the Vatican balanced *The School of Athens* (which represents Greek non-Christian philosophic thought) with his pictorial representation of the church, putting them on opposite walls. This representation of the church is called the *Disputà* for it deals with the nature of the mass. Raphael was par excellence the artist of the synthesis. But Michelangelo, on the ceiling of the Sistine Chapel in the Vatican, also combined biblical teaching and non-Christian pagan thought; he made the pagan prophetesses equal to the Old Testament prophets. Dante's writings show the same mixture.

When in Basel, Guillaume Farel (1489–1565), the Reformer in French-speaking Switzerland before Calvin, showed plainly that there was a second kind of humanism that he stood against, as well as that which had come into the church. This kind of humanism was exemplified most clearly by Erasmus of Rotterdam (1466?–1536). Erasmus helped the Reformers by editing the New Testament in the original Greek (1516) and by urging in the preface that the New Testament be translated into all the vernacular languages. Some have called the view of Erasmus and those with him

26   Michelangelo's Prophet Jeremiah and pagan prophetess of Delphi in Sistine Chapel, Vatican City. ". . . combined biblical teaching and non-Christian pagan thought." *Photos courtesy of Organizzazione Milan.*

HIEREMIAS

DELPHICA

Christian humanism, but it was less than consistent Christianity. Erasmus and his followers wanted only a limited reform of the church, in contrast to the Reformers who wanted to go back to the church as it originally was, with the authority being the Bible only. Thus Farel thoroughly cut himself off from Erasmus to make plain that he stood on principle against either form of humanism. The various branches of the Reformation had differences among themselves, but together they constituted one system—a unity— in contrast to the humanism which had come into the church on one side and to the Erasmian humanism on the outside.

The Reformation was certainly not a golden age. It was far from perfect, and in many ways it did not act consistently with the Bible's teaching, although the Reformers were trying to make the Bible their standard not only in religion but in all of life. No, it was not a golden age. For example, such overwhelming mistakes were made as Luther's unbalanced position in regard to the peasant wars, and the Reformers showed little zeal for reaching people in other parts of the world with the Christian message. Yet though they indeed had many and serious weaknesses, in regard to religious and secular humanism, they did return to the Bible's instruction and the example of the early church.

Because the Reformers did not mix humanism with their position, but took instead a serious view of the Bible, they had no problem of meaning for the individual things, the particulars; they had no nature-versus-grace problem. One could say that the Renaissance centered in autonomous man, while the Reformation centered in the infinite-personal God who had spoken in the Bible. In the answer the Reformation gave, the problem of meaning for indi- vidual things, including man, was so completely answered that the problem—as a problem—did not exist. The reason for this is that the Bible gives a unity to the universal and the particulars.

First, the Bible tells men and women true things about God. Therefore, they can know true things about God. One can know true things about God because God has revealed himself. The word *God* was not contentless to Reformation man. God was not an unknown "philosophic other" because God had told man about himself. As the Westminster Confession (1645–1647) says, when God revealed his attributes to people, the attributes are not only true

27   Statue of Farel in Neuchâtel, Switzerland. ". . . a serious view of the Bible."
Photo by Mustafa Arshad.

to people but true to God. That is, when God tells people what he is like, what he says is not just relatively true but absolutely true. As finite beings, people do not have exhaustive truth about God, but they can have truth about God; and they can know, therefore, truth about that which is the ultimate universal. And the Bible speaks to men and women concerning meaning, morals, and values.

Second, the Bible tells us true things about people and about nature. It does not give men and women *exhaustive* truth about the world and the cosmos, but it does give truth about them. So one can know many true things about nature, especially *why* things exist and why they have the form they have. Yet, because the Bible does not give exhaustive truth about history and the cosmos, historians and scientists have a job to do, and their work is not meaningless. To be sure, there is a total break between God and his creation, that is, between God and created things; God is infinite— and created things are finite. But man can know both truth about God and truth about the things of creation because in the Bible God has revealed himself and has given man the key to understanding God's world.

So, as the Reformation returned to biblical teaching, it gained two riches at once: It had no particulars-versus-universals (or meaning) problem, and yet at the same time science and art were set free to operate upon the basis of that which God had set forth in Scripture. The Christianity of the Reformation, therefore, stood in rich contrast to the basic weakness and final poverty of the humanism which existed in that day and the humanism which has existed since.

It is important that the Bible sets forth true knowledge about mankind. The biblical teaching gives meaning to all particulars, but this is especially so in regard to that particular which is the most important to man, namely, the individual himself or herself. It gives a reason for the individual being great. The ironic fact here is that humanism, which began with Man's being central, eventually had no real meaning for people. On the other hand, if one begins with the Bible's position that a person is created by God and created in the image of God, there is a basis for that person's dignity. People, the Bible teaches, are made in the image of God—they are nonprogrammed. Each is thus Man with dignity.

That Man is made in the image of God gives many important answers intellectually, but it also has had vast practical results, both in the Reformation days and in our own age. For example, in the time of the Reformation it meant that all the vocations of life came to have dignity. The vocation of honest merchant or housewife had as much dignity as king. This was strengthened further by the emphasis on the biblical teaching of the priesthood of all believers—that is, that all Christians are priests. Thus, in a very real sense, all people are equal as persons. Moreover, the government of the church by lay elders created the potential for democratic emphasis.

The Bible, however, also says that man is fallen; he has revolted against God. At the historic space-time Fall, man refused to stand in the proper relationship with this infinite reference point which is the personal God. Therefore, people are now abnormal. The Reformation saw all people as equal in this way, too—all are guilty before God. This is as true of the king and queen as the peasant. So, in contrast to the humanism of the Renaissance, which never gave an answer to explain that which is observable in people, the Bible enabled people to solve the dilemma facing them as they look at themselves: They could understand both their greatness and their cruelty.

The Bible gives a different way to come to God from that teaching which had grown up in the church through the previous centuries. The Reformers went back to the teaching of the Bible and the early church and removed the humanistic elements which had been added. The individual person, they taught, could come to God directly *by faith* through the finished work of Christ. That is, Christ's sacrifice on the cross was of infinite value, and people cannot do and need not do anything to earn or add to Christ's work. But this can be accepted as an unearned gift. It was *Sola Gratia,* grace only.

Previously, those who came into the churches were separated from what to them was the center of worship—the altar in the chancel—by a high grill of iron or wood. This was the *rood screen,* so called from the rood, or crucifix, which it often supported or which was hung above it. But with the Reformation, when the Bible was accepted in all its unique authority, these screens were often removed. In some churches the Bible was placed exactly where the screen had been, to show that the teaching of the Bible opened the way for all the people to come directly to God. One such church is in Ollon, Switzerland. You can still see where the rood screen had fit into the wall but was removed; the pulpit was then placed so that the Bible is where the rood screen had previously been.

Guillaume Farel, the early French-Swiss Reformer preached in this church, and from there and nearby Aigle the Reformation began in French-speaking Switzerland. Later, after ministries in Geneva and Lausanne, Farel preached for many years in the cathedral in Neuchâtel. The statue outside that cathedral could well be taken as the mark of the Reformation and of Christianity. This statue has Farel holding the Bible aloft. Thus it is *Sola Scriptura,* the Bible and the Bible only. This is what made all the difference to the Reformers, both in understanding the approach to God and in having the intellectual and practical answers needed in this present life.

Because of their tendency toward purifying religion from an overemphasis on visual symbols, the Reformers are often accused of being antagonistic to the arts. But the Reformation was not against art as art. To some of us the statues and paintings of the Madonna, saints, and so on may be art objects, and perhaps we wish that the people of the Reformation had taken these works and put them in a warehouse for a hundred years or so. Then they could have been brought out and put in a museum. But at that moment of history this would have been too much to ask! To the men and women of that time, these were images to worship. The men of the Reformation saw that the Bible stressed that there is only one mediator between God and man, Christ Jesus. Thus, in the pressure of that historic moment, they sometimes destroyed the images—not as works of art but as religious images which were contrary to the Bible's emphasis on Jesus as the only mediator.

We should note, however, that the Reformers usually distinguished between *cult images* and other works of art, the former alone falling under condemnation. But not even all of the cult images were destroyed. All over Europe in cathedrals and churches we can see thousands of statues which were not destroyed. The reason why some statues were destroyed is pointed out by Bernd

Moeller (1931–) in *Imperial Cities and the Reformation* (1962. English translation, 1972). He shows that in certain cases the actual donors of the images smashed them because they represented religiously that which they now rejected as unbiblical. He writes, "Those who donated an image did not merely venerate that image; those who broke an image did not merely hate it. Both the donor and the breaker of images were concerned with eternal salvation." Image breaking parallels in the area of ecology the early Christians' cutting down the sacred groves of trees which were related to the worship of pagan gods. These believers did not cut down the trees because they minimized trees or despised nature; they cut down these specific trees because of their anti-Christian religious significance. Equally, the people of the Reformation did not destroy art objects as art objects. Unlike modern man, the men of that day did not live in a splintered world. Art was an intimate part of life. What is represented had more than an aesthetic value divorced from considerations of truth and religious significance.

The proof that the Reformation was not against art *as* art is seen in the effects of the Reformation on culture. We should not forget that Lucas Cranach (1472–1553), the German painter and engraver, was a friend of Luther and painted Luther and his wife many times. Cranach also painted Luther's father. The vocal parts of the 1524 hymnbook were probably engraved by Cranach. Luther and Cranach were even the godfathers of each other's children. There is no indication at all that Luther disapproved of Cranach's painting in all the varied forms that it took.

Then, too, we can think of the music which the Reformation brought forth. There was the lively Geneva Psalter, the 1562 hymnbook made up of the Psalms. The tunes were so vivacious that some people in derision called them "Geneva Jigs." The great Theodore Beza (1519–1605), who followed Calvin as leader of the Reformation in Geneva, translated the Psalms' texts, and these were set to melodies selected or composed by Louis Bourgeois (1510–1570). Later this Psalter was used in England, Germany, the Netherlands, and Scotland, as well as in Switzerland. But it was in Luther's Germany where the effects of the Reformation on music are best seen.

Luther himself was a fine musician. He was a singer with a good tenor voice as well as an instrumentalist with skill and verve. In 1524 his choirmaster, Johann Walther (1496–1570), put out a hymnbook (*Wittenberg Gesangbuch*) which was a tremendous innovation. Walther and his friend Conrad Rupff worked on these hymns in Luther's home. Luther himself played out the tunes on his fife. The collection contained Luther's own great hymn "A Mighty Fortress Is Our God," to which he wrote both words and music. As the rood screen was removed in the churches—because with an open Bible the people had direct access to God—so also in a direct approach to God the congregations were allowed to sing again for the first time in many centuries.

We are swept back in this, as in other things, to the practice as well as the teaching of the early church. We are carried back to Ambrose (339–397), bishop of Milan and his antiphonal psalmody, as he, like Luther, wrote hymn texts and taught his congregations to sing them. Luther said in the preface to the *Wittenberg Gesangbuch,* "I wish that the young men might have something to rid them of their love ditties and wanton songs and might instead of these learn wholesome things and thus yield willingly to the good; also, because I am not of the opinion that all the arts shall be crushed to earth and perish through the Gospel, as some bigoted persons pretend, but would willingly see them all, and especially music, servants of Him who gave and created them."

Hymnwriters who later brought forth more complicated forms were Hans Leo Hassler (1564–1612) and Michael Praetorius (1571–1621). Heinrich Schütz (1585–1672) and Dietrich Buxtehude (1637–1707) should also be noted. Schütz was influenced by the baroque music of Giovanni Gabrieli (c. 1557–1612) from Venice, but in the Reformation this style took on its own character and direction. Buxtehude, the organist at Lübeck, had a profound influence on Bach. It is interesting to note that, two years before Bach came to hear Buxtehude at Lübeck, Handel (1685–1759) came there, not only intending to hear Buxtehude, but hoping to inherit Buxtehude's post. In the contract was a clause saying that the new organist was to marry Buxtehude's daughter. Handel did not take the position! The so-called *Abendmusiken* (late Sunday afternoon sacred concerts) were begun by Buxtehude, and both Handel and Bach went to hear them. The Reformation's influence

28   Martin Luther as painted by Cranach, *Poldi Pezzoli Museum,* Milan, Italy. ". . . the Reformation was not against art *as* art."

IN SILENCIO ET SPE ERIT   FORTITVDO VESTRA

on culture was not just for a favored elite but for all the people. There were also less-remembered men of the period who did remarkable work. We could think of Bach's predecessor as organist at Leipzig, Johann Kuhnau (1660–1722), who wrote biblical sonatas for the harpsichord in 1700.

Johann Sebastian Bach (1685–1750) was certainly the zenith of the composers coming out of the Reformation. His music was a direct result of the Reformation culture and the biblical Christianity of the time, which was so much a part of Bach himself. There would have been no Bach had there been no Luther. Bach wrote on his score initials representing such phrases as: "With the help of Jesus"—"To God alone be the glory"—"In the name of Jesus." It was appropriate that the last thing Bach the Christian wrote was "Before Thy Throne I Now Appear." Bach consciously related both the form and the words of his music to biblical truth. Out of the biblical context came a rich combination of music and words and a diversity with unity. This rested on the fact that the Bible gives unity to the universal and the particulars, and therefore the particulars have meaning. Expressed musically, there can be endless variety and diversity without chaos. There is variety yet resolution.

We must, of course, remember Handel who also stood in the same tradition. One naturally thinks of Handel's *Messiah* (1741), which was in the tradition of the restored Christianity in both its music and its message. Handel's religious music included not only the *Messiah* but *Saul* (c. 1738), *Israel in Egypt* (c. 1738) and *Samson* (1743). The *Messiah* could only have come forth in a setting where the Bible stood at the center. Even the order of the selections follows with extreme accuracy the Bible's teaching about the Christ as the Messiah. For example, Handel did not put the "Hallelujah Chorus" at the end, but in its proper place in the flow of the past and future history of Christ. Many modern performances often place it at the end as a musical climax, but Handel followed the Bible's teaching exactly and placed it at that future historic moment when the Bible says Christ will come back to rule upon the earth—at that point where the Bible prophetically (in the Book of Revelation) puts the cry of "King of kings and Lord of lords!" Handel probably knew Charles Wesley (1707–1788) and

29 Organ built during the time of Johann Sebastian Bach. "Bach was certainly the zenith of the composers coming out of the Reformation." *Photos by Mustafa Arshad.*

wrote the music for a hymn to original words by Wesley, "Rejoice, the Lord is King."

In passing, we should note that English church music followed the same emphasis found in the early music of Reformation Germany. A demand arose for a simplified style which would permit the words to be understood. We could mention here Thomas Tallis (c. 1505–1585) and Orlando Gibbons (1583–1625). In England as in Germany the stress was on content. Music was not incidental to the Reformation's return to biblical teaching; it was a natural outcome, a unity with what the Bible taught. What the Reformation produced musically gives us a clear affirmation that the Reformation was indeed interested in culture. As this was true in music, it was also true in visual art. We have already mentioned Cranach. We must also notice Dürer (1471–1528), Altdorfer (1480–1538), Hans Baldung-Grien (c. 1484–1545), and the Beham brothers: Hans (1500–1550) and Barthel (1502–1540).

Some of the work of Albrecht Dürer was done before the Reformation, yet he must be considered a Reformation artist. In 1521 he was in the Netherlands. (You will remember that Luther nailed his Ninety-five Theses to the door at Wittenberg on October 31, 1517.) There Dürer heard tidings that Luther had been taken captive. The rumor was false. Luther's friends had hidden him to protect his life, but most people thought he was a prisoner. Dürer was keeping a diary which he did not mean to have published. This diary is worth quoting at length (as translated by Udo Middelmann):

> On Friday before Pentecost (17th of May) in the year 1521 the news reached Antwerpen, that Martin Luther had been so treacherously taken prisoner. For when the herald of the emperor Charles had been ordered to accompany him with the emperial guard, he trusted this. But when the herald had brought him near Eisenach to an inhospitable place, he told him that he had no further need of him and rode off. Pretty soon ten riders on horseback appeared; they treacherously led away this deceived, pious man, who was illumined by the Holy Spirit and professed the true Christian faith. And is he still alive?

Or have they murdered him?—which I do not know—in that case he has suffered it for the sake of the Christian truth in that he chastized the unchristian papacy, which resists the liberation by Christ with its heavy burdens of human laws; and also for this reason has he suffered it, that we should even longer as until now be deprived and completely disrobed of all that is the fruit of our blood and sweat, and that this fruit should shamefully and blasphemously be consumed by idle folk while the thirsty, parched people die because of it.

And especially, the hardest factor for me is that God might possibly want to keep us under their false and blind teaching, which has only been composed and compiled by people whom they call fathers. Because of this, the delicious Word of God is wrongly exegeted or not at all taught in many places.

Oh God in heaven, have mercy on us. Oh Lord Jesus Christ, pray for your people, deliver us at the right time, preserve in us the right, true Christian faith, gather your widely scattered sheep by your voice, which is called the Word of God in Scripture. Help us that we might recognize this your voice and would not follow another tempting call, that would only be human imagination, so that we might never leave you, Lord Jesus Christ! . . . Oh God! You have never burdened a people so horribly with human laws as we are under the Roman chair, who desire daily to be free Christians, redeemed by your blood. Oh highest, heavenly Father! Pour into our hearts by your son Jesus Christ such light, that we might recognize which messenger we are constrained to obey, so that we might reject the burden of the others in good conscience and be able to serve you, eternal heavenly Father, with a glad and cheerful heart.

And should we have lost this man, who has written more clearly than any other that has lived in the last 140 years and to whom you have given such an evangelical spirit,

we pray you, Oh heavenly Father, that you would give
your Holy Spirit again to someone who would gather
your holy Christian Church so that we might live together again in a Christian manner and that because
of our good works all unbelievers, as there are Turks,
heathen, and Kalicutes, would desire after us of themselves and would accept the Christian faith. . . . Oh
Lord! Present us afterwards with the new, decorated
Jerusalem that descends from heaven, of which it is written in the Apocalypse, the holy pure gospel, which has
not been darkened by human doctrine.

Anyone, after all, who reads Martin Luther's books, can
see how his teaching is so clear and transparent when
he sets forth the holy gospel. Therefore these are to be
honored and ought not to be burned; unless one would
throw his opponents, who combat the truth at all times,
into the same fire together with their opinions, which
want to make Gods out of men; and one should then
proceed in this way that new printings of Luther's books
would again be available. Oh God, if Luther is dead, who
will henceforth proclaim the holy gospel with such
clarity? Oh God! What would he not have still been able
to write for us in ten or twenty more years?

In a letter to George Spalatin in 1520 Dürer wrote:

In all subservience may I ask your grace to recommend
to you the praiseworthy Dr. Luther, for the sake of the
Christian truth, for which we care more than all riches
or power of this world, for all this passes with time, only
the truth remains eternally. And help me God, that I
might get to Dr. Martinus Luther, so that I might dili-
gently picture him and etch him in copper for a lasting
memorial of this Christian man who has helped me out
of great anxieties. And I ask you, your honor, that if
Dr. Martinus produces something new in German, you
would send it to me against my money.

There are a number of things to notice in these quotations. Dürer says Luther has written more clearly than anyone for 140 years. John Wycliffe had lived from 1320 to 1384, John Huss from 1369 to 1415. Dürer's diary was written in 1521. When we subtract 140 years from this date, we arrive at 1381, which falls in the lifetime of both Wycliffe and Huss. Dürer may have had both men in mind, but probably he was thinking of Huss, for Huss's influence had remained strong in southern Germany. One thing is clear: Dürer was in the line of these men before the Reformation who had set forth many of the Reformation's basic ideas, especially the Bible as the only final authority. Notice how this fits in with what Dürer wrote about Martin Luther. A second prominent idea of Huss—that salvation did not come through the addition of man's works but through Christ and his work only—is also found echoed in the diary.

Thus Dürer was indeed a man in the stream of the Reformation when he did his great woodcuts illustrating the *Apocalypse* (1498) and his copperplate engravings of *The Knight, Death, and the Devil* (1513) and *St. Jerome in His Cell* (1514), even if he did them before Luther nailed his Theses to the door. Further, notice how he twice quotes from the Apocalypse (the last book in the Bible). This clearly ties in with his previous woodcuts and shows that even when he did them these thoughts were involved. His art is as much a cultural result of the Reformation as is Bach's music. Dürer lived at the same time as Raphael, Michelangelo and Leonardo. When he was thirteen years old, he already took nature seriously. His beautiful watercolors of flowers, rabbits, and so on were a clear exhibition that God's world has value, a real value.

I am not at all saying that the art which the Reformation produced was in every case greater as art than the art of the south. *The point is that to say that the Reformation depreciated art and culture or that it did not produce art and culture is either nonsense or dishonest.*

It is not only Christians who can paint with beauty, nor for that matter only Christians who can love or who have creative stirrings. Even though the image is now contorted, people are made in the image of God. This is who people are, whether or not they know or acknowledge it. God is the great Creator, and part of the unique mannishness of man, as made in God's image, is creativity. Thus, man as man paints, shows creativity in science and engineering and so on. Such activity does not require a special impulse from God, and it does not mean that people are not alienated from God and do not need the work of Christ to return to God. It does mean that man as man, in contrast to non-man, is creative. A person's world view almost always shows through in his creative output, however, and thus the marks on the things he creates will be different. This is so in all fields—for example, in the art of the Renaissance compared to that of the Reformation, or in the direction man's creative stirrings in science will assume, and whether and how the stirring will continue. In the case of the Reformation the art showed the good marks of its biblical base.

It was not only in Germany that the Reformation affirmed painting. The clearest example of the effects of the Reformation culture on painting is Rembrandt (1606–1669). Rembrandt had flaws in his life (as all people do), but he was a true Christian; he believed in the death of Christ for him personally. In 1633 he painted the *Raising of the Cross* for Prince Frederick Henry of Orange. It now hangs in the museum *Alte Pinakothek* in Münich. A man in a blue painter's beret raises Christ upon the cross. That man is Rembrandt himself—a self-portrait. He thus stated for all the world to see that his sins had sent Christ to the cross.

Rembrandt shows in all his work that he was a man of the Reformation; he neither idealized nature nor demeaned it. Moreover, Rembrandt's biblical base enabled him to excel in painting people with psychological depth. Man was great, but man was also cruel and broken, for he had revolted against God. Rembrandt's painting was thus lofty, yet down to earth. There was no need for him to slip into the world of illusion, as did much of the baroque painting which sprang out of the Catholic Counter-Reformation. Nature to this Dutch Reformation artist was a thing to be enjoyed as a creation of God. We can think of Rembrandt's painting *Danae* (1636) in the museum in Leningrad. This is a picture of Rembrandt's nude wife waiting in bed for him. Rembrandt himself is not in the picture. And yet as she waits for him to come from the left side, though still hidden, he is the center of the picture. There is love and gentleness here. Rembrandt understood that Christ is

30   *The Owl* and *Rhinoceron* by Dürer. ". . . a clear exhibition that God's world has value."

1508

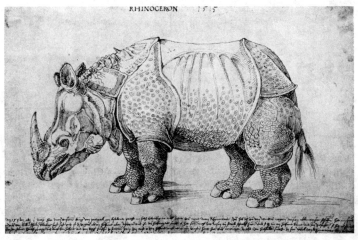

RHINOCERON 1515

the Lord of all of life. As a Christian, he lived in the midst of God's world and did not need to make himself God. Rather, he could use God's world and its form in his painting.

Many other Dutch artists stood firmly in the stream of Reformation culture. There were portrait painters, landscape painters, and still-life artists; for all of them everyday reality was seen as God's creation and thus as important. This was the right direction, a proper view of nature. Up to a certain point the development of the Renaissance in the south could have gone in a good direction or a poor one. But humanism took over—all was made autonomous and meaning was lost. In the Reformation, the right direction was regained, and nature and the whole of life were things of dignity and beauty.

In 1860 Jacob Burckhardt (1818–1897) in *The Civilization of the Renaissance in Italy* pointed out a crucial difference between the Renaissance and the Reformation. While no one now would follow Burckhardt exactly, his discussion of the contrast between the Renaissance and the Reformation is still the most remarkable one we have and seems to me to be still valid. He indicated that freedom was introduced both in the north by the Reformation and in the south by the Renaissance. But in the south it went to license; in the north it did not. The reason was that in Renaissance humanism man had no way to bring forth a meaning to the particulars of life and no place from which to get absolutes in morals. But in the north, the people of the Reformation, standing under the teaching of Scripture, had freedom and yet at the same time compelling absolute values.

Next four pages: **31**   *Raising of the Cross* by Rembrandt. ". . . a self-portrait." **32– 33**   Rembrandt etchings. ". . . people with psychological depth." *Etching photos courtesy of Rijkmuseum, Amsterdam.*   **34**   Two still lifes by Pieter Claesz. ". . . everyday reality was seen as God's creation." *Photos courtesy of Museum of Fine Arts, Boston.* Also shown is the author filming at Boston Museum of Fine Arts.

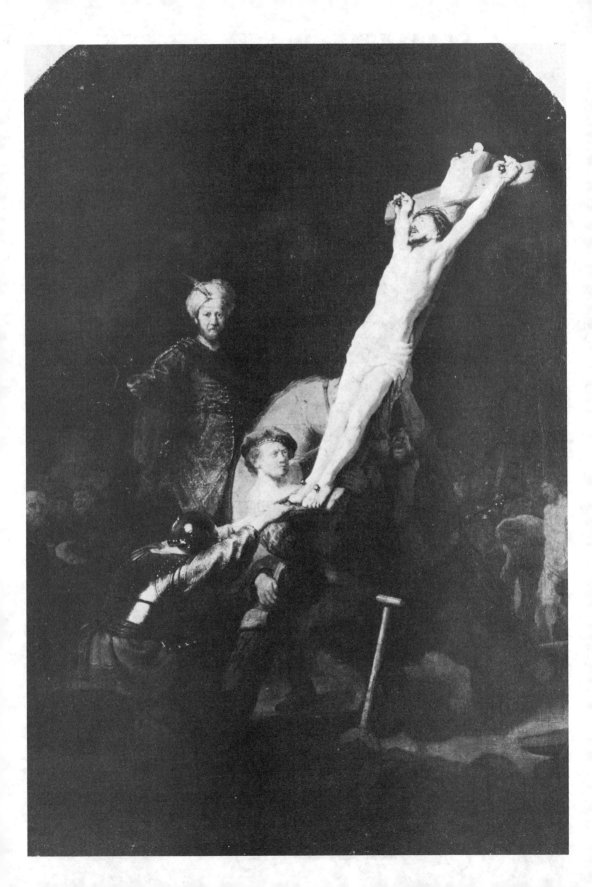

5 The Reformation— Continued

We have seen that the Reformation was neither against culture nor against art as art. Let us also note the political freedom which the return to biblical Christianity gradually brought forth. The accent here is on the word *gradually,* for all the results did not come at once. Let us emphasize again that the Reformation was no golden age; and our eyes should not turn back to it as if it were to be our perfect model. People have never carried out the biblical teaching perfectly. Nonetheless, wherever the biblical teaching has gone, even though it has always been marred by men, it not only has told of an open approach to God through the work of Christ, but also has brought peripheral results in society, including political institutions. Secondary results are produced by the preaching of the Gospel in both the arts and political affairs.

The Reformation did not bring social or political perfection, but it did gradually bring forth a vast and unique improvement. What the Reformation's return to biblical teaching gave society was the opportunity for tremendous freedom, but without chaos. That is, an individual had freedom because there was a consensus based upon the absolutes given in the Bible, and therefore real values within which to have freedom, without these freedoms leading to chaos. The world had not known anything like this before. In northern Europe, this view was seen in the form of society that resulted. The conveniently small Greek city-states for a short period of time attempted to have social and political participation for carefully defined segments of the population. And Roman law secured certain freedoms for Roman citizens—as we learn, for example, from the apostle Paul's experiences. Yet these never approached what the Reformation produced.

The basis for freedom without chaos is exhibited by Paul Robert's (1851–1923) mural which he entitled *Justice Lifts the Nations* (1905). To make his point so that it could not be missed, he painted the title on the mural itself. It is on the stairway in the old Supreme Court Building in Lausanne where the judges had to pass each time before going up to try a case. Robert wanted to remind them that the place which the Reformation gave to the Bible provided a basis not only for morals but for law. Robert pictured many types of legal cases in the foreground and the judges in their black robes standing behind the judges' bench. The problem is neatly posed: How shall the judges judge? On what basis shall they proceed so that their judgment will not be arbitrary? Above them Robert painted Justice standing unblindfolded, with her sword pointed not vertically upward but downward toward a book, and on the book is written "The Law of God." This painting expressed the sociological base, the legal base, in northern Europe after the Reformation. Paul Robert understood what the Reformation was all about in the area of law. It is the Bible which gives a base to law.

Robert was expressing at a later date what some men in the flow of the Reformation had already understood and had expressed verbally. Alexandre Vinet (1797–1847) was professor of theology at the Academy of Lausanne (now the university). He was the thinker in the canton of Vaud who stood in the stream of the Reformers who had preceded him in Switzerland. He was the foremost representative of French Protestantism in the French-speaking world of his day. He said, "Christianity is the immortal seed of freedom of the world." Switzerland's unique freedoms rest on this base. Vinet did not just talk and write about these things, but was the outspoken leader for both freedom of religious worship and freedom of the conscience in relationship to the state. A statue of Vinet with the above quote on it is situated only a few hundred feet from the old Supreme Court Building in which Robert later painted his mural.

35 *Justice Lifts the Nations* by Paul Robert in the old Supreme Court Building, Lausanne, Switzerland. ". . . freedom without chaos." *Photo by Mustafa Arshad.*

In the Anglo-Saxon world, England showed clearly the results of the Reformation, as did Holland and in varying degrees the other Reformation countries. Too often we think of law, however, only in the context of civil and criminal conduct, forgetting that law is related to the entire structure of a society, including its government. Here the return to the Bible in the Reformation had an important and beneficial influence. The exact impact in any one place or country varied according to circumstance and opportunity. But, in general, the constitutionalist ideas of a Martin Bucer (1491–1551), who was a leader of the Reformation in Strasbourg and important throughout all the Reformation countries, or a John Calvin produced results because—unlike the moribund contract ideas of the late Middle Ages—they did not lose contact with daily life.

Bucer was one of the most levelheaded and charitable Reformers and had the strongest personal influence on Calvin's deep-rooted conciliatory views in church affairs at Geneva and in church-state relations. The constitutionalist model, implicit in Presbyterian church government, was not just an example but an education in the principle of political limitation. And where, as in England, Presbyterianism as such did not triumph, its political ideas were communicated through the many complex groups which made up the Puritan element in English public life and played a creative role in trimming the power of the English kings. As a result, the ordinary citizen discovered a freedom from arbitrary governmental power in an age when in other countries the advance toward absolutist political options was restricting liberty of expression.

Thus the biblical insistence on the responsibility of people—even of monarchs—to God's law turned the political tide in those countries where the Reformation emphasis on the Bible as the only final authority took root. Elsewhere, it was natural politically for the centralizing monarchs to welcome the aid of the monarchical Roman Church in controlling political (as well as religious) heterodoxy. In England the threat of absolutism was thwarted. Here was a country where increasingly men lived without fear of arbitrary revenge.

Many good things in England came from Scotland. The clearest example of the Reformation principle of a people's political control of its sovereign is a book written by a Scot, Samuel Rutherford (1600–1661). The book is *Lex Rex:* Law Is King. When it was published in 1644, Rutherford was one of the Scottish commissioners at the Westminster Assembly in London. Later he became rector of St. Andrew's University in Scotland. What Paul Robert painted for the justices at the Supreme Court Building Samuel Rutherford had already laid down in writing in this book. Here was a concept of freedom without chaos because there was a form. Or, to put it another way, here was a government of law rather than of the arbitrary decisions of men—because the Bible as the final authority was there as the base. This went beyond the Conciliar Movement and the early medieval parliaments, for these had no base beyond inconsistent church pronouncements and the changing winds of political events.

Samuel Rutherford's work and the tradition it embodied had a great influence on the United States Constitution, even though modern Anglo-Saxons have largely forgotten him. This influence was mediated through two sources. The first was John Witherspoon (1723–1794), a Presbyterian who followed Samuel Rutherford's *Lex Rex* directly and brought its principles to bear on the writing of the Constitution and the laying down of forms and freedoms. Witherspoon, educated at Edinburgh University, became president of the College of New Jersey (now Princeton University) in 1768. He was a member of the Continental Congress from 1776 to 1779 and from 1780 to 1782. The only clergyman to sign the Declaration of Independence, he played an important role on a number of the committees of the Congress.

The second mediator of Rutherford's influence was John Locke (1632–1704), who, though secularizing the Presbyterian tradition, nevertheless drew heavily from it. He stressed inalienable rights, government by consent, separation of powers, and the right of revolution. But the biblical base for these is discovered in Rutherford's work. Without this biblical background, the whole system would be without a foundation. This is seen by the fact that Locke's own work has an inherent contradiction. His empiricism, as revealed in his *Essay Concerning Human Understanding* (1690), really leaves no place for "natural rights." Empiricism would rest everything on experience. But "natural rights" must either be innate

to the nature of man and not based on experience (thereby conflicting with the concept of empiricism) or they must have an adequate
base other than man's experience. Locke's difficulty was that he
did not have Samuel Rutherford's Christian base. He stated the
results which come from biblical Christianity without having
the base which produced them. That is, he secularized Christian
teaching.

Thomas Jefferson (1743–1826) picked up the secularized form,
often tying it into classical examples. Not all the individual men
who laid down the foundation for the United States Constitution
were Christians; many, in fact, were deists. But we should realize
that the word *Christian* can legitimately be used two ways. The
primary meaning is: an individual who has come to God through
the work of Christ. The second meaning must be kept distinct but
also has validity. It is possible for an individual to live within the
circle of that which a Christian consensus brings forth, even though
he himself is not a Christian in the first sense. This may be true in
many areas—for example, in the arts or political thought. Many
of the men who laid the foundation of the United States Constitution were not Christians in the first sense, and yet they built upon
the basis of the Reformation either directly through the *Lex Rex*
tradition or indirectly through Locke. To whatever degree a society
allows the teaching of the Bible to bring forth its natural conclusions, it is able to have form and freedom in society and
government.

So the Reformation's preaching of the Gospel brought forth two
things which were secondary to the central message of the Gospel
but nonetheless were important: an interest in culture and a true
basis for form and freedom in society and government. The latter
carries with it an important corollary, namely, that 51 percent of
the vote never becomes the final source of right and wrong in
government because the absolutes of the Bible are available to
judge a society. The "little man," the private citizen, can at any
time stand up and, on the basis of biblical teaching, say that the
majority is wrong. So, to the extent to which the biblical teaching
is practiced, one can control the despotism of the majority vote
or the despotism of one person or group.

36 Independence Hall, Philadelphia. ". . . the laying down of forms and freedoms."
National Park Service Photo.

The Reformation in northern Europe also contributed to checks and balances in government. This idea was, of course, not new in the sixteenth century. Some form of checks and balances was implicit in some medieval political thought, as we saw earlier, and a particular form of it is central to so-called Polybian republicanism, which supposedly exemplified the best elements in Greek and Roman practice. Polybian republicanism is named for Polybius (c. 198–c. 117 B.C.), a Greek who wrote a history of the growth of the Roman Republic in terms which were designed to cause his fellow Greeks to accept Roman rule. Polybian republicanism—which Niccolò Machiavelli (1469–1527) embraced—was, however, economically and politically elitist. Since Machiavelli had witnessed the destruction of Florentine republicanism, he was interested in the Polybian theory of political cycles, which involved a cyclical view of history. Machiavelli therefore wrote *The Prince,* advocating firm autocratic rule, because in his view only the dictatorial regime of the "ideal" prince could push along the cycle of political history; only the exercise of ruthlessness could improve the cycles. Machiavelli already showed in his day that ultimately the humanist Renaissance had no more of a universal in political morals than it had in personal morals. Machiavelli's *The Prince*—destined to become a handbook of political practice used by heads of state as remote in time as Benito Mussolini (1883–1945) and Adolf Hitler (1889–1945)—stands in sharp contrast to the checks-and-balances tradition encouraged by the Reformation.

The Reformers were not romantic about man. With their strong emphasis on the Fall, they understood that since every person is indeed a sinner there is a need for checks and balances, especially on people in power. For this reason, Calvin himself in Geneva did not have the authority often attributed to him. As we have seen, Calvin had been greatly influenced by the thinking of Bucer in regard to these things. In contrast to a formalized or institutional authority, Calvin's influence was moral and informal. This was so not only in political matters (in which historians recognize that Calvin had little or no direct say), but also in church affairs. For example, he preferred to have the Lord's Supper given weekly, but he allowed the will of the majority of the pastors in Geneva to prevail. Thus the Lord's Supper was celebrated only once every three months.

Each Reformation country showed the practice of checks and balances in different forms. Switzerland (whose national political life was shaped by the Reformation tradition even though not all its cantons followed the Reformation) is especially interesting in this regard. Since the mid-nineteenth century, the Swiss have separated geographically the legislative and executive parts of government from the judiciary, placing the former in Bern, the latter in Lausanne. In Great Britain came the checks and balances of a king, two Houses of Parliament, and the courts. Today the monarch has less authority than when the division of power was made, but the concept of checks and balances continues. The United States has a slightly different arrangement, but with the same basic principle. The White House covers the executive administration; Congress, in two balanced parts, is the legislature; the Supreme Court embodies the judiciary. In the Reformation countries, there was a solution to the "form" or "chaos" problem in society.

We must repeat that when Christians who came out of the Reformation tradition had more influence than they do now on the consensus in the northern European culture (which would include the United States, Canada, Australia, New Zealand, and so on), this did not mean that they achieved perfection. Even when the Reformation had more influence on generally accepted thinking than is the case today, as the centuries passed, weaknesses definitely existed and certain specific weaknesses gradually developed. At certain points the people in the stream of the Reformation were inconsistent with the biblical teaching they claimed to follow. There were many areas where the Bible was not followed as it should have been, but two are outstanding: first, a twisted view of race, and second, a noncompassionate use of accumulated wealth.

In the area of race there were two types of abuse. The first was slavery based on race; the second, racial prejudice as such. Both practices were wrong, and often both were present when Christians had a stronger influence on the consensus than they now have— and yet the church, as the church, did not speak out sufficiently against them.

The conditions on the slave ships—in which thousands died crossing the seas—the treatment slaves often received, and, in a special way, slavery based on skin color, cannot be just passed over. For complex reasons still debated by historians, Englishmen, continental Europeans, and Americans indulged in the fiction that the black man was not a person and could therefore be treated as a thing. This fiction covered their hypocrisy. Actually they harked back to Aristotle's definition of a slave as a living tool and were far removed from the biblical teaching. And in this situation the church *as* the church was all too often silent.

Today's Christians, by identification with their forebears, must acknowledge these inconsistencies in regard to a twisted view of race. We can use no lesser word than *sin* to describe those instances where the practice was (or is) so far from what the Bible directs. The most effective acknowledgment is for Christians to strive in the present to follow the Bible at these points. Of course, slavery was not only practiced in these Christian countries. In fact, in some Moslem countries, black slavery continues to the present day. But that does not lessen the wrongness of a twisted view of race in the countries where churches out of the Reformation tradition could have done more about it.

The lack of a compassionate use of accumulated wealth, especially following the Industrial Revolution, must also be faced squarely. We must not, of course, forget all the good things industrialization brought forth. The age belonged to the inventors and the engineers who harnessed first the power of water and then the power of steam. And out of that time came a steady stream of better things (one small example would be better pottery for the use of working people), and the base was laid for a greater flow of goods for people in general. If industrialization had been accompanied by a strong emphasis on the compassionate use of accumulated wealth and on the dignity of each individual, the Industrial Revolution would have indeed been a revolution for good. But all too often in England and other countries the church was silent about the Old and the New Testament's emphasis on a compassionate use of wealth. Individual efforts of charity did not excuse this silence. Following industrialization, the noncompassionate use of accumulated wealth was particularly glaring.

37 Water power and steam power. "The age belonged to the inventors." *Photos courtesy of Mary-Evans Picture Library.*

MOLA AQVARIA.
Aquarias quisquis molas antiquitus *Putat repertas, tota aberrat is via.*

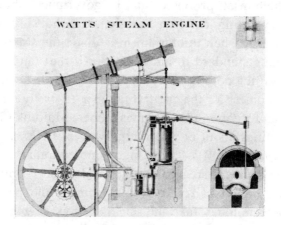

WATTS STEAM ENGINE

STEAM ENGINE

CISTERN OF COLD WATER

It was not that the majority of the people were worse off than under the previous agrarian situation, but rather that the wealth produced by the Industrial Revolution was not used with compassion. This resulted in the growth of the slums in London and other cities and industrial towns, the exploitation of children and women (who suffered especially), and the general discrepancy between the vast wealth of the few and the misery of the many (whose average working day was between twelve and sixteen hours). Seldom did the church, as the church, lift its voice against such "utilitarianism" (the teaching that utility is the ultimate appeal on all ethical questions).

It is significant that the evils of slavery and the noncompassionate use of wealth merged at this point, as slave owners used the arguments of utilitarianism to plead their cause. It must be said in fairness to Jeremy Bentham (1748–1832), the father of utilitarianism, that he himself proposed that the government should intervene to protect working children and improve housing and working conditions. But when utilitarianism is made the standard—if there is no absolute standard to judge it by or if the standard existing in the Bible is not courageously applied—then the concept of "the greatest happiness for the greatest number" is easily manipulated.

It is often forgotten that Thomas Robert Malthus (1766–1834), whose warnings about population growth in *An Essay on the Principle of Population* (1798) are much quoted today, also advocated a hands-off policy in regard to social reforms. To him, poverty is inevitable, and social reforms only increase the problems. Some of his followers today take the same position, saying, for example, that medical care for all people is an evil rather than a good. The same note came from David Ricardo (1772–1823), who in 1817 wrote the first real economics textbook *The Principles of Political Economy and Taxation*. A tragic example of the acceptance of these views was the attitude toward the Irish potato famine held by Charles Edward Trevelyan (1807–1886), who was in charge of government relief in Ireland. He withheld government assistance from the Irish on the grounds that they should help themselves and that to do otherwise would encourage them to be lazy. It was not that he lacked compassion or a social conscience (his later career shows otherwise), but that at a crucial point a sub-Christian prejudice stifled the teaching of Christ and the Bible, and sealed Ireland's doom.

These views were *not* the product of the Christian consensus, but the churches of that time must be criticized for not shouting loudly enough against these abuses. The churches could have changed things in that day if they had spoken with clarity and courage. The central reason the church should have spoken clearly and courageously on these issues is that the Bible commands it. Had the church been faithful to the Bible's teaching about the compassionate use of wealth, it would not later have lost so many of the workers. And if it had spoken clearly against the use of wealth as a weapon in a kind of "survival of the fittest," in all probability this concept as it came into secularized science would not have been so automatically accepted. Of course, the church's silence was not only a problem in England. It was equally a problem in the United States. And in the area of slavery, the United States must bear special criticism, since slavery based on race continued there until such a late date.

To keep the matter in balance: In the first place it must be said that many non-Christian influences were also at work in the culture. Likewise, many influential people who automatically called themselves Christians were not Christian at all; it was merely socially acceptable to bear the name and go through the outward forms. In the second place, many Christians *did* take a vital and vocal lead in the fight against these abuses. Many Christians struggled to bring into being the social realities that should accompany a Christian consensus. Pastors and others spoke out as prophets, often at great personal cost to themselves. The Bible makes plain that there should be effects in society from the preaching of the Gospel, and voices were raised to emphasize this fact and lives were given to illustrate it.

John Howard (1726–1790), John Wesley's friend, labored indefatigably for the reform of the prisons. A Quaker, Elizabeth Fry (1780–1845), had a profound and practical compassion for the prisoners at Newgate. The better-known Lord Shaftesbury (1801–1885) carried on an endless battle to prevent the exploitation of women and children in the mines and factories; he well understood the meaning of a compassionate use of wealth. John Wesley (1703–

1791) was himself a strong critic of slavery, and he spoke his mind bluntly, including very frank statements against the slavery he observed in the United States. John Newton (1725–1807), after he became a Christian, not only was no longer a slave trader but turned against the trade. Thomas Clarkson (1760–1846), who spoke out so clearly against the slave trade, was the son of a clergyman in the Church of England and was an admirer and historian of the Quakers.

William Wilberforce (1759–1833) was able to utilize Clarkson's pioneer work. Wilberforce fought for many years in Parliament against the slave trade, battling for the basic recognition of the black man's humanity under God. Wilberforce the Christian—and because he was Christian—was the outstanding voice in England against the slave trade. Finally slave trade was prohibited in England in 1807, and as Wilberforce was dying, slavery itself was abolished there. Slavery was forbidden throughout the British colonies in a bill passed in 1833, to be effective in 1834. The British taxpayers paid twenty million pounds sterling as compensation to the owners of the slaves. One could wish that the United States had had some outstanding Christian as consistent as Wilberforce, someone in a position of influence who could have produced the same result in the United States at the same date, or better, much before! Or better still, to have kept slavery out of the United States entirely.

The black church in the United States cannot, of course, be included in our criticism about the silence of the churches. It was giving much to the United States in many ways, including its cultural heritage—of which the wonder of its music was a part—but it had no way to speak effectively about slavery. This was especially so in those states where black slavery was practiced. Anyone with a tendency to minimize the brutality of the slavery which existed in the United States should read Charles Dickens's (1812–1870) *American Notes* (1842). He begins this portion of the book by saying, "The upholders of slavery in America—of the atrocities of which system I shall not write one word for which I have not ample proof and warrant . . . ." He then goes on to quote pages of newspaper ads which speak profoundly for themselves. Here are four examples out of the dozens which Dickens quotes: "Ran away, a negro boy about 12 years old. Had round his neck a chain dog-collar with 'De Lampert' engraved on it." "Detained at the police jail, the negro wench, Myra. Has several marks of lashing, and has irons on her feet." "One hundred dollars reward for a negro fellow, Pompoy, 40 years old. He is branded on the left jaw." "Ran away, a negro woman and two children. A few days before she went off, I burned her with a hot iron, on the left side of her face. I tried to make the letter M."

In the United States some groups did speak out. The Reformed Presbyterian Church in the United States decreed as a denomination as early as 1800 that no slave holder should be retained in their communion, and after that date no slave holder was admitted.

We should also mention the impact of the George Whitefield (1714–1770)-John Wesley revivals and the early Methodists and others who emerged from the revivals, from whom came so much emphasis on political, educational, and economic reform. In fact, the Cambridge historian J. H. Plumb (1911–) indicated that it is not too much to say that, without the influence which the Whitefield-Wesley revivals had at the grass roots, it is doubtful whether England would have avoided its own version of the French Revolution.

6 The Enlightenment

In the area of political reform, the results of the Reformation are impressive. One can think of Dickens's *Tale of Two Cities* (1859)—with Paris given over to the goddess of Reason, and London with all its inconsistencies—as having a Reformation base.

The change in England in 1688 could be and *was* bloodless. We must not discount the earlier civil wars, but the decisive change in England in 1688 was bloodless—so much so that among historians it is called the "Bloodless Revolution." At that time William III of Orange and Mary became monarchs, and it was made clear that Parliament was not a junior partner but an equal partner with the crown. This arrangement brought about the deliberate control of the monarchy within specific legal bounds.

The French philosopher Voltaire (1694–1778), often called "father of the Enlightenment," was greatly influenced by the results of this bloodless revolution in England during his time of exile there (1726–1729). The impact of the Bloodless Revolution and the ensuing freedom of public expression is shown in Voltaire's *Letters Concerning the English Nation* (1733). He wrote, "The English are the only people upon earth who have been able to prescribe limits to the power of Kings by resisting them, and who, by a series of struggles, have at last established . . . that wise government where the prince is all powerful to do good, and at the same time

120

is restrained from committing evil . . . and where the people share in the government without confusion."

While Voltaire is sometimes overflattering about English conditions, he may be excused because of the terrible contrast in France. There were indeed vast areas in France which needed righting, but when the French Revolution tried to reproduce the English conditions without the Reformation base, but rather on Voltaire's humanist Enlightenment base, the result was a bloodbath and a rapid breakdown into the authoritarian rule of Napoleon Bonaparte (1769–1821).

The utopian dream of the Enlightenment can be summed up by five words: reason, nature, happiness, progress, and liberty. It was thoroughly secular in its thinking. The humanistic elements which had risen during the Renaissance came to flood tide in the Enlightenment. Here was man starting from himself absolutely. And if the humanistic elements of the Renaissance stand in sharp contrast to the Reformation, the Enlightenment was in total antithesis to it. The two stood for and were based upon absolutely different things in an absolute way, and they produced absolutely different results.

To the Enlightenment thinkers, man and society were perfectible. And the French romantically held to this view even in the midst of the Reign of Terror. Voltaire sketched out four epochs of history, of which his own was the apex. Marquis de Condorcet (1743–1794), a mathematician, who was one of the philosophers of Voltaire's circle and who was the author of *Sketch for a Historical Picture of the Progress of the Human Mind* (1793–1794), could talk of nine stages of progress as he hid in a garret in Paris while hiding from the Terror! While hiding for his very life from Robespierre's secret police, he wrote: "We have witnessed the development of a new doctrine which is to deliver the final blow to the already tottering structure of prejudice. It is the idea of the limitless perfectibility of the human species . . . ." Later he managed to escape from Paris, was recognized, arrested, and imprisoned, dying in custody while awaiting his turn at the guillotine.

If these men had a religion, it was deism. The deists believed in a God who had created the world but who had no contact with it now, and who had not revealed truth to men. If there was a God, he was silent. And Voltaire demanded no speech from him—save when, after the Lisbon earthquake in 1755, Voltaire illogically complained of his nonintervention. The men of the French Enlightenment had no base but their own finiteness. They looked across the Channel to a Reformation England, tried to build without the Christian base, and ended with a massacre and Napoleon as authoritarian ruler.

In June 1789, the first phase of the liberal bourgeois plan of the French Revolution was at its height. Jacques-Louis David (1748–1825) depicted this in his painting *The Oath of the Tennis Court.* Here the members of the National Assembly swore to establish a constitution. Their base, consciously, was purely a humanist theory of rights. On August 26, 1789, they issued the Declaration of the Rights of Man. It sounded fine, but it had nothing to rest upon. In the Declaration of the Rights of Man what was called "the Supreme Being" equaled "the sovereignty of the nation"—that is, the general will of the people. Not only was there a contrast to England's Bloodless Revolution, but a sharp contrast with what resulted in the United States from the Declaration of Independence which was made thirteen years earlier. One had the Reformation base, the other did not.

It took two years for the National Constituent Assembly to draft a constitution (1789–1791). Within a year it was a dead letter. By that time what is often known as the Second French Revolution was in motion, leading to a bloodbath that ended with the revolutionary leaders themselves being killed.

To make their outlook clear, the French changed the calendar and called 1792 the "year one," and destroyed many of the things of the past, even suggesting the destruction of the cathedral at Chartres. They proclaimed the goddess of Reason in Notre-Dame Cathedral in Paris and in other churches in France, including Chartres. In Paris, the goddess was personified by an actress, Demoiselle Candeille, carried shoulder-high into the cathedral by men dressed in Roman costumes.

Like the humanists of the Renaissance, the men of the Enlightenment pushed aside the Christian base and heritage and looked back to the old pre-Christian times. In Voltaire's home in Ferney the picture he hung (in such a way on the wall at the foot of his bed

38 *The Oath of the Tennis Court* by David. ". . . purely a humanist theory of rights."

that it was the first thing he saw each day) was a painting of the goddess Diana with a small new crescent moon on her head and a very large one under her feet. She is reaching down to help men.

How quickly all the humanist ideals came to grief! In September 1792 began the massacre in which some 1,300 prisoners were killed. Before it was all over, the government and its agents killed 40,000 people, many of them peasants. Maximilien Robespierre (1758–1794), the revolutionary leader, was himself executed in July 1794. This destruction came not from outside the system; it was produced by the system. As in the later Russian Revolution the revolutionaries on their humanist base had only two options—anarchy or repression.

The parallels between the course of the French Revolution and the later Russian Revolution, both resting on the same base, are striking. Sometimes the French Revolution is likened to what occurred in the United States at a slightly earlier date. This is incorrect. While there were some historic crosscurrents between the United States and France, the similarities are in the Bloodless Revolution in England and the Revolution in the United States. In sharp contrast to both of these are the likenesses in the French Revolution and the later Russian Revolution. A factor in the parallel between the French Revolution and the Russian is that by 1799 Napoleon had arrived as the elite to govern France—as later Lenin, also as the elite, took over the rule of Russia.

Mention of the later Russian Revolution evokes the observation that a quite different dynamic was involved in the political fortunes of those parts of Europe structurally influenced by the restoration of biblical Christianity in the sixteenth century as compared to those not so influenced. In crude geopolitical terms, there is a contrast between the north of Europe and the south and east. Allowing for local influences, it would seem that the inspiration for most revolutionary changes in the south of Europe was a copy, but often in contorted form, of the freedoms gained from the Reformation in the north. In Italy, Giuseppe Garibaldi (1807–1882) gleaned his ideals from the north of Europe and had to carry them into the peninsula by force. In Spain, where the Inquisition continued into the eighteenth century, persecution and lack of freedom has lasted in one form or another up to our own day.

39 Symbolic engraving of the terror of the guillotine. "The government and its agents killed 40,000 people, many of them peasants."

LES FORMES ACERBES

Cette allégorique représente JOSEPH LE BON,* *posté entre les deux guillotines d'Arras et de Cambray, tenant deux calices dans lesquels il reçoit d'une main et [...]tre du sang de ses nombreuses victimes, im[...]* *[...] communes. Il est monté sur des groupes de cadavres entassés les uns sur les autres, d'un côté deux furies dignes compagnes de ce Cannibal animent des animaux moins féroces qu'elles, à dévorer les restes des malheureux qu'elles ne peuvent pl[...]* *[...] nombre de détenus de l'un et l'autre sexe, amenés sur le bord du précipice, tendent les mains au ciel, où ils aperçoivent la Convention Nationale, à qui la justice décèle la vérité, tenant deux brochures intitulées l'une les louanges de la mor[...]* *[...] prisons d'Arras, réclaves par les autres dans leurs fers, l'autre, atrocités exercées envers les femmes.» De le fond du Tableau représente des prisons et indique le résultat des exercices présentés par la société ainsi dous, répétons ce refrain d[...]*

Barbérque, direxit, ino[...]

Guerre à tous les agens du Crime! Partagez l'horreur qui m'anime.

de la Bibliothèque Impériale le [...] Avril [...] Poursuivons les jusqu'au trépas, Ils ne nous échaperont pas;

And what the Reformation produced—by native growth as in England or by borrowing as in Italy—is all in gigantic contrast to what Communist countries continue to produce. Marxist-Leninist Communists have a great liability in arguing their case because so far in no place have the Communists gained and continued in power, building on their materialistic base, without repressive policies. And they have not only stifled political freedom but freedom in every area of life, including the arts. To mention only early examples in the field of music, Igor Stravinsky (1882–1971) and Sergei Rachmaninoff (1873–1943) left Russia in order to have liberty while Sergei Prokofiev (1891–1953) and Dmitri Shostakovich (1906–) chose to stay, only to meet with constant repression.

It should not be forgotten that the Leninists, the Bolsheviks, did not make the break for freedom in Russia. That came with the "February Revolution" of 1917. Prince Georgi Lvov (1861–1925) became prime minister of the provisional government and was succeeded by Aleksandr Kerensky (1881–1970) in July. Kerensky was a social reformer but not a Leninist. Vladimir Ilyich Lenin (1870–1924), Leon Trotsky (1879–1940), and Joseph Stalin (1879–1953) did not even return to Russia until after the victory of the February Revolution. Lenin returned from Switzerland in April, Trotsky from New York in May. Stalin returned from Siberia in March. In October 1917 they took over a revolution that had been made by others, and from the beginning under Lenin they built a regime of repression.

Solzhenitsyn says in *Communism: A Legacy of Terror* (1975), "I repeat, this was March 1918—only four months after the October Revolution—all the representatives of the Petrograd factories were cursing the Communists, who had deceived them in all their promises. What is more, not only had they abandoned Petrograd to cold and hunger, themselves having fled from Petrograd to Moscow, but had given orders to machine gun the crowds of workers in the courtyards of the factories who were demanding the election of independent factory committees."

The Bolsheviks were only a small percentage of the Russian people and made up only one-fourth of the constituent assembly which had been elected in November. When the assembly met for the first time in January 1918, the Bolshevist troops dispersed it by force. That was the first and last free election in Russia. Before the Leninists took over in October, Lenin wrote a book called *The Lessons of the Paris Commune*. There he analyzed why the Paris Commune was defeated in 1871. His principal conclusion was that the Commune had not killed enough of its enemies. When Lenin came to power he acted according to this analysis and set up all the machinery for oppression.

Communists speak about "socialism" and "communism," maintaining that socialism is only the temporary stage, with a utopian communism ahead. Over a half-century has passed and not only have they not achieved the goal of "communism" anywhere, they have not even come to a free socialism. The "temporary dictatorship of the proletariat" has proven, wherever the Communists have had power, to be in reality a dictatorship by a small elite—and not temporary but permanent. No place with a communistic base has produced freedom of the kind brought forth under the Reformation in northern Europe.

Communists have had to function on the basis of internal repression. We can think of the repression begun under Lenin, as well as the Stalin purges, the Berlin Wall built in 1961 to confine the people of East Germany by force, or the disappearance of freedom in China. Externally they hold their "allies" by coercion—the clearest examples being the secret execution of thousands of Polish officers buried in Katya Forest as the Communists prepared to make Poland their "ally," and the Russian tanks in East Germany in 1953, in Hungary in 1956, and in Czechoslovakia in 1968. In Czechoslovakia the repression did not end with the tanks; later, half a million followers of Alexander Dubček (1921–) were purged from the Communist party.

Seeing the contrast between the Reformation countries and the southern European and Communist countries, we must not minimize the riches in government and society which came forth from the Reformation. Even in those places where the Reformation consensus was less consistent than it should have been, on the basis of the biblical view there were absolutes on which to combat injustice. Men like Shaftesbury, Wilberforce, and Wesley could say that the evils and injustices which they fought were absolutely wrong. And even if we must say with sorrow that all too often Christians were silent when they should have spoken out, especially in the areas of race and the compassionate use of accumulated wealth, the Christians who were silent were inconsistent with their position.

In contrast to this, humanism has no final way of saying certain things are right and other things are wrong. For a humanist, the final thing which exists—that is, the impersonal universe—is neutral and silent about right and wrong, cruelty and non-cruelty. Humanism has no way to provide absolutes. Thus, as a consistent result of humanism's position, humanism in private morals and political life is left with that which is arbitrary.

A good illustration is that at first in Russia, on the basis of Karl Marx's (1818–1883) teaching in the 1848 *Manifesto of the Communist Party,* marriage was considered a part of capitalism (private prostitution, as he expressed it) and the family was thus minimized. Later, the state decreed a code of strict family laws. This was simply an "arbitrary absolute" imposed because it worked better. There is no base for right or wrong, and the arbitrary absolutes can be reversed for totally opposite ones at any time. For the Communists, laws always have a ground only in the changing historic situation brought about by the ongoing of history.

On the biblical basis, there *are* absolutes, and therefore we can say that certain things are right or wrong, including racial discrimination and social injustice. Consider Jesus standing in front of the tomb of Lazarus. The New Testament records that Jesus not only wept but was angry. The one who claimed to be God could be angry at the abnormality of death without being angry at himself. To a Christian on the basis of what the Bible teaches, not only is death abnormal, so is the cruelty of man to man. These things did not exist as God made the world. A Christian can fight the abnormality which has resulted from man's rebellion against God without fighting the final reality of what is—that is, without fighting God. Therefore, because God exists and there are absolutes, justice can be seen as absolutely good and not as just expedient.

These matters are not just theoretical but eminently practical, as can be seen from the results produced in England and the United States in contrast to those produced in France at the time of the Enlightenment, and later in Russia.

40   The Berlin Wall. ". . . to confine the people of East Germany by force." *Photos by Mustafa Arshad.*

Den Toten der Mauer
13.8.1961 – 13.8.1971

7 The Rise of Modern Science

Two eras in history came almost simultaneously: the High Renaissance and, in contrast to it, the Reformation. A third phenomenon which we must deal with began at approximately the same time. It is often called the Scientific Revolution.

We can date the rise of modern science with Copernicus (1475–1543), the Polish astronomer, and Vesalius (1514–1564) who was Italian. But this is not to say that nothing that could be called science preceded them. The Greeks, the Arabs, and the Chinese had a deep knowledge of the world. The Chinese, however, developed few general scientific theories based on their knowledge, and medieval science largely accepted Aristotle as the ultimate authority. In the Arabic world there was much discussion in this area, but it would seem that the principles by which they comprehended the world were formed under the combined influence of Aristotelianism and Neo-Platonism. The Arabic scholars did remarkable work, especially in mathematics—in trigonometry and algebra, for example, and in astronomy. Omar Khayyam (c. 1048–c. 1122)—who is better known for his *Rubaiyat,* in which he carries to its logical conclusion the Islamic concept of fate—calculated the length of the solar year and carried algebra further than it had been taken before. But with the Arabs as with medieval Europeans, science was considered one aspect of philosophy, with the traditions of the philosophers, especially Aristotle, ruling su-

130

preme. That is, medieval science was based on authority rather than observation. It developed through logic rather than experimentation, though there were notable exceptions.

The foundation for modern science can be said to have been laid at Oxford when scholars there attacked Thomas Aquinas's teaching by proving that his chief authority, Aristotle, made certain mistakes about natural phenomena. Roger Bacon (1214–1294) was a part of this Oxford group, but the most important man was Robert Grosseteste (c. 1175–1253) who laid the philosophical foundations for a departure from Aristotelian science. Of course other factors were involved as well, but the challenge to the authority of Aristotle opened the doors for less restricted thought. This challenge to the concepts of Aristotle developed fruitfully at the University of Padua in the fifteenth and sixteenth centuries.

When the Roman Church attacked Copernicus and Galileo (1564–1642), it was not because their teaching actually contained anything contrary to the Bible. The church authorities thought it did, but that was because Aristotelian elements had become part of church orthodoxy, and Galileo's notions clearly conflicted with them. In fact, Galileo defended the compatibility of Copernicus and the Bible, and this was one of the factors which brought about his trial.

Let us return to the fact that the Renaissance and Reformation overlap the Scientific Revolution. Let me emphasize that I am not implying that the Reformation caused the rise of modern science. All I am pointing out at this point is that the High Renaissance, the Reformation, and the Scientific Revolution were simultaneous at that point in history. To put the temporal relationship into perspective, let us consider a few dates: Leonardo da Vinci lived between 1452 and 1519. Luther's Ninety-five Theses were hammered to the church door in 1517. Calvin's *Institutes* were published in 1536. In 1546 Luther died. Copernicus, the astronomer, lived from 1473 to 1543 and gave a preliminary outline of his theory in 1530—that is, that the earth went around the sun, and not the sun around the earth. In the 1540s, three things happened: first, *On the Revolutions of the Heavenly Spheres* by Copernicus was published posthumously; second, Vesalius published his book *On the Structure of the Human Body* (this book is often spoken of as

De Fabrica); third, the first edition of a Latin translation of the collected works of Archimedes (c. 287–212 B.C.) was published in 1544 in Basel. This introduced some of the mathematical methods essential to the development of modern science.

Francis Bacon lived from 1561 to 1626. He was a lawyer, essayist, and Lord Chancellor of England. Though historians now do not give him as important a place as they used to, he did, nevertheless, fight a battle against the old order of scholasticism with its slavish dependence on accepted authorities. He stressed careful observation and a systematic collection of information "to unlock nature's secrets." In 1609 Galileo began to use the newly invented telescope and what he saw and wrote about indicated that Aristotle had been mistaken in his pronouncements about the makeup of the universe. Galileo was not the first to rely on experimental evidence. Danish Tycho Brahe (1546–1601) had come to similar conclusions from observation, but Galileo articulated his findings publicly in his lifetime and in his native tongue so that all could read what he wrote. Condemned by the Roman Inquisition in 1632, he was forced to recant; but his writings continued to testify not only that Copernicus was right, but also that Aristotle was wrong.

The rise of modern science did not conflict with what the Bible teaches; indeed, at a crucial point the Scientific Revolution rested upon what the Bible teaches. Both Alfred North Whitehead (1861–1947) and J. Robert Oppenheimer (1904–1967) have stressed that modern science was born out of the Christian world view. Whitehead was a widely respected mathematician and philosopher, and Oppenheimer, after he became director of the Institute for Advanced Study at Princeton in 1947, wrote on a wide range of subjects related to science, in addition to writing on his own field on the structure of the atom and atomic energy. As far as I know, neither of the two men were Christians or claimed to be Christians, yet both were straightforward in acknowledging that modern science was born out of the Christian world view.

Oppenheimer, for example, described this in an article "On Science and Culture" in *Encounter* in October 1962. In the Harvard University Lowell Lectures entitled *Science and the Modern World* (1925), Whitehead said that Christianity is the mother of science because of "the medieval insistence on the rationality of God."

Whitehead also spoke of confidence "in the intelligible rationality of a personal being." He also says in these lectures that because of the rationality of God, the early scientists had an "inexpugnable belief that every detailed occurrence can be correlated with its antecedents in a perfectly definite manner, exemplifying general principles. Without this belief the incredible labors of scientists would be without hope." In other words, because the early scientists believed that the world was created by a reasonable God, they were not surprised to discover that people could find out something true about nature and the universe on the basis of reason.

This is a good place to emphasize some things I am *not* saying. First, the reasonableness of the created order on the basis of its creation by a reasonable God was not a distinctive emphasis of the Reformation, but was held in common by both the pre-Reformation church and the Reformers. The belief Whitehead describes would have been common to both: the heavens and earth had been created by God, and God is a reasonable God, as the Bible says he is.

Second (as was stressed when considering the art which flowed from the Reformation but should be repeated here), it is not only a Christian who can paint beauty or who has creative stirrings in the area of science. These creative stirrings are rooted in the fact that people are made in the image of God, the great Creator, whether or not an individual knows or acknowledges it, and even though the image of God in people is now contorted. This creativeness—whether in art, science, or engineering—is a part of the unique mannishness of man as made in the image of God. Man, in contrast to non-man, is creative. A person's world view, however, does show through. This includes what happens to people's creative stirrings in science. The world view determines the direction such creative stirrings will take, and how—*and whether the stirrings will continue or dry up.*

Third, not all the scientists to be considered in this section were individually consistent Christians. Many of them were, but they were all living within the thought forms brought forth by Christianity. And in this setting man's creative stirring had a base on which to continue and develop. To quote Whitehead once more, the Christian thought form of the early scientists gave them "the faith in the possibility of science."

Living within the concept that the world was created by a reasonable God, scientists could move with confidence, expecting to be able to find out about the world by observation and experimentation. This was their epistemological base—the philosophical foundation with which they were sure they could know. (*Epistemology* is the theory of knowledge—how we know, or how we know we can know.) Since the world had been created by a reasonable God, they were not surprised to find a correlation between themselves as observers and the thing observed—that is, between subject and object. This base is normative to one functioning in the Christian framework, whether he is observing a chair or the molecules which make up the chair. Without this foundation, Western modern science would not have been born.

Here one must consider an important question: Did the work of the Renaissance play a part in the birth of modern science? Of course it did. More than that, the gradual intellectual and cultural awakenings in the Middle Ages also exerted their influence. The increased knowledge of Greek thought—at Padua University, for example—opened new doors. Certainly, Renaissance elements and those of the Greek intellectual traditions were involved in the scientific awakening. But to say theoretically that the Greek tradition would have been in itself a sufficient stimulus for the Scientific Revolution comes up against the fact that it was not. It was the Christian factor that made the difference. Whitehead and Oppenheimer are right. Christianity is the mother of modern science because it insists that the God who created the universe has revealed himself in the Bible to be the kind of God he is. Consequently, there is a sufficient basis for science to study the universe. Later, when the Christian base was lost, a tradition and momentum had been set in motion, and the pragmatic necessity of technology, and even control by the state, drives science on, but, as we shall see, with a subtle yet important change in emphasis.

Francis Bacon, who could be called the major prophet of the Scientific Revolution, took the Bible seriously, including the historic Fall, the revolt of man in history. He said in *Novum Organum Scientiarum* (1620), "Man by the Fall fell at the same time from his state of innocence and from his dominion over creation. Both of these losses, however, can even in this life be in some parts repaired;

the former by religion and faith, the latter by the arts and sciences."
Notice that Bacon did not see science as autonomous. Man, including science, is not autonomous. He is to take seriously what the
Bible teaches about history and about that which it teaches has
occurred in the cosmos. Yet, upon the base of the Bible's teaching,
science and art are intrinsically valuable before both men and God.
This gave a strong impetus for the creative stirrings of science to
continue rather than to be spasmodic.

To continue with the founders of modern science: Johannes
Kepler, a German astronomer, lived between 1571 and 1630, the
same time as Galileo. He was the first man to show that the planets'
orbits are elliptical, not circular. Sir Isaac Newton (1642–1727),
while a young professor in his twenties at Cambridge University,
came to the conclusion that there is a universal force of attraction
between every body in the universe and that it must be calculable.
That force he called *gravity*. He set this forth later in *The Mathematical Principles of Natural Philosophy* (1687). This became one
of the most influential books in the history of human thought. By
experimenting in Neville's Court in Trinity College at Cambridge
University, he was also able to work out the speed of sound by
timing the interval between the sound of an object which he
dropped, and the echo coming back to him from a known distance.

Throughout his lifetime, Newton tried to be loyal to what he
believed the Bible teaches. It has been said that seventeenth-century
scientists limited themselves to the *how* without interest in the *why*.
This is not true. Newton, like other early scientists, had no problem
with the *why* because he began with the existence of a personal
God who had created the universe.

In his later years, Newton wrote more about the Bible than about
science, though little was published. Humanists have said that they
wish he had spent all of his time on his science. They think he
wasted the hours he expended on biblical study, but they really are
a bit blind when they say this. As Whitehead and Oppenheimer
stressed, if Newton and others had not had a biblical base, they
would have had no base for their science at all. That is not to say
that one must agree with all of Newton's speculations on either
metaphysics or doctrine. But the point is that Newton's intense
interest in the Bible came out of his view that the same God who

had created the universe had given people truth in the Bible. And his view was that the Bible contained the same sort of truth as could be learned from a study of the universe. Newton and these other scientists would have been astonished at a science obsessed with *how* the universe functions, but professionally failing to ask the question "Why?"

Though later he became disillusioned with science, Blaise Pascal (1623–1662) made the first successful barometer and did important work on the equilibrium of fluids. He was not content to work only in a laboratory, but took a tube of mercury up the mountain Puy de Dôme (in central France) and thus recorded the changes in the mercury level according to altitude. He was also a mathematician of note whose work hastened the development of differential calculus. By some he is also considered the greatest writer of French prose who ever lived. An outstanding Christian, he emphasized that he did not see people lost like specks of dust in the universe (which was now so much larger and more complicated than people had thought), for people—as unique—could comprehend something of the universe. People could comprehend the stars; the stars comprehend nothing. And besides this, for Pascal, people were special because Christ died on the cross for them.

René Descartes (1596–1650) was important for his emphasis on mathematical analysis and theory of science. I personally would reject his philosophic views. But he regarded himself as a good Catholic, and it was his religion which, in light of his philosophic views, saved him from solipsism—that is, from living in the cocoon of himself.

In the early days of the Royal Society of London for Improving Natural Knowledge, founded in 1662, most of its members were professing Christians. George M. Trevelyan (1876–1962) in *English Social History* (1942) writes, "Robert Boyle, Isaac Newton and the early members of the Royal Society were religious men, who repudiated the sceptical doctrines of Hobbes. But they familiarized the minds of their countrymen with the idea of law in the Universe and with scientific methods of enquiry to discover truth. It was believed that these methods would never lead to any conclusions inconsistent with Biblical history and miraculous religion; Newton lived and died in that faith." We must never think that the

41 Sir Isaac Newton engraved by Freeman (top) and Blaise Pascal by Philippe de Champagne. ". . . early scientists had no problem with the *why*." *Photos courtesy Radio Times London.*

Sir Isaac Newton

PASCAL

Christian base hindered science. Rather, the Christian base made modern science possible.

The tradition of Bacon and Newton and the early days of the Royal Society was strongly maintained right through the nineteenth century. Michael Faraday (1791–1867) made his great contributions in the area of electricity. His crowning discovery was the induction of electric current. Faraday was also a Christian. He belonged to a group whose position was: "Where the Scriptures speak, we speak; where the Scriptures are silent, we are silent." In the conviction that knowledge concerning God's creation is for all people to enjoy, and not just a professional elite, he gave famous public demonstrations of his pioneering work in electricity. James Clerk Maxwell (1831–1879), who, like Faraday, worked with electricity, was also a believer in a personal God. Indeed, the majority of those who founded modern science, from Copernicus to Maxwell, were functioning on a Christian base. Many of them were personally Christians, but even those who were not, were living within the thought forms brought forth by Christianity, especially the belief that God as the Creator and Lawgiver has implanted laws in his creation which man can discover.

But we may ask, "Isn't science now in a new stage, one in which the concept of an orderly universe is passé?" It is often said that relativity as a philosophy, as a world view, is supported by Albert Einstein's (1879–1955) theory of relativity. But this is mistaken because Einstein's theory of relativity assumes that everywhere in the universe light travels at a constant speed in a vacuum. In other words, we must say with the utmost force that nothing is less relative philosophically than the theory of relativity. Einstein himself stood implacably against any such application of his concepts. We can think of his often quoted words from the *London Observer* of April 5, 1964: "I cannot believe that God plays dice with the cosmos."

One may then ask if Einstein's views have not been proven old-fashioned by Werner Heisenberg's (1901–1976) principle of uncertainty, or indeterminacy principle (1927), and by the wide acceptance of the concept of quantum. The answer again is *no*. The principle of indeterminacy has to do with a certain area of observation, namely, the *location* of an object and its *velocity*. For example,

42   Michael Faraday conducting a public experiment. "God's creation is for all people to enjoy." *Photo courtesy of The Royal Institution.*

if we try to establish the exact position and speed of two atomic particles which are going to collide, we will never be able to determine exactly how they will rebound. The physicist cannot have an accurate *observation* of both their location and their velocity simultaneously. The quantum theory of either light or particles does not lead to the concept of chance or random universe either. For example, whether viewed as a wave or a particle, light does not function at random and it is an effect which brings forth causes. Even the far-out theoretical existence of "black holes" in space, as set forth by John G. Taylor (1931–), is based on the concept of an orderly universe and calculations resting on that concept.

If an airplane is to fly, it must be constructed to fit the order of the universe that exists. People, no matter what they have come to believe, still look for the explanation of any happening in terms of other earlier happenings. If this were not possible, not only would explanations cease, but science could not be used reliably in technology. It is possible to so function in our universe that, because there is a uniformity of natural causes, a man may travel hundreds of thousands of miles to the moon and land within a few feet of his planned destination, or he may aim an atomic weapon at a target on the other side of our planet and land it within ten feet of that target. We know we live in a universe that is much more complex than people, including scientists, once thought it to be, but that is much different from the concept of a random universe.

On the Christian base, one could expect to find out something true about the universe by reason. There were certain other results of the Christian world view. For example, there was the certainty of something "there"—an objective reality—for science to examine. What we seem to observe is not just an extension of the essence of God, as Hindu and Buddhist thinking would have it. The Christian world view gives us a real world which is there to study objectively. Another result of the Christian base was that the world was worth finding out about, for in doing so one was investigating God's creation. And people were free to investigate nature, for nature was not seen as full of gods and therefore taboo. All things were created by God and are open for people's investigation. God himself had told mankind to have dominion over nature, and as we saw from the quotation from Francis Bacon, to him science had a

43 Assembly of a satellite at the Kennedy Space Center. ". . . science could not be used." *Photo by Mustafa Arshad.*

part in this. There was a reason for continuing one's interest and pressing on.

In this setting, people's creative stirrings had a base from which to develop and to continue. To quote Bacon again, "To conclude, therefore, let no man out of weak conceit of sobriety, or in ill applied moderation, think or maintain, that a man can search too far or be too well studied in the book of God's word, or in the book of God's works." "The book of God's word" is the Bible; "the book of God's works" is the world which God has made. So, for Bacon and other scientists working on the Christian base, there was no separation or final conflict between what the Bible teaches and science.

The Greeks, the Moslems, and the Chinese eventually lost interest in science. As we said before, the Chinese had an early and profound knowledge of the world. Joseph Needham (1900–), in his book *The Grand Titration* (1969), explains why this never developed into a full-fledged science: "There was no confidence that the code of Nature's laws could ever be unveiled and read, because there was no assurance that a divine being, even more rational than ourselves, had ever formulated such a code capable of being read." But for the scientists who were functioning on a Christian base, there was an incentive to continue searching for the objective truth which they had good reason to know was there. Then, too, with the biblical emphasis on the rightness of work and the dignity of all vocations, it was natural that the things which were learned should flow over into the practical side and not remain a matter of mere intellectual curiosity and that, in other words, technology, in the beneficial sense, should be born.

What was the view of these modern scientists on a Christian base? They held to the concept of the uniformity of natural causes in an *open system,* or, as it may also be expressed, the uniformity of natural causes in a limited time span. God has made a cause-and-effect universe; therefore we can find out something about the causes from the effects. *But* (and the *but* is very important) it is an *open* universe because God and man are *outside* of the uniformity of natural causes. In other words, all that exists is not one big cosmic machine which includes everything. Of course, if a person steps in front of a moving auto, the cause-and-effect universe functions upon him; but God and people are not a part of a total cosmic machine. Things go on in a cause-and-effect sequence, but at a point of time the direction may be changed by God or by people. Consequently, there is a place for God, but there is also a proper place for man.

This carries with it something profound—that the machine, whether the cosmic machine or the machines which people make, is neither a master nor a threat—because the machine does not include everything. There is something which is "outside" of the cosmic machine, and there is a place for man to be man.

8 The Breakdown in Philosophy and Science

The point was made in chapter one that to understand where we are today in our intellectual ideas and in our day-to-day lives (including our cultural and political lives), we must trace three lines: the philosophic, the scientific, and the religious. We have done this through the preceding chapters and now have arrived at the era of modern man. As we go on to what I call *The Breakdown,* we will here consider the philosophic and scientific sides and their interrelation.

Alfred North Whitehead has remarked that the entire history of European philosophy is a series of footnotes to Plato. That goes too far. Nevertheless, Plato did understand something crucial—not only in theoretical thought but in practical life. He saw that if there are no absolutes, then the individual things (the particulars, the details) have no meaning. By particulars we mean the individual things which are about us. The individual stones on a beach are particulars. The molecules that make up the stones are particulars. The total beach is a particular. I am made up of molecules and the molecules are particulars. And I as an individual and you as an individual are particulars.

Plato understood that regardless of what kind of particulars one talks about, if there are no absolutes—no universal—then particulars have no meaning. The universal or absolute is that under which all the particulars fit—that which gives unity and meaning

144

to the whole. We can apply this in language. Apples come in many varieties, but we do not verbalize each time by running through the names of all the varieties of apples. We sum them up by the word *apples*. Likewise, there are many kinds of pears, and we sum them up with the word *pears*. On a higher level of generality there are many other varieties of fruit. But again we do not run through all these, we simply say *fruit*.

The problem, however, is not only in language but in reality: What will unify and give meaning to everything there is? Jean-Paul Sartre (1905–), the French existential philosopher, emphasized this problem in our own generation. His concept was that a finite point is absurd if it has no infinite reference point. This concept is most easily understood in the area of morals. If there is no absolute moral standard, then one cannot say in a final sense that anything is right or wrong. By *absolute* we mean that which always applies, that which provides a final or ultimate standard. There must be an absolute if there are to be *morals,* and there must be an absolute if there are to be real *values*. If there is no absolute beyond man's ideas, then there is no final appeal to judge between individuals and groups whose moral judgments conflict. We are merely left with conflicting opinions.

But it is not only that we need absolutes in morals and values; we need absolutes if our existence is to have *meaning*—my existence, your existence, Man's existence. Even more profoundly, we must have absolutes if we are to have a solid epistemology (a theory of knowing—how we know, or how we know we know). How can we be sure that what we think we know of the world outside ourselves really corresponds to what is there? And in all these layers, each more profound than the other, unless there is an absolute these things are lost to us: morals, values, the meaning of existence (including the meaning of man), and a basis for knowing.

Non-Christian philosophers from the time of the Greeks until just before our modern period had three things in common. First, they were rationalists. That is, they assumed that man (though he is finite and limited) can begin from himself and gather enough particulars to make his own universals. Rationalism rejects any knowledge outside of man himself, especially any knowledge from God.

The second point they had in common was that they took reason seriously. They accepted the validity of reason—that the mind thinks in terms of antithesis. That is, with their minds people can come to the conclusion that certain things are true while certain other things are not true, that certain things are right in contrast to other things that are wrong. The first lessons in classical logic were: **A is A** and **A is not non-A.**

Third, in addition to being rationalists who believed in the validity of reason, non-Christian philosophers prior to the eighteenth century also were optimistic. They thought they could and would succeed in their quest to establish by reason alone a unified and true knowledge of what reality is. When that happened, satisfying explanations would be on hand for everything people encountered in the universe and for all that people are and all that they think. They hoped for something which would unify all knowledge and all of life.

But three shifts came, and it was these shifts that made modern man what he is and our modern societies what they are. First, we will look at the shift in science, then the shift in philosophy, and later at the shift in theology. We have already seen that the Scientific Revolution rested on a Christian base. The early modern scientists believed in the concept of the uniformity of natural causes in an *open* system. God and man were outside the cause-and-effect machine of the cosmos, and therefore they *both* could influence the machine. To them all that exists is *not* one big cosmic machine which includes everything. The shift from modern science to what I call *modern modern science* was a shift from the concept of the uniformity of natural causes in an *open system* to the concept of the uniformity of natural causes in a *closed system*. In the latter view nothing is outside a total cosmic machine; everything which exists is a part of it.

Scientists in the seventeenth and eighteenth centuries continued to use the word *God,* but pushed God more and more to the edges of their systems. Finally, scientists in this stream of thought moved to the idea of a completely closed system. That left no place for God. But equally it left no place for man. Man disappears, to be viewed as some form of determined or behavioristic machine. Everything is a part of the cosmic machine, including people. To say this another way: Prior to the rise of modern modern science (that is, naturalistic science, or materialistic science), the laws of cause and effect were applied to physics, astronomy, and chemistry. Today the mechanical cause-and-effect perspective is applied equally to psychology and sociology.

Notice especially that the scientists who gave birth to the earlier great breakthroughs of science would not have accepted this concept. It arose not because of that which could be demonstrated by science, but because the scientists who took this new view *had accepted a different philosophic base*. The findings of science, as such, did not bring them to accept this view; rather, their world view brought them to this place. They became naturalistic or materialistic in their presuppositions.

The German philosopher Ludwig Feuerbach (1804–1872) was an early exponent of a philosophy of materialism, as was German physician Ludwig Büchner (1824–1899), whose book *Force and Matter* (1855) went into twenty-one editions and was translated into all the major languages. It is of more than passing interest that Richard Wagner (1813–1883), the German composer of opera, was reading Feuerbach as early as 1848. Wagner at this period of his life was deeply influenced by Feuerbach, and it was Wagner who encouraged Ludwig II of Bavaria to read Feuerbach. Thus the work of Feuerbach had its influence not only in abstract thought but also on the arts and on the state. Ernst Haeckel (1834–1919), a biologist at the University of Jena, wrote *The Riddle of the Universe at the Close of the 19th Century* (1899), and it became a best-seller, too. In this work Haeckel posited that matter and energy are eternal and also assumed that the human mind or soul is to be explained on the basis of materialism. He saw where this would lead and accepted that people have no freedom of will.

When people began to think in this way, there was no place for God or for man as man. When psychology and social science were made a part of a closed cause-and-effect system, along with physics, astronomy and chemistry, it was not only God who died. Man died. And within this framework love died. There is no place for love in a totally closed cause-and-effect system. There is no place for morals in a totally closed cause-and-effect system. There is no place for the freedom of people in a totally closed cause-and-effect system. Man becomes a zero. People and all they do become only a part of the machinery.

In the humanism of the High Renaissance, flowing on to maturity through the Enlightenment, man was determined to make himself autonomous. This flow continues, and by the time we come to modern modern science man himself is devoured: Man as man is dead. Life is pointless, devoid of meaning.

Büchner and Haeckel had said that matter and energy are eternal. Now the world view of materialism went on to try to explain *man* by the uniformity of cause and effect in a closed system. Charles Lyell (1797–1875), in his *Principles of Geology* (1830–1833), was the one who especially opened the door to this by emphasizing the uniformity of natural causes in the field of geology. His idea was that there were no forces in the past except those that are active now.

Charles Darwin (1809–1882) extended Lyell's concepts to the origin of biological life. In his book *The Origin of Species by Means of Natural Selection or the Preservation of Favoured Races in the Struggle for Life* (1859), Darwin set forth the concept that all biological life came from simpler forms by a process called "the survival of the fittest." Questions still exist in regard to this concept. Darwinism, Neo-Darwinism, and reductionism all have their problems explaining *how* the processes they postulate actually work. There are statistical problems as well, as has been pointed out by Murray Eden (1920–) in the 1967 article "Heresy in the Halls of Biology—Mathematicians Question Darwin" (*Scientific Research,* November 1967). This problem was also dealt with in a more technical way in Eden's article "Inadequacies of Neo-Darwinian Evolution as a Scientific Theory" which appeared in *Mathematical Challenges to the Neo-Darwinian Interpretation of Evolution* (1967). Statistical studies indicate that pure chance (randomness) could not have produced the biological complexity in the world out of chaos, in any amount of time so far suggested. "Has there been enough time for natural selection, as it is seen through the eyepieces of Darwinism or Neo-Darwinism to operate and give rise to the observed phenomena of nature? No, say these mathema-

44   Charles Darwin. ". . . problems explaining *how* the processes they postulate actually work." *Photo courtesy of* THE BETTMANN ARCHIVE INC.

ticians." In fact, we can go further; the study of statistics raises the question of whether pure chance could ever produce *an ongoing increased complexity*. If chance alone operates, *why* should that which exists (including biological structure) move toward a consistent increase of complexity?

Most importantly, no one has yet shown how man could have been brought forth from non-man solely by time plus chance. This position ends either in man's being made non-man, or in a sudden romantic explosion into a flood of words. For example, Jacob Bronowski (1908–1974) ends his book *The Ascent of Man* (1973) with such a romantic outpouring of sentences as: "We are nature's unique experiment to make the rational intelligence prove itself sounder than the reflex. Knowledge is our destiny. Self-knowledge, at last bringing together the experience of the arts and the explanation of science, waits ahead of us." The humanist thinkers, beginning from themselves autonomously, either come to the conclusion that there are no values and meaning or suddenly try to produce values and meaning out of rhetoric. Thus, there are problems of both the *how* and the *why*. The concept of an unbroken line from molecule to man, on the basis of only time plus chance, leaves these crucial questions of *how* and *why* unanswered.

Darwin's idea was popularized by Thomas Huxley (1825–1895). Herbert Spencer (1820–1903), who actually coined the phrase "survival of the fittest," extended the theory of biological evolution to all of life, including ethics. Spencer said, "The poverty of the incapable . . . starvation of the idle and those shoulderings aside of the weak by the strong . . . are the decrees of a large, far-seeing benevolence." There was no necessity to extend biological evolution to "social Darwinism." But it was natural for these men to do this because of their desire to find a unifying principle that would enable autonomous man to explain everything through naturalistic science, that is, on the basis of the uniformity of natural causes in a closed system. This had become the frame of reference by which they attempted to give unity to individual things, the particulars, to the details of the universe and to the history of man. In *Physics and Politics: Thoughts on the Application of Principles of Natural Selection and Inheritance to Political Science* (1872) Walter Bagehot (1826–1877) went even further than Spencer in applying these concepts to the advance of groups. Thus these concepts opened the door for racism and the noncompassionate use of accumulated wealth to be sanctioned and made respectable in the name of "science."

Later, these ideas helped produce an even more far-reaching yet logical conclusion: the Nazi movement in Germany. Heinrich Himmler (1900–1945), leader of the Gestapo, stated that the law of nature must take its course in the survival of the fittest. The result was the gas chambers. Hitler stated numerous times that Christianity and its notion of charity should be "replaced by the ethic of strength over weakness." Surely many factors were involved in the rise of National Socialism in Germany. For example, the Christian consensus had largely been lost by the undermining from a rationalistic philosophy and a romantic pantheism on the secular side, and a liberal theology (which was an adoption of rationalism in theological terminology) in the universities and many of the churches. Thus biblical Christianity was no longer giving the consensus for German society. After World War I came political and economic chaos and a flood of moral permissiveness in Germany. Thus, many factors created the situation. But in that setting the theory of the survival of the fittest sanctioned what occurred.

The Nazi movement was not the last result of this way of thinking. In a quieter way, and yet just as importantly, some of today's advocates of genetic engineering use the same arguments to support the position that the weak should not be kept alive through medical advances to produce a *weaker* next generation. Rather, they argue, genetic engineering should be used to propagate the fittest. Humanism had set out to make man autonomous; but its results have not been what the advocates of humanism idealistically visualized.

Having seen the shift that came in science, let us now examine the shift that came in philosophy. We have already noted that the older philosophic views were optimistic, for they assumed that people would be able through reason alone to establish a unified and true knowledge of what reality is, and that when this happened they would have satisfying explanations for everything encountered in the universe and for all that people are and think.

The history of this train of non-Christian philosophers could be pictured like this: One man would say, "Here is a circle which will give the unified and true knowledge of what reality is:" ○ . The next man would say, "No!" and cross out the circle: ⊗. Then he would say, "Here is the circle:" ○ . A third would say, "No!" cross out that circle: ⊗ and say, "Here is the circle:" ○ . And so on through the centuries. Each one showed that the previous philosophers had failed and then tried to construct his answer, which future thinkers would again show to be inadequate to contain all of knowledge and all of life.

The older philosophers did not find the circle, but they optimistically believed someone would. Then the line of crossed-out circles was broken, and a drastic shift came. It is this shift that causes modern man to be modern man.

Many scholars name René Descartes (1596–1650) as the father of modern philosophy, and no one should minimize his importance. Yet it seems to me that he should be placed among the *older* philosophers for two reasons. First, he was supremely confident that by human thought alone one could doubt all notions based on authority and could begin from himself with total sufficiency ("I think, therefore I am"). Second, he believed that mathematics would provide a unity—as a model—for all kinds of investigation. He was optimistic that mathematics and mathematical analysis, with careful deductions from these, would provide a factor which would give a unity to all knowledge. Philosophical thought is a flowing stream, and certainly Descartes had an important part in preparing for what was to follow; but in my opinion the shift came in the next century, the eighteenth.

Four men directed the shift from this older optimistic view to the modern outlook in which this optimistic hope is lost. The shift came because the humanistic ideal had failed. After all the centuries of suggested circles, the humanistic expectation of autonomous man's providing a unity to all of knowledge and all of life had stalled. People had gone round and round variations of the same answers—like going around and around a large, dark, circular room looking for a way out—and it was slowly dawning on them that there was no exit. That realization came in the eighteenth century, and with it the stance of humanistic man changed from optimism to pessimism. He gave up the hope of a unified answer.

The relative importance of these four men is open to question,

45 Adolf Hitler. ". . . the ethic of strength over weakness." *Photo courtesy of Radio Times London.*

but when the influence of these four together (with the extensions made by their followers) had been exerted, the old optimism of a unified and true knowledge on the basis of reason alone was gone. This has had an enormous effect on Western culture and society, down to the simplest man in the street. The four crucial men were Jean-Jacques Rousseau, Immanuel Kant, Georg Wilhelm Hegel, and Søren Kierkegaard.

The first, Jean-Jacques Rousseau (1712–1778), was a French-speaking Swiss from Geneva. You will remember that the humanism of the High Renaissance ran into problems because, with man's beginning only from himself, there is tension between the individual things, the particulars, and any meaning for them. We could think of it like this:

UNIVERSALS which give meaning to the particulars

PARTICULARS, including each of us as a person

By the time of Rousseau, this humanist problem developed further. With Rousseau the same problem was worded differently and may be expressed like this:

AUTONOMOUS FREEDOM

AUTONOMOUS NATURE

There were two parts to this new formulation of the old humanist problem. First, there were those who were aware that in the area of reason people were increasingly coming to the place where everything was seen as a machine, even people. At the end of his life Leonardo da Vinci had foreseen that beginning humanistically with mathematics one has only particulars and will never come to universals or meaning, but will end only with mechanics. It took humanistic thought two hundred and fifty years to arrive at the place which Leonardo had foreseen, but by the eighteenth century it had arrived. Everything is the machine, including people.

Second, Rousseau himself viewed the tension specifically at the point of society, political life, and culture. He viewed primitive man, "the noble savage," as superior to civilized man. He wrote, "If man is good by nature, as I believe to have shown him to be, it follows that he stays like that as long as nothing foreign to him corrupts him." He had a kind of "conversion" in 1749 when he concluded that the Enlightenment, with its emphasis on reason and the arts and sciences, had caused people to lose more than they had gained. So he gave up his faith in "progress."

Rousseau and his followers began to play down reason, and they saw the restraints of civilization as evils: "Man was born free, but everywhere he is in chains!" Rousseau saw the primitive as innocent and autonomous freedom as the final good. We must understand that the freedom he advocated was not just freedom from God or the Bible but freedom from any kind of restraint—freedom from culture, freedom from any authority, an absolute freedom of the individual—a freedom in which the individual is the center of the universe.

Theoretically this individual freedom would be perfectly reflected in the "general will" through the *social contract*. The utopianism of this concept was shown by the French Revolution's Reign of Terror, during which the purification of the general will meant not only the loss of freedom for the individual but the reign of the guillotine. Actually, one did not have to wait for the Reign of Terror to see the problem. It was already in Rousseau's own writing.

Rousseau's concept of autonomous freedom clashed with his own presentation when he moved from the individual to society. In *The Social Contract* (1762) he writes, "In order that the social compact may not be an empty formula, it tacitly includes the undertaking, which alone can give force to the rest, that whoever refuses to obey the general will shall be compelled to do so by the whole body. This means nothing less than that he will be forced to be free." Once more a humanistic utopianism ends in tyranny, whether in Rousseau's writing or in the Reign of Terror which carried his position to its conclusion. Robespierre, the "King of the Terror," was a doctrinaire disciple of Rousseau and rationalized his actions on Rousseau's base. It is interesting to note in this relationship of the Enlightenment and the French Revolution to Rousseau that in Voltaire's château in Ferney two life-sized statues stand perfectly balanced on the two sides of the main doorway—statues of Voltaire and Rousseau.

Rousseau's concept of freedom showed itself in many forms. For example, in his *Confessions* (1782) he argued that the best education is virtually the absence of education. This had an impact on the later education theories of self-expression which are influential in our own day. We all have our inconsistencies, but it must be mentioned that while he wrote much on education, Rousseau sent the five children born to his mistress off to orphanages. His concepts were as utopian personally as they proved to be politically. Rousseau's influence was carried not only by his prose tracts but by the operas he composed. *Le Devin du Village* (1752) played an important role in forming the style of French *opéra comique,* while his later work *Pygmalion* (produced in 1775) laid the foundation for melodrama. With his cry of "Let us return to nature," Rousseau exerted a lasting influence on the music of his time as well as on the new movements in writing and painting.

In *Rousseau and Revolution* (1967) by Will and Ariel Durant, Rousseau is portrayed as the most important influence on modern thought, and thus their book commences with him. In this instance I think they are correct. Rousseau had a profound effect on the thoughts and the lives of those who followed him. His thinking influenced that of our own day in many ways. For this reason I will spend more time on his concepts and influence than on Kant, Hegel, and Kierkegaard.

Rousseau's concept of autonomous freedom led to the Bohemian ideal, in which the hero is the man who fights all of society's standards, values, and restraints. Giacomo Puccini (1858–1924) gave this operatic expression in his most popular opera, *La Bohème* (1896). And in our own recent past this Bohemian ideal was a factor leading expressly to the genuine part of the hippie world of the 1960s.

But Rousseau did not stand alone. In Britain the Scottish philosopher David Hume (1711–1776) was working at exactly the same time. He, too, criticized reason as a method of knowing truth and defended the centrality of human experience and feeling. In his criticism of reason as a method of knowing, Hume questioned the existence of the cause-and-effect concept itself. Hume had a wide influence both on British philosophy and on the German philosopher Immanuel Kant, whom we will discuss below.

Returning to those standing in the flow of Rousseau we should consider the German poet-philosopher Johann Wolfgang von Goethe (1749–1832). Goethe equated nature and truth. Goethe

46 Voltaire and Rousseau statues in Voltaire's family home at Ferney, France. ". . . two life-sized statues stand perfectly balanced on the two sides of the main doorway." *Photo by Mustafa Arshad.*

did not just substitute nature for the Bible; for him nature was God. Here we have the vague pantheism which dominated so much of the stream of thinking at this time. Goethe became pantheistic in a conscious attempt to find a universal for all observed particulars in reality, even though those particulars were often contradictory. For example, the atrocities of the French Revolution were committed in an especially good wine year! In his naturalism—which took a vaguely pantheistic direction instead of an open materialism —Goethe romantically hoped to leave a place for man. As Goethe expressed it, nature is the ultimate sanction for all man's judgments.

Influenced by Rousseau, romanticism was born in Germany with Goethe, Johann Christoph Friedrich von Schiller (1759–1805) and Gotthold Lessing (1729–1781). All three of these men were at first followers of the Enlightenment before they turned aside to follow Rousseau. Reason was the hero of the Enlightenment; emotion became the hero of romanticism. Schiller's line, "All creatures drink in joy from nature's breast," aptly sums up this school of thought.

Beethoven (1770–1827) followed in this stream, carrying its expression into music. Beethoven's music, more than that of any composer before him, gives the impression of being a direct outpouring of his personality. In it we already feel the emphasis of modern man on self-expression. Beethoven's last quartets (1825–1826) opened the door to twentieth-century music.

The English romantic poets William Wordsworth (1770–1850) and Samuel Taylor Coleridge (1772–1834) were in the same stream. Wordsworth found his values in man's instincts rather than in learning. The English painter John Constable (1776–1837) not only painted the trees and clouds, but in some way related the nature he saw to a concept of the *moral* grandeur of the universe, thus echoing Wordsworth who wrote in "The Tables Turned,"

> One impulse from a vernal wood
> May teach you more of man,
> Of moral evil and of good,
> Than all the sages can.

It also echoes Rousseau's concept of the noble savage: That which is "natural" is morally good.

The attempt to make nature the basis of *morals* was also taken into the area of *civil law,* where it was called the Natural Law School of Jurisprudence. Its influence is still strongly felt in jurisprudence. It was an attempt in this eighteenth-century period to have principles of law, "even if there is no God." These jurists thought that a complete and perfect system of law could be constructed upon principles of natural law. But there was a serious problem in trying to construct a system of law upon nature. Nature is cruel as well as *non*cruel.

Consider the dilemma faced by Rousseau's follower Gauguin (1848–1903), the French painter who, in his hunt for total freedom, deserted his family and went to Tahiti where he tried to find it in the noble savage. After he had lived in Tahiti for a while, he found that the ideal of the noble savage was illusory. In his last great painting—*Whence Come We? What Are We? Whither Do We Go?* (1897 and 1898), which hangs in the Boston Museum of Fine Arts—he showed that man in himself has no answer to the ultimate questions—and this applies as much to primitive man as to civilized man. He painted the title directly on this painting so that no one could miss its meaning. He wrote about this painting as he was working on it, and he called it a philosophical work, comparable to the Gospel.

But what a "gospel"! In the picture is a primitive old woman dying. And Gauguin himself writes in a letter to Daniel de Montfreid, "Whither? Close to the death of an old woman, a strange stupid bird concludes: What? O sorrow, thou art my master. Fate how cruel thou art, and always vanquished. I revolt." What he found in Tahiti (where he went to find the uninhibited freedom of man, which to Rousseau and Gauguin was the "ought") turned out to be death and cruelty. When he finished this painting, he tried to commit suicide, though he did not succeed.

Or, to illustrate in another way the problem of taking nature as the moral standard, we can consider Marquis de Sade (1740–1814), who well understood the logical conclusion of this deification of nature. He knew that if nature is all, then what *is* is right, and nothing more can be said. The natural result of this was his "sadism," his cruelty, especially to women. He wrote in *La Nouvelle Justine* (1791–1797): "As nature has made us [the men] the

strongest, we can do with her [the woman] whatever we please."
There are no moral distinctions, no value system. What *is* is right.
Thus there is no basis for either morals or law.

It was one thing for the Dutch Reformation painters rejoicingly
to paint the simple things of life, for they painted in a framework
which had two parts: first, the creation of nature by a personal and
a good God; second, the present abnormality of nature because of
the Fall. But it was quite another thing to take nature as it is now
and make it the measure of goodness. For, if nature as it exists is
the standard for men to live by, cruelty becomes equal to non-
cruelty.

It should be said again that Rousseau's concept of autonomous
freedom ran head-on into a conclusion which was to become increasingly dominant as time went on. It became clear that those
who held the rationalistic position on the sole basis of their own
reason increasingly were forced to conclude that everything, including man, is a machine. But one could not hold simultaneously the
concept of everything's being a machine and the ideal of a person's
having freedom. Thus, the concept of a unified knowledge of what
reality is (on the basis of reason alone)—which almost all previous
thinkers had as their aspiration—was under great strain. By the
time of Rousseau and his followers there was a tendency for the
concepts (*everything as a machine* and *man's autonomous freedom*) to split apart and go marching off in divergent directions.

The second of the four crucial men who directed the shift from
the older optimistic view of philosophy to the modern outlook
where hope is lost was the German philosopher Immanuel Kant
(1724–1804). His books which were so important in the thought
of his day and ever since are *Critique of Pure Reason* (1781),
Critique of Practical Reason (1788), and *Critique of Judgment*
(1790). He worded the problem of his age differently from Rousseau, but it is still the same problem:

NOUMENAL WORLD—the concepts of meaning and value

PHENOMENAL WORLD—the world which can be weighed
and measured, the external world, the world of science

Kant also tried to keep these two worlds together. In fact, much
of the three books mentioned tried to solve this problem (this is

47 *Whence . . . . What . . . . Whither?* by Paul Gauguin. ". . . he found that the
ideal of the noble savage was illusory." *Photo courtesy of Museum of Fine Arts. Boston.*

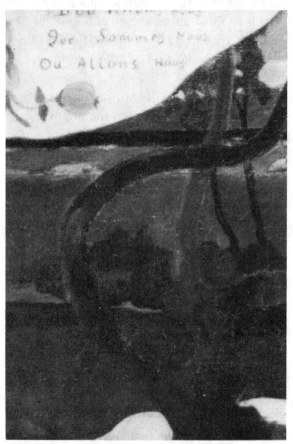

especially so of *Critique of Judgment*), but he, like Rousseau, never found any way to produce unity. With his work, the hope of a unified knowledge was on the threshold of splitting into two parts, neither having a relationship with the other. The humanist dilemma which arose in the Renaissance—of the individual things, the particulars, versus meaning and values—was now ready to explode. There was no way beginning from man alone to bring the noumenal and phenomenal worlds together.

Romanticism, which had begun with the followers of Rousseau, now developed further with a strengthened desire to believe in something—to escape—even if to do so necessitated giving up the old non-Christian philosophers' hope that people starting from themselves could by their reason find a unified answer to everything.

The third of the four significant men was another German, Georg Wilhelm Friedrich Hegel (1770–1831). His most important books are *The Phenomenology of Mind* (1807), *Science of Logic* (1812–16), *Encyclopaedia of the Philosophical Sciences* (1817), and *Philosophy of Right* (1821). From his writings it is clear that he understood the need for unity between the noumenal and phenomenal worlds. He struggled with this in a complex series of religious concepts, but he left us in reality only a flow of religious words. We can think of his words as given us by Walter Kaufmann (1921–) in his book *Hegel: Reinterpretation, Texts, and Commentary* (1965): "Not the Concept but the ecstasy, not the coldly progressing necessity of the subject matter but fermenting enthusiasm is held to be the best attitude and guide to the spread-out riches of the substance."

Hegel's intricate system puts great emphasis on the centrality of the state and the flow of history. In *The Universe Next Door* (1976) James W. Sire (1933–) summarizes Frederick Copleston's (1907–) study of Hegel in Volume 7 of *A History of Philosophy* (1963). This summary is so succinct that I will quote it, in so far as Copleston's treatment is too lengthy to quote in full: "According to Hegel, the universe is steadily unfolding and so is man's understanding of it. No single proposition about reality can truly reflect what is the case. Rather, in the heart of the truth of a given proposition one finds its opposite. This, where recognized, unfolds and stands in opposition to the thesis. Yet there is truth in both thesis and antithesis, and when this is perceived a synthesis is formed and a new proposition states the truth of the newly recognized situation. But this in turn is found to contain its own contradiction and the process goes on ad infinitum. Thus the universe and man's understanding of it unfolds dialectically. In short the universe with its consciousness—man—evolves."

The result is that all possible particular positions are indeed relativized. While it is an oversimplification of Hegel's complete position, this has led to the idea that truth is to be sought in synthesis rather than antithesis. Instead of antithesis (that some things are true and their opposite untrue), truth and moral rightness will be found in the flow of history, a synthesis of them. This concept has not only won on the other side of the Iron Curtain; it has won on this side as well. Today not only in philosophy but in politics, government, and individual morality, our generation sees solutions in terms of synthesis and not absolutes. When this happens, truth, as people had always thought of truth, has died.

The last of the four crucial men was Søren Kierkegaard (1813–1855), a Dane. He wrote both devotional and philosophical books. The latter include *Either/Or* (1843), *Philosophical Fragments* (1844), and *The Concluding Unscientific Postscript* (1846). There can and will be a continuing discussion among scholars as to whether the secular and religious thinkers who built on Kierkegaard did him justice. However, what in these can be called secular and religious Kierkegaardianism did bring to full tide the notion that reason will always lead to pessimism. That is, one must try to find optimistic answers in regard to meaning and values on an "upper level" outside of reason. Through a "leap of faith" one must try to find meaning without reason.

You will remember that in the High Renaissance, humanistic man, starting only from himself, had problems concerning the meaning or value of things and of absolutes for morals. With Rousseau it became an AUTONOMOUS FREEDOM/AUTONOMOUS NATURE problem. With Kant it was NOUMENAL WORLD/PHENOMENAL WORLD. With Kierkegaardianism it went a step further and now became:

$$\frac{\text{NON-REASON} = \text{FAITH—OPTIMISM}}{\text{REASON} = \text{PESSIMISM}}$$

So optimism will now always be in the area of non-reason.

Modern man is a man of dichotomy. By *dichotomy* we mean a total separation into two reciprocally exclusive orders, with no unity or relationship between them. The dichotomy here is the total separation between the area of meaning and values, and the area of reason. Reason leading to despair must be kept totally separate from the blind optimism of non-reason. This makes a lower and an upper story, with the lower story of reason leading to pessimism and men trying to find optimism in an upper story devoid of reason. At this point the older rationalistic thinkers (with their optimistic hope of maintaining unity between the world of reason and that of meaning and values) were left behind. This is the mark of modern man.

In our day, humanistic reason affirms that there is only the cosmic machine, which encompasses everything, including people. To those who hold this view everything people are or do is explained by some form of determinism, some type of behaviorism, some kind of reductionism. The terms *determinism* or *behaviorism* indicate that everything people think or do is determined in a machinelike way and that any sense of freedom or choice is an illusion. In one form of reductionism, man is explained by reducing him to the smallest particles which make up his body. Man is seen as being only the molecule or the energy particle, more complex but not intrinsically different.

I have never heard this expressed more clearly than when I was lecturing in Acapulco, Mexico. George Wald (1906–), a chemistry professor from Harvard University, was also there lecturing to the same group. He expressed with great force the modern concept that all things, including man, are merely the product of chance. After he had stressed over and over again that all things, beginning from the molecule and ending with man, are only a product of chance, he said, "Four hundred years ago there was a collection of molecules named Shakespeare which produced *Hamlet*." According to these theories, that is *all* that man can be. Man beginning with his proud, proud humanism, tried to make himself autonomous, but rather than becoming great, he had found himself ending up as only a collection of molecules—and nothing more.

All this is related to the question of origins: What was the beginning of everything? Ultimately, there are not many possible answers to this question. First, we could say that everything came from nothing—that is, from *really* nothing, what I call *nothing-nothing*. This means that once there was no mass, no energy, no motion, and no personality. This is theoretically a possibility, but I have never heard anyone hold this view, for it seems to be unthinkable. It follows that if we do not hold that everything has come of nothing-nothing, then something has always existed.

Second, there is the possibility of a personal beginning—that everything else was made by a personality who could bring forth the universe (the space-time continuum) when it had not existed previously in *any* form. This is not out of nothing-nothing, for the personality would have existed previously.

Third, there is the possibility of an impersonal beginning—that some form of the impersonal has existed forever, even if in a form vastly different from that which we now know. This idea of an impersonal beginning has many variations, including the use of the word *God* to mean the ultimate impersonal, as in the case of pantheism. A more accurate word than *pantheism* to describe this position is *pan-everythingism*. The word *pantheism* slips in the connotation of personality, even though, by definition, the concept excludes it. In much modern thought, all begins with the impersonality of the atom or the molecule or the energy particle, and then everything—including life and man—comes forth by chance from that.

This is really very curious because Louis Pasteur (1822–1895), the French chemist, demonstrated the impossibility of the then-accepted concept of the spontaneous generation of life—that is, life springing from nonliving things. Pasteur showed in 1864 that if the nonliving things were pasteurized, then life could not come forth. In other words, what was previously considered spontaneous generation of life from nonliving things was mistaken—life always came from living things. When pasteurization killed all the elements of life, life never came forth from the nonliving things. But then the men of that same era returned to the concept of the spontaneous generation of life by adding a new factor: long reaches of time.

This equation of the impersonal plus time plus chance producing the total configuration of the universe and all that is in it, modern people hold by faith. And if one does in faith accept this, with what final value is he left? In his lecture at Acapulco, George Wald finished with only one final value. It was the same one with which English philosopher Bertrand Russell (1872–1970) was left. For Wald and Russell and for many other modern thinkers, the final value is the biological continuity of the human race. If this is the only final value, one is left wondering why this then has importance.

Now having travelled from the pride of man in the High Renaissance and the Enlightenment down to the present despair, we can understand where modern people are. They have no place for a personal God. But equally they have no place for man as man, or for love, or for freedom, or for significance. This brings a crucial problem. Beginning only from man himself, people affirm that man is only a machine. *But those who hold this position cannot live like machines!* If they could, there would have been no tensions in their intellectual position or in their lives. But even people who believe they are machines cannot live like machines, and thus they must "leap upstairs" against their reason and try to find something which gives meaning to life, even though to do so they have to deny their reason.

This was a solution Leonardo da Vinci and the men of the Renaissance never would have accepted, even if, like Leonardo, they ended their thinking in despondency. They would not have done so, for they would have considered it intellectual suicide to separate meaning and values from reason in this way. And they would have been right. Such a solution is intellectual suicide, and one may question the intellectual integrity of those who accept such a position when their starting point was pride in the sufficiency of human reason.

9 Modern Philosophy and Modern Theology

Modern people have put various things "upstairs" in the area of non-reason in a desperate attempt to find some optimism about meaning and values. We will consider first those things the secular existential philosophers have put there, in their attempt to find meaning to life.

The existentialist who is probably best known is Jean-Paul Sartre (1905–). He held that in the area of reason everything is absurd, but nonetheless a person can authenticate himself by an act of the will; everyone should abandon the pose of spectator and act in a purposeless world. But because, as Sartre saw it, reason is separated from this authenticating, the will can act in any direction. On the basis of his teaching, you could authenticate yourself either by helping a poor old lady along the road at night or by speeding up your auto and running her down. Reason is not involved, and nothing can show you the direction which your will should take.

Albert Camus (1913–1960) was always named jointly with Sartre as one of the two leaders of French existentialism. However, Camus was never as consistent as Sartre with the presuppositions which they both held. Being less consistent, he was more human and therefore better liked by the young who were following French existentialism.

But Sartre could not live consistently with his position either. By signing the Algerian Manifesto (1960) which declared the

167

Algerian War a dirty war—that is, by making a value judgment that was not just a leap of non-reason—he destroyed his own position. This action said that man can use his reason to conclude that some things are right and some things are wrong. Sartre's later left-wing political views did the same.

Martin Heidegger (1889–1976), a German philosopher, was an existentialist who set forth basically the same idea: that answers are separated from reason. His early books are *Being and Time* (1927) and *What Is Metaphysics?* (1929). As a young man, Heidegger introduced the term *angst* (roughly meaning "anxiety") as a word defining modern man's stance before the world. This angst is not to be confused with fear. As Heidegger defined it, fear has an object, while angst is the general feeling of anxiety one experiences in the universe. It is fear without a definite object. In Heidegger's view this mood of anxiety gives people certainty of existence, and in so doing there is laid upon them a call for decision. Thus out of this mood comes meaning to life and to choice, even against one's reason. But notice: This rests on nothing more than a vague feeling of anxiety, so nebulous it does not even have a specific object. We shall see that later this view was too weak for Heidegger, and as an older man he changed his position.

Karl Jaspers (1883–1969) was a German existentialist, but he is usually thought of as Swiss because he lived and taught in Basel for so long. In some ways he has had the greatest impact on the thought and the life forms which have followed the avenue of existential thought. Jaspers suggested that we may have a "final experience" in life. To him *final experience* was a technical term. By it he meant that even though our mind tells us life is absurd, we may have some huge experience that encourages us to believe that there is a meaning to life.

The dilemma of Jaspers's existentialism can be understood clearly by an example. A young man from Holland who followed Jaspers came to study with me in Switzerland. He had had an experience in Amsterdam one night at the theatre as he watched the play *Green Pastures*. Reason had played no part, but it had been a very emotional experience, and it had given him the *hope* of some meaning to life that he had not had before. Weeks and months passed, and because no reason was involved in the experience, he could not give any words or content to it, neither to others nor to himself. To put the experience into words is impossible, for in the existential system reason is excluded from the experience. Thus, by definition, content is excluded and the possibility of putting it into words is excluded. One can only say to others or to oneself, "I had an experience." All this young man could keep on saying was, "So many months ago, I had an experience." He was gradually overwhelmed and ready to commit suicide; the feeling of meaning which had no basis in his reason gradually slipped through his fingers and, being sensitive, he was left in despair. A bitter thing indeed!

As a formal philosophical position, existentialism is growing less influential. But more and more among people generally this frame of thinking is increasing. This is so even if the people thinking this way do not know the word *existentialism*. They talk about or act upon the idea that reason leads only to pessimism. They say or act upon the concept (with varying degrees of understanding), "Let us try to find an answer in something totally separated from reason." Humanistic man tried to make himself self-sufficient and demanded that one start from himself and the individual details and build his own universals. His great hope that he could begin from himself and produce a uniformity of knowledge led him, however, to the sad place where his mind told him that he was only a machine, a bundle of molecules. Then he tried desperately to find meaning in the area of non-reason, until, with those following Jaspers, the problem became how one could be sure he would ever have a big enough *final experience* (or, even if he had one, how he could ever have another) and there was no way to be sure.

The man who followed on from that point was English—Aldous Huxley (1894–1963). He proposed drugs as a solution. We should, he said, give healthy people drugs and they can then find truth inside their own heads. They can then have the final experience any time they wish; they do not need to wait, hoping that something will happen. He first suggested this as a theoretical concept in *Brave New World* (1932), calling the all-important drug *soma*. He chose this name with care, for in Eastern Hindu myths, *soma* was the drug which kept the gods contented. Thus, in tying into Eastern thought his hope of finding a meaning for life in the area of non-reason, Aldous Huxley was already opening the door for what would be the next step.

Later Huxley went beyond the theoretical concept in *Brave New World* and openly advocated the use of drugs in *The Doors of Perception* (1956) and *Heaven and Hell* (1956). And in *The Humanist Frame* (1961), edited by his brother Julian Huxley (1887–1975), Aldous contributed the last chapter "Human Potentialities," still pushing for first-order experiences through drugs. He held this view up to the time of his death. He made his wife promise to give him LSD when he was ready to die so that he would die in the midst of a trip. All that was left for Aldous Huxley and those who followed him was truth inside a person's own head. With Huxley's idea, what began with the existential philosophers— man's individual subjectivity attempting to give order as well as meaning, in contrast to order being shaped by what is objective or external to oneself—came to its logical conclusion. Truth is in one's own head. The ideal of objective truth was gone.

This emphasis on hallucinogenic drugs brought with it many rock groups, for example, Cream, Jefferson Airplane, Grateful Dead, Incredible String Band, Pink Floyd, and Jimi Hendrix. Most of their work was from 1965 to 1968. The Beatles' *Sergeant Pepper's Lonely Hearts Club Band* (1967) also fits here. This disc is a total unity, not just an isolated series of individual songs, and for a time it became the rallying cry for young people throughout the world. It expressed the essence of their lives, thinking, and feeling. As a whole, this music was the vehicle to carry the drug culture and the mentality which went with it across frontiers which were almost impassable by other means of communication.

The next accepted version in the West of life in the area of non-reason was the religious experience of Hinduism and Buddhism. This grasping for a nonrational meaning to life and values is the central reason that these Eastern religions are so popular in the West today. Goethe, Wagner, and others had opened the door to Eastern thinking with their vague pantheism. But it came floodlike into the West with Huxley and the emphasis on drugs, for it followed naturally in the line of what people had been putting into the area of non-reason in the hope of finding meaning and values. Young people (and older ones) tried the drug trip and then turned to the Eastern religious trip. Both seek truth inside one's own head and both negate reason.

In this flow there was also the period of psychedelic rock, an attempt to find this experience without drugs, by the use of a certain type of music. This was the period of the Beatles' *Revolver* (1966) and *Strawberry Fields Forever* (1967). In the same period and in the same direction was *Blonde on Blond* (1966) by Bob Dylan.

We are seeing that many things can be put in the area of non-reason to provide an optimistic hope. Indeed it can be a highly sophisticated cultural concept. André Malraux (1901–) of France argued that art will give us the hope of some meaning to life—not the content of the art, but simply the fact that art exists. In *The Voices of Silence* (1953) Malraux showed that he understood very well that modern man is the man of no absolutes. Yet he offered art as a hope, a hope of non-reason.

Heidegger in his later years changed from his existential philosophy. His earlier existentialism had proved too weak and so he tried a new approach. His later books were *An Introduction to Metaphysics* (1953), *Essays in Metaphysics* (1957), *The Question of Being* (1956), *What Is Philosophy?* (1956), and *Discourse on Thinking* (1959). His new emphasis was clearly exhibited in his little book *What Is Philosophy?* According to the later Heidegger, because there is a being (that is, man) who speaks, who verbalizes, one can hope that the universe (that is, *Being*) has meaning. For him, this was his final cause for optimism. "Listen to the poet," he tells us in *What Is Philosophy?* It is not the content of what the poet says which is important, because the poets may contradict each other, but just the fact that poets exist.

We have also seen a tremendous rash of the occult appearing as an *upper story* hope. Though demons do not fit into modern man's concepts on the basis of his reason, many moderns would rather have demons than be left with the idea that everything in the universe is only one big machine. People put the occult in the upper story of non-reason in the hope of having some kind of meaning, even if it is a horrendous one.

Another example of what can be put in the area of non-reason is found in the thought and the art of Salvador Dali (1904–). At first Dali was a Surrealist. *Surrealism* is the uniting of Freud's concept of the existence of the unconscious with Dada—an art and life form in which all was seen as absurd. The founding group chose its very name in Zürich by opening a French dictionary at random and putting a finger down on a chance word, which happened to be the French word for rocking horse, *dada*.

Eventually, Salvador Dali abandoned Surrealism—with its acceptance of absurdity—and began his mystical paintings in which Gala, his wife, became the focal point in his leap into the area of non-reason in a hope for meaning. The first breakthrough in this period was his painting *A Basket of Bread*. He had painted in 1926 and 1945 other works with this same title; these depicted baskets of rough Spanish bread. But in 1945, he used this title for a painting of Gala with one breast exposed. He wrote her name on the picture; there is no mistaking who she is. He made her his mystical center. In some of his paintings he would portray her three or four times, often where Mary would have appeared in Roman Catholic paintings. There are a number of such paintings in the New York Cultural Center in New York City. From this time on, many of his pictures show his mystical leap into the area of non-reason.

This was the period of *Christ of Saint John of the Cross* (1951), now in the Glasgow Art Gallery, and *The Sacrament of the Last Supper* (1955), now in the National Gallery of Art in Washington. These were not paintings of the Christ of history. Rather, in them Christ is an upper story, mystical figure. They were the leap of Kierkegaardianism expressed in painting. The Christ in the *Last Supper* is a shadowy figure through whom we may look at the landscape behind. The little ships are visible through his body. This is not a body of flesh and blood in space and time. This intangible Christ which Dali painted is in sharp contrast to the bodies of the apostles who are physically solid in the picture.

Dali explained in his interviews that he had found a mystical meaning for life in the fact that things are made up of energy rather than solid mass. Because of this, for him there was a reason for a vault into an area of non-reason to give him the hope of meaning. Whether in his interviews or in these paintings, that which causes him to escape the absurdity which Surrealism presented is not reason, and it is not Christianity either; it is a blind leap into the area of non-reason.

48 *The Sacrament of the Last Supper* by Salvador Dali. ". . . Christ is an upper story, mystical figure."

One must understand that from the advent of Kierkegaardianism onward there has been a widespread concept of the dichotomy between reason and non-reason, with no interchange between them. The *lower story* area of reason is totally isolated from the optimistic area of non-reason. The line which divides reason from non-reason is as impassable as a concrete wall thousands of feet thick, reinforced with barbed wire charged with 10,000 volts of electricity. There is no interchange, no osmosis between the two parts. So modern man now lives in such a total dichotomy, wherein reason leads to despair. "Downstairs" in the area of humanistic reason, man is a machine, man is meaningless. There are no values. And "upstairs" optimism about meaning and values is totally separated from reason. Reason has no place here at all; here reason is an outcast.

This division into these two areas is the *existential methodology*. This methodology (and the existence of the dichotomy) is the hallmark of the modern stream of humanistic thinking. Once people adopt this dichotomy—where reason is separated totally from non-reason—they must then face the fact that many types of things can be put in the area of non-reason. And it really does not matter what one chooses to put there, because reason gives no basis for a choice between one thing or another.

In addition to the secular existentialism of Sartre, Camus, Jaspers, and Heidegger, Kierkegaardianism brought forth another form of existentialism: the *theological* existentialism which began with Karl Barth (1886–1968), especially with his first commentary (1919) on the New Testament book entitled *The Epistle to the Romans*. We must have profound admiration for Karl Barth in that he, as a Swiss teaching in Germany, made a public stand against Nazism in the Barman Declaration of 1934. For many years he taught at the University of Basel, was a prolific writer and has had a profound effect on the general flow of theology and intellectual thought in this generation. But in his theology Karl Barth made his own kind of dichotomy and brought the existential methodology into theology.

Back in the Middle Ages we saw that certain humanistic elements entered the church. The essence of the Reformation was the removal of these from the church's teaching. On the other hand, humanistic thinking developed in the Renaissance and again went further in the Enlightenment. The teachings of the Enlightenment became widespread in the various faculties of the German universities, and *theological* rationalism became an identifiable entity in the eighteenth century. Then gradually this came to full flood through the German theological faculties during the nineteenth century. Thus, though the Reformation had rid the church of the humanistic elements which had come into it in the Middle Ages, a more total form of humanism entered the Protestant church, and has gradually spread to all the branches of the church, including the Roman Catholic. The concept of man beginning from himself now began to be expressed in theology and in theological language. Or we can say that these theologians accepted the presuppositions of rationalism. As the Renaissance had tried to synthesize Aristotle and Christianity and then Plato and Christianity, these men were attempting to synthesize the rationalism of the Enlightenment and Christianity. This attempt has often been called *religious liberalism*.

The rationalistic theological liberalism of the nineteenth century was embarrassed by and denied the supernatural, but still tried to hold on to the historic Jesus by winnowing out of the New Testament all the supernatural elements. Let us notice, though, that they were functioning as the older *secular* thinkers had functioned: Either a thing was true or it was not. It could not be true and untrue at the same time. For example, either Christ was raised from the dead or he was not.

This came to its climax with Albert Schweitzer's (1875–1965) book *The Quest for the Historical Jesus* (1906) in which he tried to hold on to the Jesus of history. We should remember Schweitzer as an expert on Bach and a genius on the organ, and we certainly should not forget his humanitarianism in Africa, but unhappily we must also remember his place in the theological stream. *The Quest for the Historical Jesus* (especially the conclusion of the second edition which was never translated into English) showed the impossibility of ridding the New Testament of the supernatural and yet keeping any historical Jesus. The rationalistic theologians could not separate the historic Jesus from the supernatural events connected with him. History and the supernatural were too interwoven in the New Testament. If one retained any of the historical Jesus, one had to keep some of the supernatural. If one got rid of all the supernatural, one had no historical Jesus. Albert Schweitzer himself was left with what has often been called a poetic ethical pantheism.

Ever since theology accepted the presupposition of rationalism, it has followed, always a few years later, the shifting form of humanistic thought. Thus, as humanistic thought in general was first optimistic about finding out the answers to life by reason starting from man alone (but with Kierkegaardianism shifted to pessimism and accepted the *existential methodology* and its dichotomy) so liberal theology did the same. With Karl Barth the existential methodology and the dichotomy were accepted in theology. After the older theological liberalism had failed, Barth stepped into the vacuum with his Kierkegaardian theology.

Karl Barth held until the end of his life the "higher critical" views of the Bible which the nineteenth-century liberal theologians held, and thus he viewed the Bible as having many mistakes. But he then taught that a religious "word" breaks through from it. This was the theological form of existentialism and the dichotomy. In other words, the existential methodology was applied to theology. This meant that theology had now been added to all the other things which had been put into the area of non-reason.

Following the advent of the existential methodology there arose the neo-orthodox existential theology, which says that the Bible in the area of reason has mistakes but nonetheless can provide a religious experience in the area of non-reason. Neo-orthodox theologians do not see the Bible as giving truth which can be stated in contentful propositions, especially regarding the cosmos and history, that is, as making statements which are open to any verification. And for many of them the Bible does not give moral absolutes either. For these theologians, it is not faith in something; it is faith in faith.

But this finally brings them to the place where the word *God* merely becomes the *word* God, and no certain content can be put into it. In this many of the established theologians are in the same position as George Harrison (1943–) (the former Beatles' guitarist) when he wrote "My Sweet Lord" (1970). Many people thought he had come to Christianity. But listen to the words in the background: "Krishna, Krishna, Krishna." Krishna is one Hindu name for God. This song expressed no content, just a feeling of religious experience. To Harrison, the words were equal: Christ or Krishna. Actually, neither the word used nor its content was of importance.

Many of the established theologians also came to the place where the word *God* had no certain content; but one can use the word *God* and other religious words as the basis for a contentless religious experience within which reason has no place. J. S. Bezzant (1897–), a Cambridge don, in the volume *Objections to Christian Belief* (1964) gave his opinion of the neo-orthodox position (though he himself was an old-fashioned liberal): "When I am told that it is precisely its immunity from proof which secures the Christian proclamation from the charge of being mythological, I reply that immunity from proof can 'secure' nothing whatever except immunity from proof, and call nonsense by its name." He understood neo-orthodoxy very well.

The new liberal theology, because it says that the Bible does not touch the cosmos or history, has no real basis for applying the Bible's values in a historic situation, in either morals or law. Everything religious is in the area of non-reason, and since reason has no place there, there is no room for discussion; there are only arbitrary pronouncements. Immanuel Kant could not bring together the noumenal and the phenomenal worlds, and the new theologian has no way logically to bring his personal arbitrary values into a historic situation. Or to say it another way: Sartre said that in an absurd world we can authenticate ourselves by an act of the will; but, as we saw, because reason has no place in this we can help people or hurt them. Similarly, because the pronouncements of these theologians about morals or law are arbitrary, in a different mood they, too, can be totally reversed.

The new theologians also have no way to explain why evil exists, and thus they are left with the same problem the Hindu philosophers have; that is, they must say that finally everything that *is* is equally in God. In Hindu thought one of the manifestations of God is Kali, a feminine representation of God with fangs and skulls hanging about her neck. Why do Hindus picture God this way? Because to them everything that exists now is a part of what has always been, a part of that which the Hindus would call "God"— and therefore cruelty is equal to non-cruelty. Modern humanistic man in both his secular and his religious forms has come to the same awful place. Both have no final way to say what is right and what is wrong, and no final way to say why one should choose non-cruelty instead of cruelty.

Paul Tillich (1886–1965) of Harvard Divinity School was one of the outstanding neo-orthodox theologians. A student related to me that when Tillich was asked just before his death in Santa Barbara, California, "Sir, do you pray?" he answered, "No, but I meditate." He was left only with the word *God,* with no certainty that there was anything more than just the word or that the word equaled anything more than the pantheistic pan-everythingism. The God-is-dead theology which followed Tillich concluded logically that if we are left only with the word *God,* there is no reason not to cross out the word itself.

But for many modern liberal theologians (even if they do not say that God is dead), certain other things *are* dead. Because they do not accept that God in the Bible and in the revelation in Christ has given man truth which may be expressed in propositions, for them all *content* about God is dead and all assurance of a *personal* God is dead. One is left with the connotation of religious words without content, and the emotion which certain religious words still bring forth—and that is all.

The next step is that these highly motivating religious words out of our religious past, but separated from their original content and context in the Bible, are then used for manipulation. The words became a banner for men to grab and run with in any arbitrary direction—either shifting sexual morality from its historic Christian position based on the Bible's and Christ's teaching, or in legal and political manipulation.

Modern people and modern theology, in trying to start from man alone, are left where the brilliant German philosopher Friedrich Nietzsche (1844–1900) found himself. Nietzsche in the 1880s was the first one who said in the modern way that God is dead, and he understood well where people end when they say this. If God is dead, then everything for which God gives an answer and meaning is dead. And this is true whether it is a secular man or a modern theologian who says, "God is dead." It is also equally true whether the modern theologian says, "God is dead," or whether he reacts

49 Kali. ". . . and cruelty is equal to non-cruelty." *Photo by Mustafa Arshad.*

against those theologians who say that God is dead, but he continues to use an existential methodology. He himself is left with all *content* about God being dead and all assurance of God as *personal* being dead. The final result is the same.

I am convinced that when Nietzsche came to Switzerland and went insane, it was not because of venereal disease, though he did have this disease. Rather, it was because he understood that insanity was the only philosophic answer if the infinite-personal God does not exist.

I know well the beautiful village of Sils Maria in the Swiss Engadine, where Nietzsche spent his summers and did much work from 1881 to 1888. His house is still there. And on the lovely peninsula of Chasté a quotation from Nietzsche is inscribed on a plaque on a great rock. The following is an English translation from the German (by Udo Middelmann):

> Oh man! Take heed
>   of what the dark midnight says:
> I slept, I slept—from deep dreams I awoke:
> The world is deep—and more profound than day
>   would have thought.
> Profound in her pain—
> Pleasure—more profound than pain of heart,
> Woe speaks; pass on.
> But all pleasure seeks eternity—
>   a deep and profound eternity.

Surrounded by some of the most beautiful scenery in the world, Nietzsche knew the tension and despair of modern man. With no personal God, all is dead. Yet man, being truly man (no matter what he says he is), cries out for a meaning that can only be found in the existence of the infinite-personal God, who has not been silent but has spoken, and in the existence of a personal life continuing into eternity. Thus Nietzsche's words are profound: "But all pleasure seeks eternity—a deep and profound eternity."

Without the infinite-personal God, all a person can do, as Nietzsche points out, is to make "systems." In today's speech we would call them "game plans." A person can erect some sort of structure, some type of limited frame, in which he lives, shutting himself up in that frame and not looking beyond it. This game plan can be one of a number of things. It can sound high and noble, such as talking in an idealistic way about the greatest good for the greatest number. Or it can be a scientist concentrating on some small point of science so that he does not have to think of any of the big questions, such as why things exist at all. It can be a skier concentrating for years on knocking one-tenth of a second from a downhill run. Or it can as easily be a theological word game within the structure of the *existential methodology*. That is where modern people, building only on themselves, have come, and that is where they are now.

10 Modern Art, Music, Literature, and Films

Modern pessimism and modern fragmentation, have spread in three different ways to people of our own culture and to people across the world. *Geographically,* it spread from the European mainland to England, after a time jumping the Atlantic to the United States. *Culturally,* it spread in the various disciplines from philosophy to art, to music, to general culture (the novel, poetry, drama, films), and to theology. *Socially,* it spread from the intellectuals to the educated and then through the mass media to everyone.

In spreading socially, modern pessimism left isolated a certain age group of the middle class which still thought in the old ways. Though many in the group had no sufficient base for doing so, nevertheless through inertia they continued to act as though values did exist for them. But as their children were educated, the children were injected with the new thought, and the *generation gap* came into being. Members of the new generation saw that many of their parents had no base for the values that they said they held. Many of their parents were governed only by a dead tradition; they acted largely out of habit from the past.

As time has gone on, people in Western culture have become surrounded by an almost monolithic consensus. That is to say, the same basic dichotomy—in which reason leads to pessimism and all optimism is in the area of non-reason—surrounds us on every side and comes to us from almost every quarter. In the various disciplines, the first place this perspective was taught was in philosophy, of which we have already spoken at length. Then it was presented through art, then through music, then through general culture, and finally through theology.

After philosophy proper, the second vehicle was art. In art the way was prepared by a curious twist in the way naturalists were painting. The viewer comes to the painting and in one way sees what the artist pictures, but in another way asks himself, "Is there any meaning to what I am looking at?" The art had become sterile.

The breakthrough came with the Impressionists Claude Monet (1840–1926) and Pierre Auguste Renoir (1841–1919), who were soon followed by Camille Pissarro (1830–1903), Alfred Sisley (1839–1899), and Edgar Degas (1834–1917), all of them great artists. These men painted *only* what their eyes brought them, but this left the question as to whether there was a reality behind the light waves reaching the eyes. They called it "following nature." After 1885 Monet carried this to its logical conclusion, and reality tended to become a dream. We could think of Monet's series of poplar trees, for example, *Poplars at Giverney, Sunrise* (1888) now in the Museum of Modern Art in New York, and *Poplars at Epte* (1890), now in the Tate Gallery in London. As reality tended to become a dream, Impressionism as a movement fell apart. With Impressionism the door was open for art to become the vehicle for modern thought.

Then came the post-Impressionists who attempted to solve the problem by trying to find the way back to reality, to the absolute behind the individual things. They felt the loss of universals, tried to solve the problem, and in the end they failed. It is not that these painters were always consciously painting their philosophy of life, but rather that in their work as a whole their world view was often reflected. The great post-Impressionists were Paul Cézanne (1839–1906), Vincent Van Gogh (1853–1890), Paul Gauguin (1848–1903), and Georges Seurat (1859–1891).

These men had great talent as painters, and some of their paintings have great beauty. To read the letters of Vincent Van Gogh is to weep for the pain of this sensitive man. But we must also stress their place in culture, as art became the vehicle for modern man's view of the fragmentation of truth and life.

As philosophy had moved from unity to a fragmentation, this fragmentation was also carried into the field of painting. The fragmentation shown in post-Impressionist paintings was parallel to the loss of a hope for a unity of knowledge in philosophy. It was not just a new technique in painting. It expressed a world view. Cézanne reduced nature to what he considered its basic geometric forms. In this he was searching for a universal which would tie all kinds of particulars in nature together. Nonetheless, this gave nature a fragmented, broken appearance. In *Bathers* (c. 1905, now in the National Gallery in London), there is much freshness and vitality, much in the balance of the picture as a whole. However, in this painting Cézanne brought the appearance of fragmented reality not only to his painting of nature but to man himself. Man, too, was presented as fragmented.

From this point onward one could either move to the extreme of an ultranatural naturalism, such as the photo-realists, or to the extreme of freedom, whereby reality becomes so fragmented that it disappears, and man is left to make up his own personal world. In 1912 abstract Expressionist painter Wassily Kandinsky (1866–1944) wrote an article entitled "About the Question of Form" in *The Blue Rider* saying that, since the old harmony (a unity of knowledge) had been lost, only two possibilities remained—extreme naturalism or extreme abstraction. Both, he said, were equal.

Gertrude Stein (1874–1946), an American author living in Paris, was important at this time. It was at her home that many artists and writers met and talked of these things, hammering out in talk the new ideas—many of them long before they personally became famous. Picasso initially met Cézanne at her home.

Pablo Picasso (1881–1973) brought together the fragmentation of Cézanne along with Gauguin's concept of the noble savage, and he added the form of the African masks which had just become popular in Paris. With this mixture he painted *Les Demoiselles d'Avignon* (1906–1907). This painting, now in the Museum of Modern Art in New York, marked the birth of "modern art."

In great art the technique fits the world view being presented, and this new technique of fragmentation fits the world view of

Next two pages: **50** *Poplars at Giverney* by Claude Monet. ". . . reality tended to become a dream." **51** The author while filming *Bathers* by Cézanne in National Gallery, London. ". . . a fragmented, broken appearance." *Photo by Mustafa Arshad.*

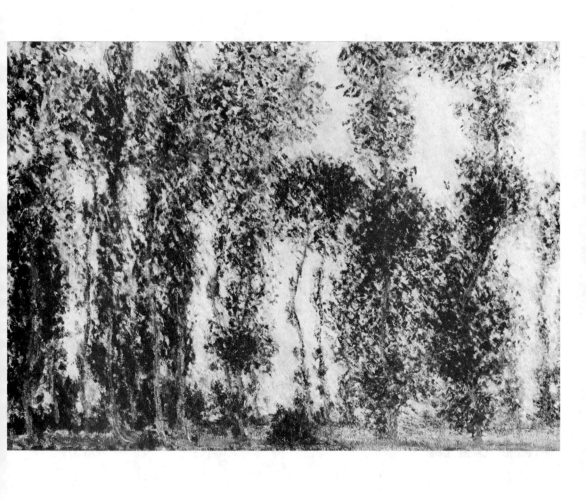

modern man. The technique expressed well the concept of a fragmented world and fragmented man. What David Douglas Duncan (1916–) says in his book *Picasso's Picassos* (1961) about a certain set of Picasso's pictures in Picasso's private collection, is in a way a summing up of much of Picasso's work: "Of course, not one of these pictures was actually a portrait but his prophecy of a ruined world." It was a complete break with the art of the Renaissance which had been founded on man's humanist hope. In *Les Demoiselles d'Avignon* people were made to be less than people; the humanity had been lost.

But it is fascinating that Picasso could not really live with this loss. When he fell in love with Olga, and later Jacqueline, Picasso did not consistently paint them in a fragmented way. Rather, at crucial points in their relationship, he painted them with all his genius as they really were with all their humanity. He had many mistresses, but these were the two women he married. It is interesting that Jacqueline kept one of these paintings in her private sitting room. Duncan says of this lovely picture, "Hanging precariously on an old nail driven high into one of La Californie's [Picasso and Jacqueline's home] second floor sitting room walls, a portrait of Jacqueline Picasso reigns supreme. The room is her domain. . . . Painted in oil with charcoal, the picture has been at her side since shortly after she and the maestro met. . . . She loves it and wants it nearby." Then, too, when Picasso painted his children when they were young, he also often departed from his broken, fragmented technique.

Note that I am not saying that humanity or gentleness is never present in the techniques of modern art, but that as these techniques advanced, humanity was increasingly fragmented—as we shall see, for example, with Marcel Duchamp. The artists carried the idea of a fragmented reality onto the canvas. But at the same time, being sensitive men, the artists realized where this fragmented reality was taking man, that is, to the absurdity of all things.

Hans Arp (1887–1966), an Alsatian sculptor, wrote a poem which appeared in the final issue of the magazine *De Stijl* (The Style) which was published by the *De Stijl* group of artists led by Piet Mondrian and Theo van Doesburg. Mondrian (1872–1944) was the best-known artist of this school. He was not of the Dada school which accepted and portrayed absurdity. Rather, Mondrian was hoping to paint the absolute. Hans Arp, however, was a Dadaist artist connected with *De Stijl*. His poem "Für Theo Van Doesburg," translated from the German, reads:

> the head downward
> the legs upward
> he tumbles into the bottomless
> from whence he came
>
> he has no more honour in his body
> he bites no more bite of any short meal
> he answers no greeting
> and is not proud when being adored
>
> the head downward
> the legs upward
> he tumbles into the bottomless
> from whence he came
>
> like a dish covered with hair
> like a four-legged sucking chair
> like a deaf echotrunk
> half full half empty
>
> the head downward
> the legs upward
> he tumbles into the bottomless
> from whence he came.

Dada carried to its logical conclusion the notion of all having come about by chance; the result was the final absurdity of everything, including humanity.

The man who perhaps most clearly and consciously showed this understanding of the resulting absurdity of all things was Marcel Duchamp (1887–1969). He carried the concept of fragmentation further in *Nude Descending a Staircase* (1912), one version of which is now in the Philadelphia Museum of Art—a painting in which the human disappeared completely. The chance and fragmented concept of what *is* led to the devaluation and absurdity of all things. All one was left with was a fragmented view of a life

52   *Les Demoiselles d'Avignon* by Picasso, Museum of Modern Art in New York City (top) and the author with film crew. ". . . expressed well the concept of a fragmented world." *Photos by Mustafa Arshad.*

which is absurd in all its parts. Duchamp realized that the absurdity of all things includes the absurdity of art itself. His "ready-mades" were any object near at hand, which he simply signed. It could be a bicycle wheel or a urinal. Thus art itself was declared absurd.

The historical flow is like this: The philosophers from Rousseau, Kant, Hegel and Kierkegaard onward, having lost their hope of a unity of knowledge and a unity of life, presented a fragmented concept of reality; then the artists painted that way. It was the artists, however, who first understood that the end of this view was the absurdity of all things. Temporally these artists followed the philosophers, as the artists of the Renaissance had followed Thomas Aquinas. In the Renaissance it was also philosophy, followed by the painters (Cimabue and Giotto), followed by the writers (Dante). This was the same order in which the concept of fragmented reality spread in the twentieth century. The philosophers first formulated intellectually what the artists later depicted artistically.

Jackson Pollock (1912–1956) is perhaps the clearest example in the United States of painting deliberately in order to make the statement that all is chance. He placed canvases horizontally on the floor and dripped paint on them from suspended cans swinging over them. Thus, his paintings were a product of chance. But wait a minute! Is there not an order in the lines of paint on his canvases? Yes, because it was not really chance shaping his canvases! The universe is not a random universe; it has order. Therefore, as the dripping paint from the swinging cans moved over the canvases, the lines of paint were following the order of the universe itself. The universe is not what these painters said it is.

The third way the idea spread was through music. This came about first in classical music, though later many of the same elements came into popular music, such as rock. In classical music two streams are involved: the German and the French.

The first shift in German music came with the last Quartets of Beethoven, composed in 1825 and 1826. These certainly were not what we would call "modern," but they were a shift from the music prior to them. Leonard Bernstein (1918–) speaks of Beethoven as the "new artist—the artist as priest and prophet." Joseph Machlis (1906–) says in *Introduction to Contemporary Music* (1961), "Schönberg took his point of departure from the final Quartets of

Next two pages: 53 *Nude Descending a Staircase* by Marcel Duchamp. ". . . the human disappeared completely." *Photo by Mustafa Arshad.* 54 Duchamp's "ready-made" called *Bicycle Wheel.* ". . . any object near at hand." *Photo courtesy of Philadelphia Museum of Art.*

Beethoven." And Stravinsky said, "These Quartets are my highest articles of musical belief (which is a longer word for love, whatever else), as indispensable to the ways and meaning of art, as a musician of my era thinks of art and has to learn it, as temperature is to life."

Beethoven was followed by Wagner (1813–1883); then came Gustav Mahler (1860–1911). Leonard Bernstein in the *Norton Lectures* at Harvard University in 1973 says of Mahler and especially Mahler's Ninth Symphony, "Ours is the century of death and Mahler is its musical prophet . . . . If Mahler knew this [personal death, death of tonality, and the death of culture as it had been] and his message is so clear, how do we, knowing it too, manage to survive? Why are we still here, struggling to go on? We are now face to face with the truly ultimate ambiguity, which is the human spirit—the most fascinating ambiguity of all . . . . We learn to accept our mortality; yet we persist in our search for immortality . . . . All this ultimate ambiguity is to be heard in the finale of Mahler's Ninth." Notice how closely this parallels Nietzsche's poem on page 180. This is modern man's position. He has come to a position of the death of man in his own mind, but he cannot live with it, for it does not describe what he is.

Then came Schoenberg (1874–1951), and with him we are into the music which was a vehicle for modern thought. Schoenberg totally rejected the past tradition in music and invented the "12-tone row." This was "modern" in that there was perpetual variation with *no resolution*. This stands in sharp contrast to Bach who, on his biblical base, had much diversity but always resolution. Bach's music had resolution because as a Christian he believed that there will be resolution both for each individual life and for history. As the music which came out of the biblical teaching of the Reformation was shaped by that world view, so the world view of modern man shapes modern music.

Among Schoenberg's pupils were Alban Berg (1885–1935), Anton Webern (1883–1945) and John Cage (1912–). Each of these carried on this line of non-resolution in his own way. Donald Jay Grout (1902–) in *A History of Western Music* speaks of Schoenberg's and Berg's subject matter in the modern world: ". . . isolated, helpless in the grip of forces he does not understand, prey to inner conflict, tension, anxiety and fear." One can understand that a music of non-resolution is a fitting expression of the place to which modern man has come.

In *Introduction to Contemporary Music* Joseph Machlis says of Webern that his way of placing the weightier sounds on the offbeat and perpetually varying the rhythmic phrase imparts to his music its indefinable quality of "hovering suspension." Machlis adds that Karlheinz Stockhausen (1928–), and the German Cologne school in general, take up from Webern with the formation of electronic music which "generates, transforms and manipulates sounds electronically." Stockhausen produced the first published score of electronic music in his *Electronic Studies*. A part of his concern was with the element of chance in composition. As we shall see, this ties into the work of John Cage, whom we will study in more detail below. But first let us look at the French stream.

The French shift began with Claude Debussy (1862–1918). His direction was not so much that of non-resolution but of *fragmentation*. Many of us enjoy and admire much of Debussy's music, but he opened the door to fragmentation in music and has influenced most of the composers since, not only in classical music but in popular music and rock as well. Even the music which is one of the glories of America—black jazz and black spirituals—was gradually infiltrated.

It is worth reemphasizing that this fragmentation in music is parallel to the fragmentation which occurred in painting. And again let us say that these were not just changes of technique; they expressed a world view and became a vehicle for carrying that world view to masses of people which the bare philosophic writings never would have touched.

John Cage provides perhaps the clearest example of what is involved in the shift in music. Cage believed the universe is a universe of chance, and to express this he produced music by chance. He tried carrying this out with great consistency. For example, at times he flipped coins to decide what the music should be. At other times he erected a machine that led an orchestra by chance motions so that the orchestra would not know what was coming next. Thus there was no order. Or again, he placed two conductors leading the same orchestra, separated from each other by a partition, so that what resulted was utter confusion. There is a close tie-in again to

55 Reenactment of one of Jackson Pollock's methods of painting "by chance" and *Convergence* by Pollock. ". . . painting deliberately in order to make the statement that all is chance."

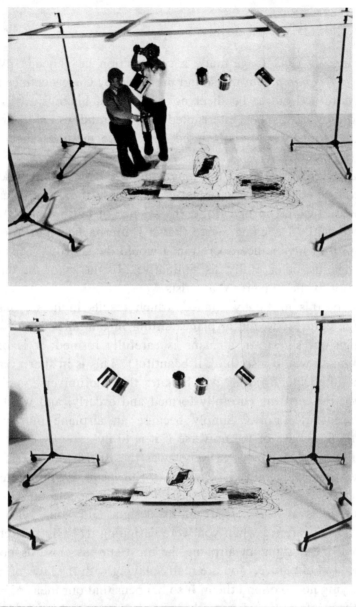

painting; in 1947 Cage made a composition he called *Music for Marcel Duchamp*. But the sound produced by Cage's chance music always turned out to be sheer noise. Some of his music was composed only of silence (interrupted only by random environmental sounds), but as soon as he used his chance methods sheer noise was the outcome.

But Cage also showed that one cannot live on such a base, that the chance concept of the universe does not fit the universe as it is. Cage is an expert in mycology, the science of mushrooms. And he himself said, "I became aware that if I approached mushrooms in the spirit of my chance operation, I would die shortly." Mushroom picking must be carefully discriminative. His theory of the universe does not fit the universe that exists.

All of this music by chance, which results in noise, makes a strange contrast to the airplanes sitting in our airports or slicing through our skies. An airplane is carefully formed; it is orderly (and many would also think it beautiful). This is in sharp contrast to the intellectualized art which states that the universe is chance. Why is the airplane carefully formed and orderly, and what Cage produced utter noise? Simply because an airplane must fit the orderly flow lines of the universe if it is to fly!

Sir Archibald Russel (1905–) was the British designer for the Concorde airliner. In a *Newsweek:* European Edition interview (February 16, 1976) he was asked: "Many people find that the Concorde is a work of art in its design. Did you consider its esthetic appearance when you were designing it?" His answer was, "When one designs an airplane, he must stay as close as possible to the laws of nature. You are really playing with the laws of nature and trying not to offend them. It so happens that our ideas of beauty are those of nature. Every shape and curve of the Concorde is arranged so it will conform with the natural flow as conditioned by the laws of nature. That's why I doubt that the Russian supersonic airplane is a crib of ours. The Russians have the same basic phenomena imposed on them by nature as we do."

Cage's music and the world view for which it is the vehicle do not fit the universe that is. Someone might here bring in Einstein, Werner Heisenberg's principle of uncertainty and quantum, but we have considered them on page 138, and so will not repeat the discussion here. The universe is not what Cage in his music and Pollock in his painting say it is. And we must add that Cage's music does not fit what people are, either. It has had to become increasingly spectacular to keep interest; for example, a nude cellist has played Cage's music under water.

A further question is: Is this art really art? Is it not rather a bare philosophic, intellectual statement, separated from the fullness of who people are and the fullness of what the universe is? The more it tends to be only an intellectual statement, rather than a work of art, the more it becomes anti-art.

The fourth vehicle for these ideas is what I will call general culture. By this, I mean poetry, the novel, drama, and cinema. In the Anglo-Saxon world, the introduction in poetry came with T. S. Eliot's (1888–1965) "The Waste Land," which was published in 1922. Here he matched a fragmented message to a fragmented form of poetry. The end of the fifth (and last) section of "The Waste Land" reads:

> *Le Prince d'Aquitaine à la tour abolie.*
> These fragments I have shored against my ruins
> Why then Ile fit you.
> Hieronymo's mad againe.
> Datta. Dayadhvam. Damyata.
>   Shantih shantih shantih.

In this poem he opened the door to modern poetry the way Picasso opened the way to a fragmented concept of life in his painting *Les Demoiselles d'Avignon*. It is interesting that later when Eliot became a Christian, his form of writing, although it did not become "old-fashioned," did change. We will pick up elements of general culture later in this chapter, especially the uniquely twentieth-century art form—the cinema. Popular music, such as the elements of rock, brought to the young people of the entire world the concept of a fragmented world—and optimism only in the area of non-reason. And poetry, drama, the novel, and especially films carried these ideas to the mass of people in a way that went beyond the other vehicles we have considered.

All of this gives us today an almost monolithic consensus, an almost unified voice shouting at us a fragmented concept of the universe and of life. And as it comes at us from every side and with many voices, it is difficult not to be infiltrated by it. We and our children now get this message from every side—from art, music, general culture, modern theology, the mass media, and often even comic books. Perhaps cinema, especially in the sixties, proclaimed this message in a way that spread it most widely. But in order to understand its unique contribution we must first consider other developments in philosophy.

Formal philosophy, as such, has tended to sicken, if not die, for modern people. As we have seen, modern modern science put aside the epistemological base of early science—this early base being that, because the world was created by a reasonable God, man can find out about the universe by reason. Then, when this Christian base was abandoned, scientists tried to make the philosophy of *positivism* their philosophic base for knowing.

Positivism had been worked out in the first half of the nineteenth century by the French philosopher Auguste Comte (1798–1857) and was developed as the base for science by Herbert Spencer (1820–1903). Related to John Locke's (1632–1704) empiricism, positivism is a naive philosophy which basically says that you look at an object and there it is. The data which reaches you through your senses enables you to know the object in a straightforward and uncomplicated way.

But some years ago people began to realize that science did not really look at an object with total objectivity. In the *Journal of the Franklin Institute* (1936) Albert Einstein pointed out that man makes choices out of the multitude of sense data which comes to him. In other words, there is a subjective element involved in the scientific process. Michael Polanyi (1891–1976), who retired from Manchester University in 1958 and since that time had taught in many universities, in his book *Personal Knowledge: Towards a Post-Critical Philosophy* (1958) destroyed the naive view of positivism. Polanyi pointed out that the observer is always there and always makes the conclusions, and he is never entirely neutral.

And with this, positivism is no longer a viable base for knowing. In science a man arranges the experiment; he has a grid in his thinking into which he fits his observations and makes the conclusions. The positivism I knew when I was younger, which was so very, very strong in the universities of Europe and America, is now dead. No longer are those holding this view so sure of the relationship between themselves and the object they are observing.

There is another profound objection to positivism, namely, that on the basis of this philosophic system there is no reason for certainty that the data reaching the observer is really data and not just illusion. This was no problem when Christianity was the basis, with a view of the universe as created by a God of reason, and people created by the same reasonable God to live in that universe. But without the Christian base, what assurance do people have that what reaches them through the senses corresponds to what is "out there"? Humanism in the Renaissance had not been able to find a way to impart meaning and value to the individual things, the particulars. By the time of the death of positivism, humanism had no base for certainty in knowing.

Interestingly, the artists had seen the problem before the philosophers and scientists, for positivism was parallel to Impressionism. As we have said, the Impressionists painted what they saw, but this left the question of whether there was reality behind the light waves reaching their eyes. Monet took the next step in 1885 and reality tended to be obscured. Thus there was a time when the artists were ahead of both philosophers and scientists. Without the Christian base, neither artists nor philosophers nor scientists had a base which would bear the needed weight in the area of how we can be sure we can know.

What then has happened to science? In brief, science, as it is now usually conceived, has no epistemological base—that is, no base for being sure that what scientists think they observe corresponds to what really exists. It should be noted, however, that even though they have no such base in their own system, yet in both science and day-by-day knowing, there *is* a correspondence between the external world and ourselves, for God indeed made the subject and object to be in a proper relationship, just as our lungs fit this atmosphere on the earth. Thus, men can go on learning about the universe. But the point is that the humanist has no base for knowing *within his own philosophic system*. His optimism about knowing the external world is weakened.

In this setting modern modern science tends increasingly to

become one of two things: either a high form of technology, often with a goal of increasing affluence, or what I would call *sociological science*. By the latter I mean that, with a weakened certainty about objectivity, people find it easier to come to whatever conclusions they desire for the sociological ends they wish to see attained.

One example is Edmund Leach (1910–), a Reith Lecturer and well-known teacher of anthropology at Cambridge University. In *The New York Review of Books* (1966) Leach said that in the past there have been two views of evolution: either that all men came from the same starting place, or that there were different starting places and different starting times from prehuman biological forms. This second concept usually carries with it the idea that the races which are the oldest are the most advanced. Leach said that he chose the first concept because the second led to racism. Speaking of this second concept, he said that "this view of race is utterly useless for any purpose whatsoever except for ammunition for deplorable political causes." This is what I would call *sociological science*: choices being made on the basis of the sociological consequences which would result. With the weakening of certainty about knowing the objective, external world, the ideal of *objectivity* in science is weakened.

This is parallel to a change among the news makers. As their concept of truth becomes more relative, the ideal of *objectivity* in the news columns in contrast to the editorial pages is increasingly diminished. Thus, the loss of a philosophic base for truth and the certainty of knowing has the practical result of making for a *sociological science* and a *sociological news medium*—both available for use by manipulators. And this is especially potent with science because of the almost "religious" belief which people have developed about the objectivity—and thus the certainty—of the results of science.

Returning to philosophy as such, after positivism, came *linguistic analysis*. This is a philosophy that deals with the analysis of language. Two philosophies were then dominant: existentialism and linguistic analysis. But to me neither are philosophies; both are antiphilosophies.

Existentialism deals with the big questions, but separates the attempted answers from reason, placing them in the area of non-reason. By contrast, linguistic analysis examines language on the basis of reason—only to discover gradually that analysis of language leads neither to values nor to facts. Language leads only to language, and linguistic analysis thus never gets to the big questions. Consequently, existentialism and linguistic analysis are both anti-philosophies in that neither gives the basis people need for the answers to the big and fundamental questions. Not only do they not give the answers people need, but each in its own way generates confusion about meaning and values. There were other less influential philosophies as well, but they gave no more definitive answers. Formal philosophy had left a vacuum.

The important concepts of philosophy increasingly began to come not as formal statements of philosophy but rather as expressions in art, music, novels, poetry, drama, and the cinema—those things we spoke of as general culture earlier in the chapter. As an example, Sartre's and Camus' existentialism came not so much through formal philosophical statements as in their novels. Consider Sartre's *Nausea* (1938), and Camus' *The Stranger* (1942) and *The Plague* (1947), and also Simone de Beauvoir's (1908–) *L'Invitée* (1943).

Especially in the sixties the major philosophic statements which received a wide hearing were made through films. These philosophic movies reached many more people than philosophic writing or even painting and literature. Among these films were *The Last Year at Marienbad* by Alain Resnais (1961), *The Silence* by Ingmar Bergman (1963), *Juliet of the Spirits* by Federico Fellini (1965), *Blow-Up* by Michelangelo Antonioni (1966), *Belle de Jour* by Luis Buñel (1967) and *The Hour of the Wolf* by Ingmar Bergman (1967). They showed pictorially (and with great force) what it is like if man is a machine and also what it is like if man tries to live in the area of non-reason. In the area of non-reason man is left without categories. He has no way to distinguish between right and wrong, or even between what is objectively true as opposed to illusion or fantasy.

A good example is Antonioni's *Blow-Up*. The advertisement for the film read: "Murder without guilt, love without meaning." Antonioni was portraying how, in the area of non-reason, there are no certainties concerning moral values, and no human categories either. *Blow-Up* had no hero. Compare this with Michelangelo's

David—that statement of humanist pride in the Renaissance. Man had set himself up as autonomous, but the end result was not Michelangelo's *David,* but Antonioni's non-hero. All there is in the film is the camera which goes "click, click, click," and the human has disappeared. The main character snaps pictures of individual things, particulars. One might point out, for example, the models he snaps; all their humanity and meaning are gone.

After a scene in which clowns play tennis without a ball, there is at the end of the film a reverse zoom shot in which the man who is the central character disappears entirely, and all that remains is the grass. Man is gone. Modern people, on their basis of reason, see themselves only as machines. But as they move into the area of non-reason and look for their optimism, they find themselves separated from reason and without any human or moral values.

Some of the films of this period went even further as, for example, *Juliet of the Spirits, The Last Year at Marienbad, The Hour of the Wolf* and *Belle de Jour.* They were saying something even more profound: For modern people, as they leap into the area of non-reason to try to find optimism without reason, not only are there no human or moral categories but there is no certainty, no categories upon which to distinguish between reality and illusion.

Bergman provides a clear case here. In 1963 he directed *The Silence.* In a filmed interview he said he had come to conclude that God is dead; therefore there is only silence in the universe. Thus, he made this film. Then followed *The Hour of the Wolf* (1967) where one cannot tell the difference between what is real and what is fantasy. Was what was presented really happening or was it in the mind of one of the characters? This same problem was involved in the films *Juliet of the Spirits, The Last Year at Marienbad,* and *Belle de Jour.* One could view these films a hundred times and there still would be no way to be sure what was portrayed as objectively true and what was part of a character's imagination. If people begin only from themselves and really live in a universe in which there is no personal God to speak, they have no final way to be sure of the difference between reality and fantasy or illusion.

But Bergman (like Sartre, Camus, and all the rest) cannot really live with his own position. Therefore in *The Silence* the background music is Bach's Goldberg Variations. When he was asked in the

56 Movie posters from *Blow-Up, Silence,* and *Hour of the Wolf.* ". . . the major philosophic statements which received a wide hearing were made through films.

Michelangelo Antonioni's
first English-language film

Antonioni's camera never flinches.
At love without meaning. At murder without guilt.
At the dazzle and the madness of London today.

Vanessa Redgrave

BLOW-UP

David Hemmings
Sarah Miles

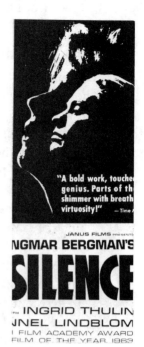

"A bold work, touched... genius. Parts of th... shimmer with breath... virtuosity!"
— Time A...

JANUS FILMS presents
NGMAR BERGMAN'S

SILENCE

... INGRID THULIN
...NEL LINDBLOM
...I FILM ACADEMY AWARD
FILM OF THE YEAR. 1963

INGMAR BERGMAN'S

"The Hour Of The Wolf" is the hour between night and dawn. It is the hour when most people die, when sleep is deepest, when nightmares are most real. It is the hour when the sleepless are haunted by their deepest fear, when ghosts and demons are most powerful. "The Hour Of The Wolf" is also the hour when most children are born.

"HOUR OF THE WOLF"

MAX VON SYDOW • LIV ULLMANN
DISTRIBUTED BY LOPERT PICTURES CORPORATION

filmed interview about music, he said that there is a small holy part of the human being where music speaks. He added that as he was writing *The Silence* he had the Goldberg Variations playing in his house and that this music interfered with what was being set forth in that film.

On the Christian base it is possible to know why music speaks. Man is not the product of chance. Man is made in the image of God, and on this basis, it is understandable why music *is* music to man. On the basis of revelation—the Bible and the revelation of God through Christ—there is not ultimate silence in the universe, and there are certainties of human values and moral values and categories to distinguish between illusion and fantasy. And there is a reason why man is man. But not for these modern people with a humanist position.

These philosophic films have spoken clearly about where people have come. Modern people are in trouble indeed. These things are not shut up within the art museums, the concert halls and rock festivals, the stage and movies, or the theological seminaries. People function on the basis of their world view. Therefore, society has changed radically. This is the reason—and not a less basic one— that it is unsafe to walk at night through the streets of many of today's cities. As a man thinketh, so is he.

11 Our Society

Gradually, that which had become the basic thought form of modern people became the almost totally accepted viewpoint, an almost monolithic consensus. And as it came to the majority of people through art, music, drama, theology, and the mass media, values died. As the more Christian-dominated consensus weakened, the majority of people adopted two impoverished values: *personal peace* and *affluence*.

Personal peace means just to be let alone, not to be troubled by the troubles of other people, whether across the world or across the city—to live one's life with minimal possibilities of being personally disturbed. Personal peace means wanting to have my personal life pattern undisturbed in my lifetime, regardless of what the result will be in the lifetimes of my children and grandchildren. Affluence means an overwhelming and ever-increasing prosperity—a life made up of things, things, and more things—a success judged by an ever-higher level of material abundance.

For several generations the fragmented concept of knowledge and life which had become dominant was taught to the young by many of the professors in universities around the world. All too often when the students of the early sixties asked their parents and others, "Why be educated?" they were told, in words if not by implication, "Because statistically an educated man makes so much more money a year." And when they asked, "Why make more money?" they were told, "So that you can send *your* children to the university." According to this kind of spoken or implied answer, there was no meaning for man, and no meaning for education.

Much of the mass media popularized these concepts, pouring them out in an endless stream so that a whole generation from its birth has been injected with the teaching that reason leads to pessimism in regard to a meaning of life and with reference to any fixed values. This had been that generation's atmosphere. It had no personal memory of the days when Christianity had more influence on the consensus. Those in the universities saw themselves as little computers controlled by the larger computer of the university, which in turn was controlled by the still-larger computer of the state.

The work ethic, which had meaning within the Christian framework, now became ugly as the Christian base was removed. Work became an end in itself—with no reason to work and no values to determine what to do with the products of one's work. And suddenly, in 1964 at the University of California at Berkeley, the students carried these ideas about the meaninglessness of man out into the streets. Why should anybody have been surprised? Many of the teachers taught the ultimate meaninglessness of man and the absence of absolutes, but they themselves lived inconsistently by depending on the memory of the past. Was it not natural that one generation would begin to live on the basis of what they had been taught? And at Berkeley in 1964 the results were visible, full blast.

Because the only hope of meaning had been placed in the area of non-reason, drugs were brought into the picture. Drugs had been around a long time, but, following Aldous Huxley's ideas, many students now approached drug taking as an ideology, and some, as a religion. They hoped that drugs would provide meaning "inside one's head," in contrast to objective truth, concerning which they had given up hope. Psychologist Timothy Leary (1920–), Gary Snyder (1930–), author-philosopher Alan Watts (1915–1973), and poet Allen Ginsberg (1926–) were all influential in making drugs an ideology. Timothy Leary, for example, said that drugs were the sacraments for the new religion. Of course, as we have seen in a previous chapter, this drug taking was really only one

57 Drug taking. ". . . many students now approached drug taking as an ideology." *Photos by Rex Features.*

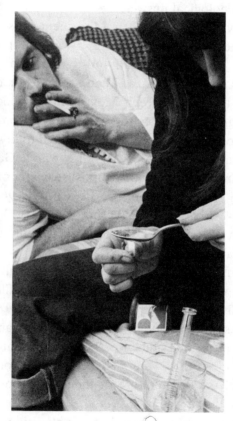

more leap, an attempt to find meaning in the area of non-reason. Charles Slack (1929–), writing of his long relationship with Leary, reported in *Timothy Leary, the Madness of the Sixties and Me* (1974) that Leary had said to him, "Death to the mind, that is the goal you must have. Nothing else will do."

The utopian dream of the turned-on world was that if enough people were on drugs, the problems of modern civilization would be solved. With this in mind there was talk of introducing LSD into the drinking water of the cities. This was not vicious, for the people suggesting it really believed that drugs were the door to Paradise. In 1964 and for some years after, the hippie world really believed this ideological answer.

At Berkeley the Free Speech Movement arose simultaneously with the hippie world of drugs. At first it was politically neither left nor right, but rather a call for the freedom to express any political views on Sproul Plaza. Then soon the Free Speech Movement became the Dirty Speech Movement, in which freedom was seen as shouting four-letter words into a mike. Soon after, it became the platform for the political New Left which followed the teaching of Herbert Marcuse (1898–). Marcuse was a German professor of philosophy related to the neo-Marxist teaching of the "Frankfurt School," along with Theodor Adorno (1903–1969), Max Horkheimer (1895–) and Jürgen Habermas (1929–). When he became the inspiration of the New Left, he was teaching at the University of California at San Diego.

For some time, young people were fighting against their parents' impoverished values of personal peace and affluence—whether their way of fighting was through Marcuse's New Left or through taking drugs as an ideology. The young people wanted more to life than personal peace and affluence. They were right in their analysis of the problem, but they were mistaken in their solutions.

The peak of the drug culture of the hippie movement was well symbolized by the movie *Woodstock*. Woodstock was a rock festival held in northeastern United States in the summer of 1969. The movie about that rock festival was released in the spring of 1970. Many young people thought that Woodstock was the beginning of a new and wonderful age. The organizer claimed, "This is the beginning of a new era. It works!" But the drug world was already ugly, and it was approaching the end of its optimism, although the young people did not yet know it. Jimi Hendrix (1942–1970) himself was soon to become a symbol of the end. Black, extremely talented, inhumanly exploited, he overdosed in September 1970 and drowned in his own vomit, soon after the claim that the culture of which he was a symbol was a new beginning. In the late sixties the ideological hopes based on drug taking died.

At Altamont, California, in December 1969, the Rolling Stones had a festival. They brought in the Hell's Angels to police the grounds in return for a certain amount of beer. But a man was killed, and *Rolling Stone* magazine in its next issue reported, "Our age of innocency is gone." Soon afterward (August 1970) 250,000 people came to a music festival on the Isle of Wight in the English Channel. It, too, ended in utter ugliness, and from that time on drug taking changed.

Unhappily, the result was not that fewer people were taking drugs. As the sixties drew to a close and the seventies began, probably more people were taking some form of drug, and at an ever-younger age. But taking drugs was no longer an ideology. That was finished. Drugs simply became the escape which they had been traditionally in many places in the past.

In the United States the New Left also slowly ground down, losing favor because of the excesses of the bombings, especially in the bombing of the University of Wisconsin lab in 1970, where a graduate student was killed. This was not the last bomb that was or will be planted in the United States. Hard-core groups of radicals still remain and are active, and could become more active, but the violence which the New Left produced as its natural heritage (as it also had in Europe) caused the majority of young people in the United States no longer to see it as a hope. So some young people began in 1964 to challenge the false values of personal peace and affluence, and we must admire them for this. Humanism, man beginning only from himself, had destroyed the old basis of values, and could find no way to generate with certainty any new values. In the resulting vacuum the impoverished values of personal peace and affluence had come to stand supreme. And now, for the majority of the young people, after the passing of the false hopes of drugs as an ideology and the fading of the New Left, what remained? Only *apathy* was left. In the United States by the beginning of the seventies, *apathy* was almost complete. In contrast to the political activists of the sixties, not many of the young even went to the polls to vote, even though the national voting age was lowered to eighteen. Hope was gone.

After the turmoil of the sixties, many people thought that it was so much better when the universities quieted down in the early seventies. I could have wept. The young people had been right in their analysis, though wrong in their solutions. How much worse when many gave up hope and simply accepted the same values as their parents—personal peace and affluence. Now drugs remain, but only in parallel to the older generation's alcohol, and an excessive use of alcohol has become a problem among the young people as well. Promiscuous sex and bisexuality remain, but only in parallel to the older generation's adultery. In other words, as the young people revolted against their parents, they came around in a big circle—and often ended an inch lower—with only the same two impoverished values: their own kind of personal peace and their own kind of affluence.

In some places the Marxist-Leninist line or the Maoist line took over. This was not so true in the United States, but these ideologies have become a major factor in Europe, South America, and other parts of the world. But Marxist-Leninism is another leap into the area of non-reason—as idealistic as drug taking was in its early days. The young followed Marxism in spite of clear evidence that oppression was not an excess of Stalin, but was and is an integral part of the system of communism.

No one has made this more clear than Alexander Solzhenitsyn (1918–) in *The Gulag Archipelago* (Vol. I, 1974). He takes great pains to point out that the foundations of lawless expediency were firmly established by Lenin. Summarizing the trials up through 1922 and looking ahead to the famous "showcase trials" of 1937, Solzhenitsyn asks, "What, then, were they surprised at in 1937? Hadn't all the foundations of lawlessness been laid?" But if this preceded Stalin, it is clear that it also survived him. Solzhenitsyn says that the salamander, by which he means the prison-camp network, is still alive. In *The Gulag Archipelago* (Vol. II, 1975) he says that the prison camps held up to fifteen million inmates at

58 News photos of Woodstock. "But the drug world . . . was approaching the end of its optimism." *Photos by Rex Features.*

a time, and he estimated that from the Revolution to 1959 a total of sixty-six million prisoners died.

Even if this salamander is not so obviously voracious now, Solzhenitsyn is not appeased. He correctly identifies the root cause of the lawless expediency as the willingness to assure internal security at any cost. And he sees that when his contemporaries now urge him to "let bygones be bygones" they are making the same choice. "Dwell on the past and you'll lose an eye," they say. Solzhenitsyn adds, "But the proverb goes on to say: 'Forget the past and you'll lose both eyes.' "

Tellingly, he compares the West German effort since World War II to track down and punish major, known Nazi criminals (of which 86,000 had been convicted by 1966) with the total absence of such a procedure both in East Germany as regards Nazis and in Russia as regards the active agents of the officially condemned crimes of Stalin. He selects Molotov as a symbol of this mentality—a man who lives on comfortably, "a man who has learned nothing at all, even now, though he is saturated with our blood and nobly crosses the sidewalk to seat himself in his long, wide automobile." Reflecting upon these facts, Solzhenitsyn writes, "From the most ancient times justice has been a two-part concept: virtue triumphs and vice is punished." In contrast, Solzhenitsyn concludes about Russia, "Young people are acquiring the conviction that foul deeds are never punished on earth, that they always bring prosperity." He then adds, "It is going to be uncomfortable, horrible, to live in such a country!" And this is the case not only in Russia but wherever communism has attained power. China probably has less internal freedom than Russia.

Communists have also used external oppression: Think of Hungary and Czechoslovakia. I'll never forget the day—November 4, 1956—when Hungary was taken over. Listening in Switzerland to my shortwave radio, I heard the students repeatedly pleading in the English language for help, hoping the outside world would listen. I have a newspaper picture of one of the girls arrested in Hungary. It is a portrait of a lovely Hungarian girl on trial. Her name was Ilond Troth. She was hanged in July 1957. I keep her picture to remember: "Forget the past and you will lose both eyes."

How romantic, in a negative sense, is the leap into the area of

Next two pages: **59** Prague, 1968. ". . . external oppression." *Photos courtesy of* GAMMA *and* POPPERFOTO. **60** Ilond Troth at her trial. ". . . hanged in July 1957."

non-reason to Marxist-Leninism! It is a different kind of leap from that of the existentialist and others we considered in the previous chapters, but it, too, is without a base in reason. Materialism, the philosophic base for Marxist-Leninism, gives no basis for the dignity or rights of man. Where Marxist-Leninism is not in power it attracts and converts by talking much of dignity and rights, but its materialistic base gives no basis for the dignity or rights of man. Yet it attracts by its constant talk of idealism.

To understand this phenomenon we must understand that Marx reached over to that for which Christianity *does* give a base—the dignity of man—and took the words as words of his own. The only understanding of idealistic sounding Marxist-Leninism is that it is (in this sense) a Christian heresy. Not having the Christian base, until it comes to power it uses the words for which Christianity does give a base. But wherever Marxist-Leninism has had power, it has at no place in history shown where it has not brought forth oppression. As soon as they have had the power, the desire of the majority has become a concept without meaning.

As we said in the first chapter, men have presuppositions and will live more consistently with these presuppositions than even they themselves know. People's presuppositions rest upon that which they consider to be the truth of what exists. With a whole state consciously resting upon philosophic materialism, there is no base for "communism with a human face," for which have pleaded some of the reformers in Poland, Czechoslovakia, and other Communist controlled countries (and some Communists in non-Communist controlled countries).

In 1975 when André Malraux was asked if there really can be communism with a human face, he pondered a while and then replied, "Historical experience suggests that there can't be." With no base for the dignity of the individual, only arbitrary expediency gives whatever dignity is given. And being only arbitrary, expediency can twist and turn at will. Men tend to act ultimately with remarkable consistency to their presuppositions, their world view. To forget this in regard to a system which consciously rests on the philosophic base of materialism will be to lose not only two eyes, but also one's head.

Countries which have a different base, for example, a Christian one (or at least one with the memory of a Christian foundation) may indeed act most inconsistently and horribly. But when a state with a materialistic base acts arbitrarily and gives no dignity to man, internally or externally, it is being consistent to its basic presuppositions and principles. To accept Marxist-Leninism is indeed a leap into the area of non-reason. It is its own kind of Nietzsche game plan, a setting of limits as to what one will observe, and a refusal to look outside of these boundaries lest the system be brought down like a house of cards. This does not make Marxist-Leninism less of a danger, and it is also necessary to take into account the resurgence of the old-line Communist parties, especially in some of the European countries where they are either legal or underground.

There are two streams of Marxist-Leninism: first, those who hold it in an idealistic form as a leap against all reason—listening to the words which have been lifted as a Christian heresy, the words of dignity and rights—and who close their eyes to the intrinsic oppression of the system as a system; second, the old-line Communists who hold an orthodox communistic ideology. "Danny the Red" (Daniel Cohn-Bendit), who led the student riots in France in May 1968 and who is still a Marxist, in an interview in 1975 made the distinction between these two groups. He spoke of the old-line Communists in terms of "orthodox Communist ideology" and "bureaucratic structure of the type existing in the Soviet Union."

If personal peace and affluence would seem available under communism, no one can be sure what many of the young people and older ones, too, will do. The two streams of Marxist-Leninism of which we have spoken could flow together at a crucial point and produce political results which would be irreversible.

In the United States many other practical problems developed as man's desire to be autonomous from God's revelation—in the Bible and through Christ—increasingly reached its natural conclusions. Sociologically, *law is king* (Samuel Rutherford's *Lex Rex*) was no longer the base whereby one could be ruled by law rather than the arbitrary judgments of men and whereby there could be wide freedoms without chaos. Any ways in which the system is still working is largely due to the sheer inertia of the continuation of the past principles. But this borrowing cannot go on forever.

As we have seen, there is a danger that without a sufficient base modern modern science will become *sociological science;* so civil law has moved toward being *sociological law.* Distinguished jurist and Supreme Court Justice Oliver Wendell Holmes, Jr. (1841–1935) took a long step in this direction. In *The Common Law* (1881) Holmes said that law is based on experience. Daniel H. Benson (1936–), assistant professor of law at the Texas Tech University School of Law quotes Holmes: "Truth is the majority vote of that nation that could lick all others." In a 1926 letter to John C. H. Wu, Holmes wrote, "So when it comes to the development of a *corpus juris* the ultimate question is what do the dominant forces of the community want and do they want it hard enough to disregard whatever inhibitions may stand in the way." This is very different from Samuel Rutherford's biblical base and from Paul Robert's painting in which Justice points to "The Word of God."

Frederick Moore Vinson (1890–1953), former Chief Justice of the United States Supreme Court, spelled out this problem by saying, "Nothing is more certain in modern society than the principle that there are no absolutes." All is relative; all is experience. In passing, we should note this curious mark of our age: The only absolute allowed is the absolute insistence that there is no absolute.

Roscoe Pound (1870–1964) wrote in *Jurisprudence* (1959): "The Greek philosophers sought to find some assured basis of social control other than tradition and the habit of obedience on the one hand, or the will of the politically supreme for the moment on the other hand. They conceived they had found such a basis in the analogy of the constant and universal phenomena of physical nature." In the days of Rousseau, Goethe, and Constable, when nature was being venerated, there was a concerted attempt to make nature the base for law. It is called Natural Law or the Law-of-Nature School of Jurisprudence. Roscoe Pound writes about the men identified with this approach: "Jurists of the 18th century Law-of-Nature School conceived that a complete and perfect system of law might be constructed upon principles of natural (i.e., ideal) law which were discoverable by reason." This was a part of Enlightenment optimism.

But, as we have seen, nature provides no sufficient base for either morals or law, because nature is both cruel and noncruel. Gradually, the hope that nature would give a fixed value in law was abandoned, and instead (as Pound quotes French jurist and legal philosopher Joseph Charmont [1859–1922]) by the start of the twentieth century, law rooted in nature only had a variable content. A Jewish-Christian lawyer once wrote to me that, as he considered the serious meaning of the Nuremberg war-crimes trials, "I knew then that no moral law was written on a blade of grass, in a drop of water, or even in the stars. I realized the necessity of the Divine Immutable Law as set forth in the Sacred Torah, consisting of definite commandments, statutes, ordinances and judgments."

Man has failed to build only from himself autonomously and to find a solid basis in nature for law, and we are left today with Oliver Wendell Holmes's "experience" and Frederick Moore Vinson's statement that nothing is more certain in modern society than that there are no absolutes. Law has only a variable content. Much modern law is not even based on precedent; that is, it does not necessarily hold fast to a continuity with the legal decisions of the past. Thus, within a wide range, the Constitution of the United States can be made to say what the courts of the present want it to say— based on a court's decision as to what the court feels is sociologically helpful at the moment. At times this brings forth happy results, at least temporarily; but once the door is opened, anything can become law and the arbitrary judgments of men are king. Law is now freewheeling, and the courts not only interpret the laws which legislators have made, but make law. *Lex Rex* has become *Rex Lex*. Arbitrary judgment concerning current sociological good is *king*.

As arbitrary absolutes characterize communistic rule, so there is a drift in this direction on our side of the Iron Curtain as well. *This means that tremendous changes of direction can be made and the majority of the people tend to accept them without question— no matter how arbitrary the changes are or how big a break they make with past law or past consensus.*

It is worth considering at length, as an example, the United States Supreme Court ruling concerning the human fetus, the unborn baby. On January 22, 1973, the United States Supreme Court ruled that every woman in the United States has the right to an abortion during the first three months of pregnancy, with no discussion. In the second three months abortion is allowed if the state agrees it is healthy for the mother to have the abortion. During the second three months, as in the first three months, the fetus does not enter into consideration. Even during the last three months the fetus does not have effective protection under the law, because the word *health* (of the mother) has been given a very wide meaning.

To quote Joseph P. Witherspoon (1916–), professor of jurisprudence at the University of Texas School of Law, in the *Texas Tech Law Review,* Volume six, 1974–1975: "In this 1973 decision the Court . . . held that the unborn child is not a person within the meaning and protection of the term 'person' utilized in the fourteenth amendment so as to strip all unborn children of all constitutional protection for their lives, liberty, and property." In Britain the law allows pregnancies to be terminated up to the twenty-eighth week. There are several things to notice here.

This is a totally arbitrary absolute. First, it is *medically* arbitrary. *Our Future Inheritance: Choice or Chance?* (1974) is a book put out in England to inform the public about the questions of genetics which are immediately before us at this point of history. It is based on a series of working papers produced with the cooperation of scientists in a number of fields, including some scientists from the United States. It is in favor of abortion. However, the book says that the question about when human life begins is open: "It [abortion] can be carried out before the foetus becomes 'viable'— although when that is, is in itself an arguable point." It further states that "a biologist might say that human life started at the moment of fertilization when the sperm and the ovum merge."

The arbitrary nature of the decision *medically* is underlined by the fact that one section of the book accepts the destruction of the fetus by abortion, yet another section focuses on the question of whether it is ethical to fertilize the ovum with a sperm *in vitro* (in the laboratory) when at our present stage of technology it is certain to live for only a very limited number of days. The problem is that after fertilization it has "the full genetic potential for becoming a human being and will become one if implantation [in the womb] and gestation are successful. At what stage of development should the status of a patient be attributed to the embryo or foetus?" Here the question is raised whether the six-day-old fetus should be considered "a patient." In another place the book argues for fertilization in the laboratory on the basis that, since we help a baby who is prematurely born, should we not be willing to help "the complete development of a baby outside the body"? This is preceded by the sentence: "Assistance for the premature baby would, by most, be considered one of the basic duties of society." And in the argument for a total development outside the body the concept of the *premature baby* is carried back to the time of fertilization. What does this make the abortion of a five-and-one-half-month-old baby? It certainly has "the full genetic potential for becoming a human being."

I am making only one point here: Both the ruling by the United States Supreme Court and the British law were purely arbitrary *medically*. They established an arbitrary absolute which affects millions of embryos, when *medically* the matter is so open that the asking of ethical questions about a fertilized ovum of only seven days is considered valid, and when *medically* the question concerning the seven-day-old fertilized ovum rests on the fact that it has "the full genetic potential for becoming a human being." So when the official *Supreme Court Reporter* (Vol. 410) says that the unborn are not recognized in the law as persons, here is a *medical* arbitrary absolute with a vengeance—and at the point of human life.

Second, it is not only arbitrary medically but *legally*. The ruling set up an arbitrary absolute by disregarding the intent of the Thirteenth and Fourteenth Amendments of the Constitution. Quoting Professor Witherspoon again:

> Thus, the failure of the Court in Roe v. Wade [the abortion case] to have examined into the actual purpose and intent of the legislature in framing the fourteenth amendment and the thirteenth amendment to which it was so closely related and supplementary thereof when it was considering the meaning to be assigned to the concept of "person" was a failure to be faithful to the law or to respect the legislature which framed it. Careful research of the history of these two amendments will

61 The author and his film crew at the Supreme Court Building, Washington, D.C. ". . . to strip all unborn children of all constitutional protection." *Photo by Mustafa Arshad.*

demonstrate to any impartial investigator that there is overwhelming evidence supporting the proposition that the principal, actual purpose of their framers was to prevent any court, and especially the Supreme Court of the United States, because of its earlier performance in the *Dred Scott* case, or any other institution of government, whether legislative or executive, from ever again defining the concept of person so as to exclude any class of human beings from the protection of the Constitution and the safeguards it established for the fundamental rights of human beings, including slaves, peons, Indians, aliens, women, the poor, the aged, criminals, the mentally ill or retarded, and children, including the unborn from the time of their conception.

Supreme Court Justice White in his dissent to the Court's action stated, "As an exercise of raw judicial power, the Court perhaps has authority to do what it does today; but in my view its judgment is an improvident and extravagant exercise of the power of judicial review that the Constitution extends to this Court." Upon this arbitrary ruling *medically* and *legally,* the Supreme Court invalidated the law on this subject of abortion of almost every one of the states in the Union.

Further, this arbitrary decision is at complete variance with the past Christian consensus. In the pagan Roman Empire, abortion was freely practiced, but Christians took a stand against it. In 314 the Council of Ancyra barred from the taking of the Lord's Supper for ten years all who procured abortions or made drugs to further abortions. Previously the Synod of Elvira (305–306) had specified excommunication till the deathbed for these offenses. The arbitrary absolutes of the Supreme Court are accepted against the previous consensus of centuries, as well as against past law. *And (taking abortion as an example) if this arbitrary absolute by law is accepted by most modern people, bred with the concept of no absolutes but rather relativity, why wouldn't arbitrary absolutes in regard to such matters as authoritarian limitations on freedom be equally accepted as long as they were thought to be sociologically helpful?* We are left with *sociological law* without any certainty of limitation.

By the ruling of the Supreme Court, the unborn baby is not counted as a person. In our day, quite rightly, there has been a hue and cry against some of our ancestors' cruel viewing of the black slave as a non-person. This was horrible indeed—an act of hypocrisy as well as cruelty. But now, by an arbitrary absolute brought in on the humanist flow, millions of unborn babies of every color of skin are equally by law declared non-persons. Surely this, too, must be seen as an act of hypocrisy.

The door is open. In regard to the fetus, the courts have arbitrarily separated "aliveness" from "personhood," and if this is so, why not arbitrarily do the same with the aged? So the steps move along, and euthanasia may well become increasingly acceptable. And if so, why not keep alive the bodies of the so-called neo-morts (persons in whom the brain wave is flat) to harvest from them body parts and blood, when the polls show that this has become acceptable to the majority? Dr. Willard Gaylin (1925–) discussed this possibility in *Harper's* (September 1974) under the title, "Harvesting the Dead." Law has become a matter of averages, just as the culture's sexual mores have become only a matter of averages.

As the Christian consensus dies, there are not many sociological alternatives. One possibility is hedonism, in which every man does his own thing. Trying to build a society on hedonism leads to chaos. One man can live on a desert island and do as he wishes within the limits of the form of the universe, but as soon as two men live on the island, if they are to live in peace, they cannot both do simply as they please. Consider two hedonists meeting on a narrow bridge crossing a rushing stream: Each cannot do his own thing.

A second possibility is the absoluteness of the 51-percent vote. In the days of a more Christian culture, a lone individual with the Bible could judge and warn society, regardless of the majority vote, because there was an absolute by which to judge. There was an absolute for both morals and law. But to the extent that the Christian consensus is gone, this absolute is gone as a social force. Let us remember that on the basis of the absoluteness of the 51-percent vote, Hitler was perfectly entitled to do as he wished if he had the popular support. On this basis, law and morals become a matter of averages. And on this basis, if the majority vote supported it, it would become "right" to kill the old, the incurably ill, the insane

—and other groups could be declared non-persons. No voice could be raised against it.

Alfred Charles Kinsey (1894–1956), a biologist-sociologist at the Institute for Sex Research at Indiana University produced his influential *Sexual Behavior of the Human Male* (1948) and *Sexual Behavior of the Human Female* (1953). These were based on 18,500 interviews. Kinsey made that which is "right" in sex a matter of statistics. Many people read his books because at that date they were far more titillating than other books accepted as respectable. However, their real impact was the underlying conception that sexual right and wrong depend only on what most people are doing sexually at a given moment of history. This has become the generally accepted sexual standard in the years since. Modern man has done the same thing in law.

As we saw in the first chapter, the Greeks found that society—the *polis*—was not a strong enough final authority to build upon, and it is still not strong enough today. If there are no absolutes, and if we do not like either the chaos of hedonism or the absoluteness of the 51-percent vote, only one other alternative is left: one man or an elite, giving authoritative arbitrary absolutes.

Here is a simple but profound rule: *If there are no absolutes by which to judge society, then society is absolute.* Society is left with one man or an elite filling the vacuum left by the loss of the Christian consensus which originally gave us form and freedom in northern Europe and in the West. In communism, the elite has won its way, and rule is based upon arbitrary absolutes handed down by that elite. Absolutes can be *this* today and *that* tomorrow. If Mao equals the law, then the concept of a continual cultural revolution, "The Great Leap Forward," may be in order one year and very much out of order the next. Arbitrary absolutes can be handed down and there is no absolute by which to judge them.

So far, two elites have put themselves forward, offering to fill the vacuum in our culture. The first was Marcuse's New Left, which has waned in influence. It no longer provides the live possibility for action which it did for a time. Then John Kenneth Galbraith (1908–) offered his form of the elite. Like the students at Berkeley, this economist has said that we live in a poor culture. Galbraith suggested an elite composed of intellectuals (especially the academic and scientific world) plus the government. In June 1975, 2,000 "futurists" met for the Second General Assembly of the World Future Society in Washington, D.C. Socioeconomist Robert Theobald (1929–) endorsed the concept of "sapientary authority," a social structure in which wise men selected by merit would be deeply involved in the governmental decision-making process. "It's naive," declared Theobald, "to deny the necessity for some kind of competent elite."

Daniel Bell (1919–), professor of sociology at Harvard University, sees an elite composed of select intellectuals. He writes in *The Coming of Post-Industrial Society* (1973), in the chapter entitled "Who Will Rule," that "the university—or some other knowledge institute—will become the central institution of the next hundred years because of its role as the new source of innovation and knowledge." He says that crucial decisions will come from government, but more and more the decisions of both business and government will be predicated on government-sponsored research, and "because of the intricately linked nature of their consequences, [the decisions] will have an increasingly technical character." Society thus turns into a technocracy where "the determining influence belongs to technicians of the administration and of the economy." Bell sees that in the final analysis the whole state—its business, its education, its government, even the daily pattern of the ordinary man's life—becomes a matter of control by the technocratic elite. They are the only ones who know how to run the complicated machinery of society and they will then, in collusion with the government elite, have all the power necessary to manage it.

Bell's most astute warning concerns the ethical implications of this situation: "A post-industrial society cannot provide a transcendent ethic . . . . The lack of a rooted moral belief system is the cultural contradiction of the society, the deepest challenge to its survival." He adds that in the future men can be remade, their behavior conditioned, or their consciousness altered. The constraints of the past vanish. To the extent that Bell's picture of this future is fulfilled, Galbraith's form of the elite will be the actuality.

Humanism has led to its natural conclusion. It has ground down to the point Leonardo da Vinci visualized so long ago when he realized that, starting only from man, mathematics leads us only to particulars—and particulars lead only to mechanics. Humanism had no way to find the universal in the areas of meaning and values. As my son, Franky, put it, "Humanism has changed the Twenty-third Psalm:

> They began—I am my shepherd
> Then—Sheep are my shepherd
> Then—Everything is my shepherd
> Finally—Nothing is my shepherd."

There is a death wish inherent in humanism—the impulsive drive to beat to death the base which made our freedoms and our culture possible.

In ancient Israel, when the nation had turned from God and from his truth and commands as given in Scripture, the prophet Jeremiah cried out that there was death in the city. He was speaking not only of physical death in Jerusalem but also a wider death. Because Jewish society of that day had turned away from what God had given them in the Scripture, there was death in the *polis,* that is, death in the total culture and the total society.

In our era, sociologically, man destroyed the base which gave him the possibility of freedoms without chaos. Humanists have been determined to beat to death the knowledge of God and the knowledge that God has not been silent, but has spoken in the Bible and through Christ—and they have been determined to do this even though the death of values has come with the death of that knowledge.

We see two effects of our loss of meaning and values. The first is degeneracy. Think of New York City's Times Square—Forty-second and Broadway. If one goes to what used to be the lovely Kalverstraat in Amsterdam, one finds that it, too, has become equally squalid. The same is true of lovely old streets in Copenhagen. Pompeii has returned! The marks of ancient Rome scar us: degeneracy, decadence, depravity, a love of violence for violence's sake. The situation is plain. If we look, we see it. If we see it, we are concerned.

But we *must* notice that there is a second result of modern man's loss of meaning and values which is more ominous, and which many people do not see. This second result is that the elite will exist. Society cannot stand chaos. Some group or some person will fill the vacuum. An elite will offer us arbitrary absolutes, and who will stand in its way?

Will the silent majority (which at one time we heard so much about) help? The so-called silent majority was, and is, divided into a minority and a majority. The *minority* are either Christians who have a real basis for values or those who at least have a memory of the days when the values were real. The *majority* are left with only their two poor values of personal peace and affluence.

With such values, will men stand for their liberties? Will they not give up their liberties step by step, inch by inch, as long as their own personal peace and prosperity is sustained and not challenged, and as long as the goods are delivered? The life-styles of the young and the old generations are different. There are tensions between long hair and short, drugs and non-drugs, whatever are the outward distinctions of the moment. But they support each other sociologically, for both embrace the values of personal peace and affluence. Much of the church is no help here either, because for so long a large section of the church has only been teaching a relativistic humanism using religious terminology.

I believe the majority of the silent majority, young and old, will sustain the loss of liberties without raising their voices as long as their own life-styles are not threatened. And since personal peace and affluence are so often the only values that count with the majority, politicians know that to be elected they must promise these things. Politics has largely become not a matter of ideals— increasingly men and women are not stirred by the values of liberty and truth—but of supplying a constituency with a frosting of personal peace and affluence. They know that voices will not be raised as long as people have these things, or at least an illusion of them.

Edward Gibbon (1737–1794) in his *Decline and Fall of the Roman Empire* (1776–1788) said that the following five attributes marked Rome at its end: first, a mounting love of show and luxury (that is, affluence); second, a widening gap between the very rich and the very poor (this could be among countries in the family of nations as well as in a single nation); third, an obsession with sex; fourth, freakishness in the arts, masquerading as originality, and enthusiasms pretending to be creativity; fifth, an increased desire to live off the state. It all sounds so familiar. We have come a long road since our first chapter, and we are back in Rome.

12 Manipulation and the New Elite

As we consider the coming of an elite, an authoritarian state, to fill the vacuum left by the loss of Christian principles, we must not think naively of the models of Stalin and Hitler. We must think rather of a *manipulative* authoritarian government. Modern governments have forms of manipulation at their disposal which the world has never known before. We will examine a number of these methods and theories of manipulation, concentrating first on the psychological techniques, then on techniques associated with biological science, and finally on the new ways in which some of the media are influencing behavior.

First, one could mention the determinists, who say man has no freedom in his choices. For example, we can think of Sigmund Freud's (1856–1939) *psychological determinism,* B. F. Skinner's (1904–) *sociological determinism* through conditioning, and Francis Crick's (1916–) *chemical,* that is, *genetic determinism.*

Freud's determinism rests upon the child's relationship to its mother during the early portion of its life. He taught that this sets the pattern of the child's psychological makeup.

The ideas of sociological determinism, primarily involving conditioning (behaviorism), were widely discussed after B. F. Skinner published *Beyond Freedom and Dignity* (1971). His thesis was that all that people are can be explained by the way their environment has conditioned them. Since society plays a specially important role in that environment, society can and should use positive stimuli to bring about the society it wants. That this was meant not only to be a theory but to be put into use is shown by his earlier book, *Walden Two* (1948), a novel.

In *Walden Two* Skinner's utopia was a totally conditioned society. The director, T. E. Frazier, manipulated everyone to control all the details of the society. He made the people think that they wanted what he had decided they and society itself should be. In this and all other forms of determinism, man dies. In fact, Skinner himself acknowledged that what is being abolished is man. He says, "To man qua [as] man we readily say good riddance."

Skinner (like Bertrand Russell and George Wald) retains only the value of biological continuity: "Survival is the only value according to which a culture is eventually to be judged, and any practice that furthers survival has survival value by definition." But like other people we have considered, Skinner cannot live on the basis of his own system. He lives inconsistently on the memory of Christian values for which his system has no place.

The Christian position is *not* that there is no element of conditioning in human life, but rather that by no means does conditioning explain what people are in their totality. To a determinist, however, if one removed all the bundle of conditioning in man, there would be no man *as* man. Christianity rejects this. It insists that each individual person exists as a being created in the image of God, and that therefore each person is an ongoing entity with dignity. To proud, humanist man, who demands to be autonomous, technology of one kind or another is to be used to get rid of the limitations of nature, *including human nature,* which autonomous man finds insufferably confining. There is here a tension in modern people, especially perhaps among students: Modern people want to be free to shape their own destiny, and yet they think they know they are determined.

The sadism of Marquis de Sade is the specter standing behind any determinist because the basis of de Sade's sadism was his concept of determinism. De Sade's position was that what is, is right; and if a person holds *any* form of determinism, he must agree that de Sade's conclusion is the only logical one. This is not to say that the determinists always carry their position to de Sade's logical conclusion, but it is the conclusion. In any form of determinism, what is considered right or acceptable is arbitrary.

Modern determinists have not presented only abstract theories. Rather, there have been two practical results. First, and most important, as their ideas about what people are have been increasingly accepted, people consciously or unconsciously have opened themselves to being treated as machines and treating other people as machines. Second, each theory of determinism has carried with it a method of manipulation. So even though many—even most—people may reject the concept that man is totally a product of psychological, sociological, or chemical conditioning, manipulation by these methods is still very much a live possibility. In fact, these techniques are all at the disposal of authoritarian states, and they are in some degree already being used.

Some people might say that these deterministic ideas are only science fiction, but this is not so. T. George Harris (1924–), who reviewed Skinner's book in *Psychology Today* (August 1971), said, "Nobody would panic at Skinner's attack upon our idea of freedom if he were only talking. But he has a program, and followers to push it." Voices have been raised against Skinner's views and against behaviorism in general. For example, Noam Chomsky's (1928–) 1959 article in *Language* spoke out against one of Skinner's earlier books, *Verbal Behavior* (1957). But the behaviorists are numerous and, as Harris said, they have a program and followers to push it. Those who hold behavioristic concepts are often in positions of influence. For example, they often control education down to the lowest grades. Articles in the press constantly remind us that behaviorism dominates various university psychology departments. This professor or writer or then another comes into fashion and later becomes less important, but behaviorism is an ongoing and progressing factor in society.

The pressure toward the development of manipulative techniques comes through strongly in current biological research and development. We see this clearly in the outlook of Francis Crick (1916–), who received the 1962 Nobel Prize in Physiology and Medicine—along with James D. Watson and Maurice Wilkins—for breaking the DNA code. The Spring 1971 issue of *Washington University Magazine* carries an article by Crick entitled "Why I Study Biology." He gives a call for full genetic engineering at once and tells us what is his basic motive for studying biology:

> My own motivation, which I have only touched on up to now, is rather elsewhere. It is difficult to say it in a few words. If you had to find a simple description of why I do biological reseach, it is for philosophical and what you might call religious reasons.

A crucial part of the view of life that he expounds, as we can clearly see from what he writes, is the idea that man can be essentially reduced to the chemical and physical properties that go to make up the DNA template. Philosophically, therefore, Francis Crick is a reductionist, that is, one who would reduce man to an electrochemical machine. Such a view soon leads to the idea that man can and should be manipulated and even controlled.

In this article he mentions the fact that, when he was in California visiting a university, he met a charming girl who asked him about his birthdate and talked to him about astrology and the Age of Aquarius. He also noted that the bookstores were heavily stocked with books on the occult. Here is his reaction:

> . . . . I think one has to say that scientifically, astrology really is complete nonsense. I have tried very hard to think of a way in which it could make some sense and it's too much. I wonder whether people who feel that way should be at a university.

Who, then, is going to be allowed in the universities? What he is suggesting is not just that the content of astrology is wrong or meaningless, but he raises the question as to whether people with such views should be in a university.

Francis Crick continues:

> The major conclusion which one draws from present day biology is the importance of natural selection. The essence of natural selection, and this is the thing that people find very hard to accept, is that it's motivated by

chance events. It is not pre-programmed but is driven by
chance events. You can make an argument that chance
is the only real source of true novelty.

Natural selection is not programmed; it is generated by chance.
A little further on in the article, however, Dr. Crick says, "You
cannot lay down a general trend [for the course of evolution];
natural selection is cleverer than that. It will think of combinations
and ways of doing things which haven't been foreseen." The language here is interesting because it attributes a sort of personality
to natural selection.

In *The Origin of the Genetic Code* (1968) Crick begins to
spell *nature* with a capital *N* about halfway through the book,
and in *Of Molecules and Men* (1967) he refers to nature as "she."
In other words, he personalizes what by definition is impersonal
according to his own system. Why? Because he can't stand the
implications of impersonality, and because this kind of semantic
mysticism gives relief to people caught in the web of the impersonal.
By his own definition Crick lives in an impersonal universe, but
by the connotation of the language he uses, Crick personalizes the
impersonal universe and calls natural selection "clever" and says it
will "think." Such language takes the pressure off, and people fail
to understand what they have read.

Dr. Crick says that his scientific enterprise is governed by a basic
religious stance. And while he recognizes that the particular stance
he takes is antireligious in conventional terms, ". . . it is a religious
attitude because it's concerned with religious problems." He is right.
What Crick is doing is bringing forth a faith system based on the
prestige of science—even though the suggestions being made have
no logical relationship to that on which the prestige rests.

Later in the article Crick turns to the area of mental behavior
and how it is determined. He says, "We'd like to know more about
mental health—how much is genetically determined and how much
depends on the environment. We'd also like to know the same
thing for intelligence and creativity." Is it not clear here how man
suddenly disappears? There are only two factors: (1) heredity and
(2) environment. Is it 90 percent of one and 10 of the other?
Or the other way around? It makes no difference. Either factor

or both together are mechanical. Man has a genetic code. He has an environment which influences that which comes as a product of the genetic code. That's all people are.

In the last section of the article, he begins a new topic: "This leads us to the area of which I'm least at home in because it is not my particular temperament: the question of biology and politics." What is the state to do about biology? Crick tells us:

> . . . . We all know, I think, or are beginning to realize, that the future is in our own hands, that we can, to some extent, do what we want.
>
> Now what is happening at the moment? What is happening is that we know that with technology we can make life easier for human beings; we can make changes. What we are really doing is learning to tinker with the system. But there is very little thinking at the fundamental level as to what sort of people we would like to have. In the long term, that is the question you are bound to come up with. I think that you have to realize that in many contexts what will happen if we go on in the present way is not what people actually want.
>
> . . . . It's the aim of medical research to try to cure as many diseases as possible, in particular cancer and heart conditions. Those are probably the major killers. But what is going to happen under that situation? What is going to happen essentially is that you can easily work out the age distribution, under a stable population, from the death rate. It means that gradually the population is going to become very old. What medical research is aiming for at the moment is to make the world safe for senility.

Crick is really saying: Let's adjust the humanitarian concept of medicine. Furthermore, let's begin now. The article continues:

> . . . . It's going to be the people now between fifteen and twenty-five who are going to have to face it, so they may as well start thinking about it now.

. . . . We've just seen that the discussion as to how many people there should be in the world has now, as it were, become quite acceptable. It is not acceptable, at the moment, to discuss who should be the parents of the next generation, who should be born, and who should have children. There's a general feeling that if we are all nice to each other and if everybody has 2.3 children, everything will pan out. I don't think that is true. For good genetic reasons, even though you have more medical care, transplantation of organs, and all these things, it would be an unhealthy biological situation. Some group of people should decide that some people should have more children and some should have fewer . . . . You have to decide who is to be born.

Biology is indeed a revolutionary subject when you look at it in this way. It is, in fact, *the* major revolutionary subject. It is the one that's going to make the new concepts which will come into social thinking. Biology is not simply, as it were, what you can do with herds of cattle. There are much more intricate things involving people at the psychological level interacting in society, but I don't think you're going to solve all these problems by just tinkering with the genetic material. I think it will turn out that thinking along these lines will have to take place, and if you don't do it in this country, it will start in another country.

Francis Crick closes "Why I Study Biology" in this way:

This comes to probably the basic thing that I would say. That really what is wanted is education—an education at the level of younger people. It's nice to read articles in *Time* and *Life,* but if you learn something when you're in school, you're forced to learn it in a more regular way. You absorb it, to some extent, at a more impressionable period; you're made to do exercise on it. And I think really there should be some thinking if we're to take this new view of looking at man.

The author obviously wishes to bring the subject of the biological nature of man and the acceptability of human engineering down into the education of even the lower grades.

If man is what Francis Crick says he is, then he is only the sum of the impersonal *plus* time *plus* chance; he is nothing more than the energy particle extended and more complex. Our own generation can thus disregard human life. On the one end we kill the embryo through abortion—and on the other end we will introduce euthanasia for the old. The one is already here and the door is opened for the other.

Thus, Francis Crick is one of those who put a strong emphasis on the immediate use of the full range of "genetic engineering"— with some group of people deciding who should be the parents of the next generation, who should be born, and who should have children. Too often the subject of genetic engineering is approached in an atmosphere of spectacularism, in a "Sunday Supplement" frame of mind. But men like Crick must be taken seriously as an influence in the area of biological manipulation. Crick is not alone in his view that modern medicine is a menace since it keeps the weak alive to breed a less-than-best next generation. A chancellor of one of the Swiss universities took this for the theme of his inaugural speech some years ago.

The question of genetic engineering, however, must be seen in a balanced way, for by no means are all those involved as extreme as those to whom I have referred. The British book I mentioned before, *Our Future Inheritance: Choice or Chance?* (1974), tries to set forth a balanced view, though it seems to me that the title itself is slanted toward accepting genetic engineering: *Choice* sounds so much better than *chance*. The book has special importance because of the many scientists whose working papers were the basis for it. The following few pages are largely based on material from this book or issues which are raised by the material in it.

As we evaluate genetic engineering, it must be said first that certain things are *not* immediately at hand, for example, a baby grown entirely outside of the body (*in vitro*) or the making of endless duplicates of one individual without male and female elements (cloning). However, these phenomena may be possible later, and so are part of the whole question, ethically and practically.

Some things, for example, transplants, *are* immediately at hand. The most successful have been kidney transplants.

This surely is a breakthrough for which we can be glad, but even this medical achievement creates problems. In order to justify the early taking of the needed kidneys and other organs, the criterion for death is now generally accepted as a flat brain wave over a twenty-four-hour period. This is not an ethical problem in itself, but as we have seen, the door is opened for keeping bodies alive indefinitely (where there is a flat brain wave but where the organs all continue to function) to harvest their blood and organs for transplants and experimentation. The problem is clear: Without the absolute line which Christianity gives for the distinctiveness of people, even things which can be good in themselves lead to human-ness being increasingly lost.

Another example of this problem is the curing of childlessness which is caused by an infertile husband. Such childlessness often can be cured by artificial insemination using the husband's sperm (A.I.H.). Surely this is a help to many couples. But what about A.I.D. (sperm by a donor, another man)? Where is the boundary condition? *Our Future Inheritance: Choice or Chance?* says that under present laws in Britain the child born is illegitimate, and in the United States judges in some divorce cases have ruled A.I.D. children the illegitimate products of adultery, denying custody rights to the husband or relieving him of financial-support obliga-tions. And what is the next step? The book answers, "Perhaps the most sensible suggestion made is that the concept of legitimacy be removed entirely." If this suggestion were followed, morals would be shifted, and once more humanness would be weakened. What the family is, is weakened. What will be the relationship of parents and children? In the book this change in morals and laws is to be made upon the basis of "social hindrance." This is what I have called *sociological law*.

Any of us would be glad for methods of genetic changes which would cure genetic disease and help individuals. However, remov-ing these things from the uniqueness which Christianity gives to people, and from the Christian absolutes, tends to lead to an increas-ing loss of humanness, even in the milder forms. In the call for full genetic engineering the door is wide open for the most far-reaching manipulation. The call concerns who should have children and what kind of children they should have. It is a call for a group in society to determine what kind of people is wanted, and a call to set out to make them genetically. It is striking that James D. Watson (1928–), who along with Francis Crick received the Nobel Prize in 1962 for breaking the DNA code, spoke out for exercising the greatest caution. He warned a congressional committee of the dangers of experiments in these areas and sounded the same note of warning in *The Atlantic* (May 1971) under the title "Moving Towards the Clonal Man, Is That What We Want?"

On every side people are taught that people are only machines, and as they are so taught their resistance to manipulation in all these ways is weakened, step by step. Modern man has no real boundary condition for what he *should* do; he is left only with what he *can* do. Moral "oughts" are only what is sociologically accepted at the moment. In this setting will today's unthinkable still be unthinkable in ten years?

Man no longer sees himself as qualitatively different from nonman. The Christian consensus gave a basis for people being unique, as made in the image of God, but this has largely been thrown away. Thus there tends, even with the good things, to be a progressive fracturedness in the practice of life as human life. Remember, too, that for a long time in philosophy, and popularly in some of the mass media, people have been taught that truth as objective truth does not exist. All morals and law are seen as relative. Thus people gradually accept the *idea* of manipulation, and a bit more gradually open themselves to accept the *practice* of the varying forms of manipulation.

We can also mention Jacques Monod's (1910–1976) *Chance and Necessity* (1971). Here all values are up for grabs. Monod's theory that everything is a product of chance did not rest on his scientific work but rather on the fact that he followed the philosophy of Camus. With Monod science blurs into speculation, thus giving his work, for many people, the authority of his proper scientific prestige, when in reality no necessary relationship exists between the book's speculative and scientific portions. Monod argues correctly that on the basis of nature there is no way man can derive the *ought* from the *is*. For him the *is* is merely what is naturally there, what has willy-nilly come by chance. Therefore, since what *is* gives no clue to what ought to be, we must choose our values arbitrarily. Once people accept this mentality, it is much easier to impose arbitrary absolutes.

Arthur Koestler (1905–) suggested that a chemical element be developed to bring man into a place of tranquility (*Horizon Magazine,* Spring 1968). Based on his view of evolution, he postulates that man has three brains from his past: the brain of the reptile, the brain of the horse, and the unique human brain. Koestler urges the discovery of a chemical that will somehow bring peace between these brains and thus rid man of aggression. Essentially, he is calling for a supertranquilizer. He suggests the possibility that some community would put this in its drinking water, thus forcing all people to accept it. This actually is little different from the suggestion made by those who held the idealistic drug-taking concept of using the drinking water to give LSD to the residents of large cities. The principle involved is no different.

Newspapers reported that Kermit Krantz (1923–), head of the Gynecology and Obstetrics Department of the University of Kansas, urged in October 1969 that the pill to control birth be put into the world's drinking supplies to control population. Some others have suggested that the government could then dispense as it chose another drug to nullify what was in the water, so the state could decide who would be able to have babies. It all sounds very much like the ugliness portrayed in C. S. Lewis's (1898–1963) *That Hideous Strength* (1945). But this is not fiction; it is today's news, as is evidenced by news stories on the work of such men as José M. Delgado, Kenneth B. Clark, and Russel V. Lee.

José M. Delgado (1915–) of Yale University has been one of the men using sensors in the brains of monkeys and human epileptics to control their behavior. In a speech to the UNESCO Committee on Human Aggression, Delgado said that we will see a revolution in medicine's treating aggressiveness by these means in the next few years—a revolution which will be as great as the revolution in the treatment of infectious diseases with antibiotics a few years ago. The future society, he says, will be psycho-civilized with E.S.B. (Electrical Stimulating of the Brain).

Kenneth B. Clark (1914–), the American social psychologist, when president of the American Psychological Association in 1971, suggested that all political leaders should have to take antiaggression pills. Then the leaders *could not* be aggressive. More recently he has advocated "psychotechnology," that is, experiments with brain control.

Newspapers reported that Clinical Professor Emeritus Russel V. Lee (1895–) of Stanford University Medical School, suggested that all public officials should be required to have a comprehensive psychological test each year. Then, in the case of high federal officials, when the testers decided it was necessary, the finding should be transmitted to a committee of Congress which could recommend that the official be removed from office. Both Clark and Lee were forgetting a small thing—that the man who dispensed the pills or who controlled the psychological testing would be king.

In the light of this discussion about social manipulation, three questions arise. First, who will control the controllers? Second, what will happen now that people have no boundary condition indicating what they *should* do in contrast to what they *can* do? Third, if mankind is only what modern people say it is, why does man's biological continuation have value?

Stories on all these techniques for manipulation have been given important space in the mass media. And the more these are absorbed without analysis, the more they open the way for men to think of themselves differently, and the more manipulation becomes acceptable. It is no secret from many articles and from Valeriy Tarsis's (1900–) book *Ward 7: An Autobiographical Novel* (1965) that in Russia political prisoners are put in mental wards to be "reconditioned." A person who does not agree with the social order is declared "ill" and becomes a non-person, lost in the mental hospital and no longer possessing civil rights. But let us not assume that conditioning must be as crude as that of Ward 7. As we have seen, there are suggestions for the emergence of an elite to manipulate society on this side of the Iron Curtain. And the technical breakthroughs necessary to make this possible have largely been accomplished. Any modern authoritarian government has almost endless means of manipulation.

We can think of subliminal influence as a further example. It is possible to flash something over and over again on a TV or movie screen at such a fast rate that, while a viewer doesn't know he has seen it, it still has a strong influence upon him. In one experiment an audience was told, subliminally, to purchase a certain soft drink. People did not know they had seen these repeated messages, and yet when the film was over the supplies of this soft drink in the neighborhood were soon exhausted. This technique is banned by law in Western countries, but in totalitarian states why should it not be used? Even in the Western world only a law stands between us and its use; and we must not forget the drift in law toward that which is considered the sociological good at that moment. There would be no way of knowing if subliminal TV messages were beginning to be used.

Actually, TV manipulates viewers just by its normal way of operating. Many viewers seem to assume that when they have seen something on TV, they have seen it with their own eyes. It makes the viewer think he has actually been on the scene. He *knows,* because his own eyes have seen. He has the impression of greater direct objective knowledge than ever before. For many, what they see on television becomes more true than what they see with their eyes in the external world.

But this is not so, for one must never forget that every television minute has been edited. The viewer does not see the event. He sees an edited form of the event. It is not the event which is seen, but an *edited symbol* or an *edited image* of the event. An aura and illusion of objectivity and truth is built up, which could not be totally the case even if the people shooting the film were completely neutral. The physical limitations of the camera dictate that only one aspect of the total situation is given. If the camera were aimed ten feet to the left or ten feet to the right, an entirely different "objective story" might come across.

And, on top of that, the people taking the film and those editing it often do have a subjective viewpoint that enters in. When we see a political figure on TV, we are not seeing the person as he necessarily is; we are seeing, rather, the image someone has decided we should see. And if Leni Riefenstahl's (1902–) *Triumph of the Will,* a documentary on the 1934 Nazi rally at Nuremberg, could be a terrifyingly effective propaganda vehicle as it was for that

62 Media reporting on events. ". . . not the event which is seen but an *edited symbol." Photo by Mustafa Arshad.*

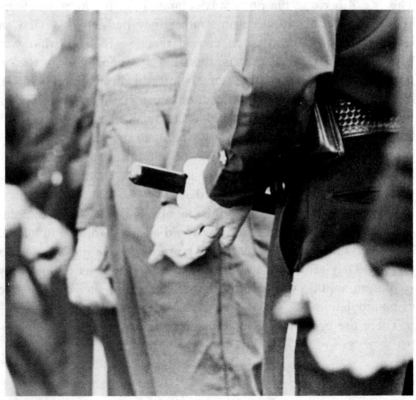

authoritarian government, what can a properly managed TV schedule, with its edited illusion of reality, be as it enters every home and is watched for endless hours by both young and old?

With an elite providing the arbitrary absolutes, not just TV but the general apparatus of the mass media can be a vehicle for manipulation. There is no need for collusion or a plot. All that is needed is that the world view of the elite and the world view of the central news media coincide. One may discuss if planned collusion exists at times, but to be looking only for the possibility of a clandestine plot opens the way for failing to see a much greater danger: that many of those who are in the most prominent places of influence and many of those who decide what is news do have the common, modern, humanist world view we have described at length in this book. It is natural that they act upon this viewpoint, with varying degrees of consciousness of what they are doing, and even varying degrees of consciousness of who is using whom. Their world view is the grid which determines their presentation.

A good example is that much of the press (and many diplomats, too) saw and spoke against Hitler's repressions much sooner (in fact, years sooner) than Stalin's repressions were acknowledged. This is not because the press was communistic, for most members of the press certainly were not; rather they had a world view, a set of presuppositions, which caused them to look at what was happening in Hitler's Germany and what was happening in Russia through two entirely different sets of glasses. Edward Behr (1926–), *Newsweek*'s European regional editor—in reviewing Oliver Todd's *The Ducks of Camau* in 1975—sets forth the problem well: ". . . the liberal dilemma: how to be against injustice . . . and yet remain lucid enough to combat the authoritarian forms of government that, through the revolutionary process, replace such injustice with tyranny of a different order."

And not all the media need to be involved in order for manipulation to be effective. In fact, rarely would all the media be involved. *It is always unfair to say simply "the press" or "the media" do this or that.* They are never to be all lumped together as though they were a monolithic whole. Nonetheless, the media can be a vehicle of manipulation.

There are certain news organizations, newspapers, news magazines, wire services, and news broadcasts which have the ability to generate news. They are the *news makers,* and when an item appears in them it *becomes* the news. This ability to generate news rests upon a kind of syndrome or psychology or mind-set, not only in the journalistic fraternity but also in influential circles comprised of congressmen, other government officials, and professors. The influence is not necessarily based on circulation, but rather on its reputation with the right people. This is at times consciously cultivated; for example, certain news outlets release their big stories to the wires and the radio and TV networks before the "big story" hits the newsstands.

Not only do these news makers make certain things news—in contrast to that which gets "lost"—but the color they put on the news tends to be picked up as well. Often this tone is set by starting off with what is called a "hard lead," the first sentence of a news article which is supposed to sum up the story in an eye-catching way. If this is subtly slanted, the tone of the whole story tends to be set, and it becomes the stained-glass window through which that story and perhaps even related stories are comprehended.

To put this in terms we have used before, just as we now tend to have *sociological science* and *sociological law,* we tend to have *sociological news.* Here, too, objectivity tends to be lost. One of the old ideals of journalism was objectivity, but, as White House correspondent Forrest Boyd (1921–) of Mutual Broadcasting remarked to me, "Objectivity has taken a beating in recent years." The distinction between the news columns and the editorial page has, in many of the most influential papers, become much less clear. An ideological position that has nothing to do with the item under review can even be dragged into the society section or into the movie reviews. The news makers obviously have tremendous power, and if either the elite captures them or if because of their world view they and the elite coincide, then the media is a ready vehicle for manipulative authoritarianism.

Finally we must not forget the manipulative capacity of the high-speed computer. As a tool it is useful but neutral. It can be used for good purposes or equally for harm. It is not only helpful in scientific and business procedures but even now is useful in medicine to make more rapid diagnoses.

Yet the possibility of information storage, beyond what men and governments ever had before, can make available at the touch of a button a man's total history (including remarks put on his record by his kindergarten teacher about his ability and character). And with the computer must be placed the modern scientific technical capability which exists for wholesale monitoring of telephone, cable, Telex, and microwave transmissions which carry much of today's spoken and written communications. The combined use of the technical capability of listening in on all these forms of communications with the high-speed computer literally leaves no place to hide and little room for any privacy.

And as in the case with subliminal TV, what will happen as the pressures on society mount? What will protect us from computer control? To say it another way, what use will the present totalitarian countries make of the high-speed computers being made available to them at the present time?

The question, however, is not limited to the use to which present totalitarian regimes will put the computer. The question is what will all these available manipulating techniques mean in our own countries? We must not think of an overnight change, but rather of a subtle trend by the leadership toward greater control and manipulation of the individual. Of course, some might feel uncomfortable about this increased control and manipulation in a relativistic age, but where would they draw a line? Many who talk of civil liberties are also committed to the concept of the state's responsibility to solve all problems; so in a time of overwhelming pressures (and with the modern loss of any qualitative distinction between man and non-man) at some point the feeling of uncomfortableness will be submerged.

What of tomorrow? In the United States, for example, a manipulating authoritarian government could come from the administrative side or from the legislative side. A public official in the United States serving at the highest level has wisely said, "Legislative dictatorship is no better than executive tyranny." And one would have to add that with the concept of variable law and with the courts making law, it could come from the judicial side as well. The Supreme Court has the final voice in regard to both administrative and legislative actions, and with the concept of variable law the judicial side could become more and more the center of power. This could well be called "the imperial judiciary." Cut away from its true foundation, the power of the Court is nothing more than the instrument of unlimited power. This is especially so when it is tied into what Oliver Wendell Holmes called "the dominant forces of the community" (*see* page 217).

Or control could come from a semiofficial organization such as has been suggested both in Britain and in the United States to meet the threat of civil chaos, or even from an international institution. And as a thinkable possibility, control could be imposed by a foreign power in the "right" mix of strength on their side and weakness on the other.

Of course, the makeup of the government in other countries is different. But that is only a minor detail and does not change the basic thrust of the possibility of a manipulative, authoritarian government arising from some part of the government in that particular country. As the memory of the Christian consensus which gave us freedom within the biblical form increasingly is forgotten, a manipulating authoritarianism will tend to fill the vacuum.

The central message of biblical Christianity is the possibility of men and women approaching God through the work of Christ. But the message also has secondary results, among them the unusual and wide freedoms which biblical Christianity gave to countries where it supplied the consensus. When these freedoms are separated from the Christian base, however, they become a force of destruction leading to chaos. When this happens, as it has today, then, to quote Eric Hoffer (1902–), "When freedom destroys order, the yearning for order will destroy freedom."

At that point the words left *or* right *will make no difference. They are only two roads to the same end. There is no difference between an authoritarian government from the right or the left: the results are the same.* An elite, an authoritarianism as such, will gradually force form on society so that it will not go on to chaos. And most people will accept it—from the desire for personal peace and affluence, from apathy, and from the yearning for order to assure the functioning of some political system, business, and the affairs of daily life. That is just what Rome did with Caesar Augustus.

13 The Alternatives

Overwhelming pressures are being brought to bear on people who have no absolutes, but only have the impoverished values of personal peace and prosperity. The pressures are progressively preparing modern people to accept a manipulative, authoritarian government. Unhappily, many of these pressures are upon us now.

Economic breakdown.   Modern society's inability to find a solution to the problem of inflation without causing economic recession opens the door wide for economic breakdown. Each cycle of inflation, attempted control, the threat of economic recession, and finally, released control, has increased inflation, yet *politically,* with most people dominated by the concept of an ever-expanding affluence, it is difficult or impossible to face the danger of economic recession. Thus, each threat of economic recession opens the door for the next higher state of inflation. At a certain point economic breakdown seems all too possible.

I cannot get out of my mind the uncomfortable parallel to the Germans' loss of confidence in the Weimar Republic just before Hitler, which was caused by unacceptable inflation. History indicates that at a certain point of economic breakdown people cease being concerned with individual liberties and are ready to accept regimentation. The danger is obviously even greater when the two main values so many people have are personal peace and affluence.

War or the serious threat of war—*between the expansionist, imperialistic, communistic countries and the West.* Alistair Cooke (1908–) in *America* (1973) has said it well: "What is fiercely in dispute between the Communist and non-Communist nations today is the quality and staying power of American civilization." I would only add that not only America but the West in general is involved. Will the West be able to stand against the totalitarian nations now that the Christian base of the Western freedoms is largely gone? Obviously this could be related to point one—the possibility of economic breakdown in the West.

Pressure from the communistic countries could come in any of several ways or a combination of them: *militarily* by a strong East acting against a less militarily strong West over a crisis arising somewhere in the world; *economically* in the event of breakdown in the West; or *politically* through the takeover of the southern European countries by the old-line Communist parties in those countries. The latter could come suddenly with open collusion with Russia and its military power, or it could come subtly and slowly with apparent reasonableness, until a time of crisis and showdown. There is a surge by the old-line Communist parties in southern Europe, and it is important to note that these are the countries which never had the biblical base which the northern countries had after the Reformation. The freedoms in these countries were imported, not homegrown.

In this mix the threat of war, especially atomic war, would cause those who have only the values of personal peace and prosperity to be ready for almost any kind of authoritarian government which would be able to remove the threat of war, particularly if (as Augustus did in ancient Rome) it was brought in while seemingly keeping the outward forms of constitutionality. The atomic bomb is a special threat to a generation that has so largely turned away from the existence of an objective God and which therefore believes that only man exists to watch with intelligence the sun set or the birds fly.

Nevil Shute's (1899–1960) novel *On the Beach* (1952) still speaks with relevance. In it he envisions a time after the atom bombs have fallen, when no person is left alive. Lights will be left burning for a time in the cities, but no person will be there to see them. Not long ago, men thought there might be conscious life on Mars. It has been said that when Charlie Chaplin, speaking not as a clown but as a philosopher, heard that there is no conscious life there he said, "I'm lonely." And to the many thinkers for whom the only final value is the biological survival of the human race, the atom bomb brings a special pressure to give up almost anything in order for the threat of war to be even slightly minimized.

The chaos of violence—especially random or political violence and indiscriminate terrorism, in an individual nation or in the world.   Both in individual nations and in the overall world the widespread use of political terrorism has become one of the phenomena of the age. Random and indiscriminate terrorism is even more frightening. Similarly alarming are the indications that terrorist organizations from all over the world have in some way coordinated their efforts. We have already seen indications of how people give up liberties when they are faced with the threat of terrorism.

The radical redistribution of the wealth of the world.   Redistributing the world's wealth would be accompanied by at least two things. First, there would be a lowering of prosperity and affluence among those individuals and countries which have come to take an ever-increasing level of prosperity for granted. Recent history has shown us how quickly nations and individuals change their principles toward other nations and other individuals when this becomes a threat. Second would come a redistribution of power in the world. In a descending spiral of prosperity and world power, a manipulating authoritarian government might be easily welcomed, in the hope that such a government would somehow soften the unpleasant results caused by a lessening of prosperity and world power.

A growing shortage of food and other natural resources in the world.   This last point is apt to become increasingly important.

As the Christian consensus dies in countries where it has previously existed, we must expect that it will make a difference not only within the nations themselves but also in their compassion for others. What will be left will be not compassion but only utilitarianism. Not that the record has ever been perfect, but we can expect open pragmatism increasingly to take the place of the partial compassion which has existed. A growing food shortage is apt to constitute an increasing pressure to cause people to drift along with a growing authoritarianism which promises solutions. As insecurity grows, greed—with the goals of personal peace and affluence at any price—grows.

If these pressures do continue to mount, which seems probable, do you think people, young or old, will at great cost to themselves, at the cost of their present personal peace and affluence, stand up for liberty and for the individual? Countries that have never had a Christian Reformation base will be the first to bow to authoritarianism. Already a growing number in Asia and Africa have gone this way. Men in the Western governments, who were themselves often modern men, did not understand that freedom without chaos is not a magic formula which can be implanted anywhere. Rather, being modern men, it was their view that, because the human race had evolved to a certain level by some such year as 1950, democracy could be planted anywhere from outside. They had carefully closed their eyes to the fact that freedom without chaos had come forth from a Christian base. They did not understand that freedom without chaos could not be separated from its roots.

And when these outward forms are imposed on a world view that would have never produced freedom without chaos in the first place, people will not stand when the pressures increase. Reports in the newspapers remind us that in many countries where democracy has been imposed from outside or from the top downward authoritarianism has increasingly become the rule of the day. One could make a long list of such countries.

Jiro Tokuyama, managing director of the Nomuro Research Institute, the largest interdisciplinary research organization in Japan, wrote in *Newsweek:* "Whereas Western religions are based on beliefs in an everlasting, absolute God, the Japanese . . . did not perceive the presence of such a permanent being. Instead they believed that what is right changes with the times and changing situations." Tokuyama well understood that the world view of a people will determine its private morals and its form of society.

Furthermore, when these nations which have no base for democratic procedures in their own countries gather in international organizations and form a majority in them, we are foolish to think that they will not function in the way they do in their own countries, even if this means functioning illegally against the constitutions or the charters of those organizations. This is true not only of the United Nations but of the whole range of such bodies. We can expect the tyranny of the majority in the midst of the winds of political change.

Let us hasten to say that freedom of the individual is not magic in the countries with a Reformation background either. As the memory of the Christian base grows ever dimmer, freedom will disintegrate in these countries as well. The system will not simply go on, divorced from its founding roots. And the drift will tend to be the same, no matter what political party is voted in. When the principles are gone, there remains only expediency at any price.

Most of the leaders of the countries which used to have a Christian base are now "modern" men. Happily there are notable exceptions, but they are exceptions. The attempt to be autonomous —to be independent from God and from what he has taught in the Bible and from the revelation of God in Christ—affects the political leaders as well as the university professors and the common people. Most of these leaders, too, think in terms of synthesis instead of fixed standards and absolutes and this shows in political actions both at home and in foreign affairs.

Synthesis has won on both sides of the Iron Curtain: People see no fixed, final right or wrong, but only a mixture in public dealing as well as in private morals, in foreign affairs as well as in internal matters. This is especially so of the intellectuals who have understandingly carried the abandonment of the Christian base toward its logical conclusion. But it is also true of those who have been influenced by this thought without analyzing it. Pragmatism, doing what seems to work without regard for fixed principles of right or wrong, is largely in control. In both international and home affairs, expediency—at any price to maintain personal peace and affluence at the moment—is the accepted procedure. Absolute principles have little or no meaning in the place to which the decline of western thought has come.

But we must have a disquieting memory—the memory of British Prime Minister Neville Chamberlain signing the Münich Pact with Hitler on September 30, 1938, at the cost of Czechoslovakia and at the cost of all that followed, in the illusion of attaining "peace in our time." Winston Churchill's (1874–1965) words in the House of Commons after the Münich Pact was signed now sound prophetic: "[The people] should know that we have sustained a defeat without a war . . . they should know that we have passed an awful milestone in our history . . . and that the terrible words have for the time being been pronounced against the Western democracies: 'Thou art weighed in the balance and found wanting.' And do not suppose this is the end. This is only the beginning of the reckoning. This is only the first sip, the first foretaste of a bitter cup which will be proffered to us year by year unless, by a supreme recovery of moral health and martial vigor, we arise again and take our stand for freedom as in the olden times."

It is unfortunate that no leader of vision was available after the crisis of war to warn the West that the moral battle was being lost in a new way. After the war 50,000 Cossacks were forcibly thrust back into Russia against their wishes, to be killed and imprisoned by Stalin. Solzhenitsyn asked in *Gulag Archipelago,* "What military or political reason can there have been for the delivery to death at Stalin's hands of these hundreds of thousands?" In *Communism: A Legacy of Terror* Solzhenitsyn said that one and a half million Soviet citizens who did not want to return to Communist Russia were turned over by force to Stalin to be exterminated. And in *The Last Secret* (1974) by Nicholas Bethell (1938–), a British senior staff officer who supervised the hand-over of the Cossacks is said to have told Bethell, "There is nothing we can do to help these poor wretches now, but we can at least learn something from their fate."

But the years that have passed show no sign that such a lesson has been learned. Without the base for right and wrong, but only a concept of synthesis, pragmatism, and utilitarianism, what will *not* be given up, both inside of nations or in foreign affairs, for the sake of *immediate* peace and affluence? The weak humanistic ideals are not and will not be enough in our own generation or for the future. Remember from the first chapter the little Roman bridge that would stand when people walked over it, but would break under the weight of a truck? If further economic recessions come, if fear of the loss of personal peace and prosperity increases, if wars and threats of wars intensify, if violence and terrorism spread, if food and other resources in the world become ever scarcer—and all of these are more than possible—then the trend is speeded up. As these things come upon people who have only the values of personal peace and affluence, they will crush them as a six-wheeled truck will crush the little bridge.

In such circumstances, it seems that there are only two alternatives in the natural flow of events: first, imposed order or, second, our society once again affirming that base which gave freedom without chaos in the first place—God's revelation in the Bible and his revelation through Christ. We have seen in the previous chapters many of the implications of an imposed order. But rather than throwing up our hands and giving in, we should take seriously the second alternative.

Christian values, however, cannot be accepted as a superior utilitarianism, just as a means to an end. The biblical message is truth and it demands a commitment to truth. It means that everything is not the result of the impersonal plus time plus chance, but that there is an infinite-personal God who is the Creator of the universe, the space-time continuum. We should not forget that this was what the founders of modern science built upon. It means the acceptance of Christ as Savior and Lord, and it means living under God's revelation. Here there are morals, values, and meaning, including meaning for people, which are not just a result of statistical averages. This is neither a utilitarianism, nor a leap away from reason; it is the truth that gives a unity to all of knowledge and all of life. This second alternative means that individuals come to the place where they have this base, and they influence the consensus. *Such Christians do not need to be a majority in order for this influence on society to occur.*

In about A.D. 60, a Jew who was a Christian and who also knew the Greek and Roman thinking of his day wrote a letter to those who lived in Rome. Previously, he had said the same things to Greek thinkers while speaking on Mars Hill in Athens. He had spoken with the Acropolis above him and the ancient marketplace below him, in the place where the thinkers of Athens met for discussion. A plaque marks that spot today and gives his talk in the common Greek spoken in his day. He was interrupted in his talk in Athens, but his Letter to the Romans gives us without interruption what he had to say to the thinking people of that period.

He said that the integration points of the Greek and Roman world view were not enough to answer the questions posed either by the existence of the universe and its form, or by the uniqueness of man. He said that they deserved judgment because they knew that they did not have an adequate answer to the questions raised by the universe or by the existence of man, and yet they refused, they suppressed, that which is the answer. To quote his letter: "The retribution of God is revealed from heaven against all ungodliness and unrighteousness of men, who suppress the truth in unrighteousness. Because that which is known of God is evident within them [that is, the uniqueness of man in contrast to non-man], for God made it evident to them. For the invisible things of him since the creation of the world are clearly seen, being perceived by the things that are made [that is, the existence of the universe and its form], even his eternal power and divinity; so that they are without excuse."

Here he is saying that the universe and its form and the mannishness of man speak the same truth that the Bible gives in greater detail. That this God exists and that he has not been silent but has spoken to people in the Bible and through Christ was the basis for the return to a more fully biblical Christianity in the days of the Reformers. It was a message of the possibility that people could return to God on the basis of the death of Christ alone. But with it came many other realities, including form and freedom in the culture and society built on that more biblical Christianity. The freedom brought forth was titanic, and yet, with the forms given in the Scripture, the freedoms did not lead to chaos. And it is this which can give us hope for the future. It is either this or an imposed order.

As I have said in the first chapter, people function on the basis of their world view more consistently than even they themselves may realize. The problem is not outward things. The problem is having, and then acting upon, the right world view—the world view which gives men and women the truth of what is.

A Special Note

This special note is primarily for Christians. First, let us remember what is the hallmark of the present generation of humanistic thinking. It is the acceptance of the dichotomy, the separation of optimism about meaning and values from the area of reason. Once this separation is accepted, what an individual puts in the area of non-reason is incidental. The mark of the present form of humanistic thinking is this *existential methodology*.

As Christians, we must not slip into our own form of existential methodology. We do this if we try to keep hold of the value system, the meaning system, and the "religious matters" given in the Bible, while playing down what the Bible affirms about the cosmos, history, and specific commands in morals. We are following our own form of existential methodology if we put what the Bible says about the cosmos, history, and absolute commands in morals in the realm of the culturally oriented. If we do this, the generation which follows will certainly be undercut as far as historic Christianity is concerned. But also, if we ourselves bear the central mark of our generation, we cannot at this moment in history be the voice we should be to our poor and fractured generation; we cannot be the restorative salt which Christians are supposed to be to their generation and their culture if in regard to the Scriptures we, too, are marked by the existential methodology. If we are so marked, we then have no real absolute by which to help, or by which to judge, the culture, state, and society.

Second, as Christians we are not only to *know* the right world view, the world view that tells us the truth of what *is,* but consciously to *act* upon that world view so as to influence society in all its parts and facets across the whole spectrum of life, as much as we can to the extent of our individual and collective ability.

Third, as we look back to the time of slavery and the time after the Industrial Revolution, we are thankful for Christians such as Elizabeth Fry, Lord Shaftesbury, William Wilberforce, and John Wesley who spoke out and acted publicly against slavery and against the noncompassionate use of accumulated wealth. I wonder if Christians of the future will be thankful that in our day we spoke out and acted against abuses in the areas of race and the noncompassionate use of wealth, *yet simultaneously and equally* balanced this in speaking out and acting also against the special sickness and threat of our age—the rise of authoritarian government? That is, will we resist authoritarian government in all its forms regardless of the label it carries and regardless of its origin? The danger in regard to the rise of authoritarian government is that Christians will be still as long as their own religious activities, evangelism, and life-styles are not disturbed.

We are not excused from speaking, just because the culture and society no longer rest as much as they once did on Christian thinking. Moreover, Christians do not need to be in the majority in order to influence society.

But we must be realistic. John the Baptist raised his voice, on the basis of the biblical absolutes, against the personification of power in the person of Herod, and it cost him his head. In the Roman Empire the Christians refused to worship Caesar along with Christ, and this was seen by those in power as disrupting the unity of the Empire; for many this was costly.

But let us be realistic in another way, too. If we as Christians do not speak out as authoritarian governments grow from within or come from outside, eventually we or our children will be the *enemy* of society and the state. No truly authoritarian government can tolerate those who have a real absolute by which to judge its arbitrary absolutes and who speak out and act upon that absolute. This was the issue with the early church in regard to the Roman Empire, and though the specific issue will in all probability take a different form than Caesar-worship, the basic issue of having an absolute by which to judge the state and society will be the same.

Here is a sentence to memorize: *To make no decision in regard to the growth of authoritarian government is already a decision for it.*

The title of this book and film series *How Should We Then Live?* comes from the watchman passage in Ezekiel 33:1–11, 19. The title is contained in verse 10.

Again the word of the Lord came unto me, saying,

Son of man, speak to the children of thy people, and say unto them, When I bring the sword upon a land, if the people of the land take a man of their coasts, and set him for their watchman:

If when he seeth the sword come upon the land, he blow the trumpet, and warn the people;

Then whosoever heareth the sound of the trumpet, and taketh not warning; if the sword come, and take him away, his blood shall be upon his own head.

He heard the sound of the trumpet, and took not warning; his blood shall be upon him. But he that taketh warning shall deliver his soul.

But if the watchman see the sword come, and blow not the trumpet, and the people be not warned; if the sword come, and take any person from among them, he is taken away in his iniquity; but his blood will I require at the watchman's hand.

So thou, O son of man, I have set thee a watchman unto the house of Israel; therefore thou shalt hear the word at my mouth, and warn them from me.

When I say unto the wicked, O wicked man, thou shalt surely die; if thou dost not speak to warn the wicked from his way, that wicked man shall die in his iniquity; but his blood will I require at thine hand.

Nevertheless, if thou warn the wicked of his way to turn from it; if he do not turn from his way, he shall die in his iniquity; but thou hast delivered thy soul.

Therefore, O thou son of man, speak unto the house of Israel;

Thus ye speak, saying, If our transgressions and our sins be upon us, and we pine away in them, *how should we then live?*

Say unto them, As I live, saith the Lord God, I have no pleasure in the death of the wicked; but that the wicked turn from his way and live: turn ye, turn ye from your evil ways; for why will ye die, O house of Israel?

. . . But if the wicked turn from his wickedness, and do that which is lawful and right, *he shall live thereby.*

This book is written in the hope that this generation may turn from that greatest of wickednesses, the placing of any created thing in the place of the Creator, and that this generation may get its feet out of the paths of death and may live.

Chronological Index

(Numbers in parentheses indicate page references in text)

259

Topical Index

Aachen: Palatine Chapel, 44, 46

Abortion: legal rulings as examples of sociological law, 218–223; contradictions in arguments for, 219–222; and euthanasia, 223, 235; in Roman Empire, 222

Absolutes. *See* Universals

Absolutism, 108

Abstraction in painting, 184

Absurd, The: as defined by Sartre, 145, 167–68; and Jaspers, 168–69; and *Dada,* 172, 187–88; and Duchamp, 188

Acapulco (Mexico): conference at, 164

Adorno, Theodor: and Neo-Marxism, 208

Adultery: parallel to promiscuity, 210; whether A.I.D. constitutes, 236

Aerodynamics: proceeds on basis of orderly universe, 140

Affluence: as a modern absolute value, 205, 227, 245; chap. 13 *passim;* rationale for higher education, 205; challenged by young people in 1960s, 209; in decline of Rome, 227. *See also* Peace

Africa: Schweitzer's work in, 175; influence of masks on Picasso, 184; authoritarianism in new nations of, 248

A.I.D. (Artificial Insemination by Donor): problem of, 236

Aigle (Switzerland): Reformation at, 88

A.I.H. (Artificial Insemination by Husband), 236

Alberti, Leone Battista, 62

Alcuin of York, 44

Algerian Manifesto: and Sartre, 167

Altamont: rock festival, 209

Altdorfer, Albrecht, 94

Ambrose of Milan, 30, 43, 90

America. *See* United States

American Psychological Association: president cited, 239

Amsterdam (Netherlands), 168; Kalverstraat in, 226

Anarchy: repression and, 124; hedonism as form of, 223; imposed order the inevitable response to, 245

Ancyra, Council of, 224

Andrea da Firenze, 52

Angst: and Heidegger, 168; in music of Schoenberg and Berg, 193

Antithesis: as principle of thought, 146; undermined by Hegel, 162–63

Antonioni, Michelangelo: film *Blow-Up* as philosophical statement, 201–02

Antwerp: Dürer at, 94

Aosta, 23

Apathy, 245; in Rome, 29; as sole response to young people after the 1960s, 209–10

Aquarius, Age of, 231

Aquinas, Thomas: assimilation of Aristotle, 43, 74; life, thought, and influence, 51, 57, 81, 82, 190; teachings attacked at Oxford, 131

Arab science, 130, 142

Arbitrary absolutes: in humanist and materialist thought and practice, 128, 218–22, 224, 238; the 51 percent vote, 224; and the elite, 227

Archimedes: Latin translation of collected works published, 132

Architecture: Gothic, 40, 47–48; Romanesque, 46; Renaissance, 62

Aristotle, 58; in Thomism, 43, 52, 74; philosophy proscribed, 52; in Christian theology, 43, 52, 74, 175; as symbol of particulars in Raphael's *School of Athens,* 52, 74; definition of a slave, 114; and science, 130–31; thought challenged by pioneers of modern science, 131

Arnolfo (di Cambio), 47

Arp, Hans: poem in *De Stijl,* 187–88

Select Bibliography

As the heading suggests, the following list of books and articles is not intended as a complete bibliographical guide to the complex and multidimensional argument set forth in the text. Rather, in the spirit of a responsible declaration of one's immediate sources, it is, first of all and mainly, an alphabetical listing of works actually mentioned in the text and second, mention of other works which are related to the same areas of thought. Even so, for a subject as vast as the development of Western civilization—one in which I have been keenly absorbed for many years—it is impossible to remember, let alone do full justice to, all the writings which have helped to form my opinions.

Parentheses after a title indicate the original, primary date of publication where this date is of significance. Wherever possible, the publisher and date is supplied for an edition which is currently in print.

Alberti, Leone Battista. *On Painting and on Sculpture* (1435). New York: Phaidon, 1972.

Anderson, F. M., ed. *Constitutions and Other Select Documents Illustrative of the History of France, 1789–1907*. 2nd rev. & enl. ed. 1908. New York: Russell & Russell, 1967.

Anderson, J. N. D. *Christianity: The Witness of History*. Downers Grove, Ill.: Inter-Varsity, 1970.

Apel, Willi, ed. *Harvard Dictionary of Music*. Cambridge, Mass.: Harvard University Press, 1969.

Archimedes. *Opera* (1543).

Arp, Hans. "Für Theo Van Doesburg." *De Stijl,* January 1932.

Augustine, St. *The City of God* (413–426). 2 vols. New York: Dutton, 1945.

Ayer, A. J. *What I Believe*. 1966.

Bacon, Francis. *The New Organon* (1620). New York: Bobbs, 1960.

Bagehot, Walter. *Physics and Politics*. Thoughts on the Application of the Principles of Natural Selection and Inheritance to Political Science (1872). Lexington, Mass.: Gregg Intl. Pub. Ltd., 1971.

Balsdon, J. P. V. D. *Life and Leisure in Ancient Rome*. New York: McGraw-Hill, 1969.

Barth, Karl. *The Epistle to the Romans* (1919). New York: Oxford University Press, 1933.

Beauvoir, Simone de. *L'Invitée*. New York: French & European, 1943.

281

Bell, Daniel. *The Coming of Post-Industrial Society*. A Venture in Social Forecasting. New York: Basic Books, 1973.

Benda, Julien. *The Treason of the Intellectuals* (1928). Translated by Richard Aldington. New York: Norton, 1969.

Bernstein, Leonard. *Norton Lectures* at Harvard University, 1973.

Bethell, Nicholas. *The Last Secret*. New York: Basic Books, 1974.

Bezzant, J. S. "Intellectual Objections." *Objections to Christian Belief*. Vidler, ed. 1963.

Blamires, Harry. *The Christian Mind*. New York: Seabury, 1963.

Boccaccio, Giovanni. *The Decameron* (c. 1350). Translated by Richard Aldington. New York: Doubleday, 1949.

Bonjour, E.; Offler, H. S.; and Potter, G. R. *A Short History of Switzerland*. New York: Oxford University Press, 1952.

Boorstin, Daniel. *Image; or, What Happened to the American Dream*. New York: Atheneum, 1962.

Borsook, Eve. *Florence*. 1973.

Boyd, Forrest. *Instant Analysis: Confessions of a White House Correspondent*. Richmond, Va.: John Knox, 1974.

Brinton, Crane, ed. *Portable Age of Reason Reader*. New York: Viking, 1956.

Bronowski, Jacob. *The Ascent of Man*. Boston: Little, Brown, 1973.

Brown, Colin. *Philosophy and the Christian Faith*. Downers Grove, Ill.: Inter-Varsity, 1969.

Büchner, Ludwig. *Force and Matter* (1855).

Bulteau, L'Abbé. *Monographie de la Cathédrale de Chartres* (1887–92). Vol. I.

Burckhardt, Jacob. *The Civilization of the Renaissance in Italy* (1860). New York: Phaidon, 1952.

Burgess, Anthony. *The Clockwork Orange*. New York: Norton, 1963.

Calvin, John. *The Institutes of the Christian Religion* (1536, 1559). Edited by John T. McNeill. 2 vols. Philadelphia: Westminster, 1960.

Camus, Albert. *The Stranger*. New York: Knopf, 1946.

———. *The Plague*. New York: Knopf, 1948.

Canons of the Council of Ancyra. *Sacrorum Conciliorum Nova*. Vol. 2. Edited by Mansi.

Cellini, Benvenuto. *Autobiography* (1558f.). Translated by J. Bull. Baltimore: Penguin, 1956.

Chomsky, Noam. Review of *Verbal Behavior* by B. F. Skinner. *Language* 35 (Jan.–March, 1959):26–58.

Clark, Kenneth. *Civilisation: A Personal View*. New York: Harper & Row, 1969.

Condorcet, Marquis Antoine Nicolas de. *Sketch for a Historical Picture of the Progress of the Human Mind* (1793–4). Atlantic Highlands, N.J.: Humanities, 1955.

Constant, Pierre. *Les Hymnes et Chansons de la Révolution Française* (1901).

Cooke, Alistair. *Alistair Cooke's America*. New York: Knopf, 1973.

Copernicus, Nicholas. *De Revolutionibus Orbium Coelestium* (1543). New York: Johnson Reprint Corp., 1973.

Copleston, Frederick. *A History of Philosophy*. 8 vols. Paramus, N.J.: Paulist-Newman, 1946–1966.

Crick, Francis. *Of Molecules and Men*. Seattle: University of Washington Press, 1967.

———. *Origins of the Genetic Code*. 1968.

———. "Why I Study Biology." *Washington University Magazine*, Spring 1971, pp. 20–24.

Dante, Alighieri. *La Vita Nuova* (*The New Life*) (1293). Bloomington, Ind.: Indiana University Press, 1973.

———. *The Divine Comedy* (1300–1320). Translated by J. B. Fletcher. New York: Columbia University Press, 1951.

Darwin, Charles. *The Origin of Species by Means of Natural Selection or the Preservation of Favoured Races in the Struggle for Life* (1859). New York: Oxford University Press, 1963.

Darwin, Charles. *The Descent of Man* (1871). Philadelphia: R. West, 1902.

David, Hans T. and Mendel, Arthur, eds. *The Bach Reader*. A Life of Bach in Letters and Documents. New York: Norton, 1945.

Dickens, Charles. *American Notes* (1842). Baltimore: Penguin Books, 1972.

————. *A Tale of Two Cities* (1859). Gloucester, Mass.: Peter Smith, 1957.

Drew, Donald. *Images of Man*. Downers Grove, Ill.: Inter-Varsity, 1974.

Duncan, David B. *Picasso's Picassos*. New York: Harper & Row, 1961.

Durant, Will and Ariel. *The Age of Reason Begins*. New York: Simon & Schuster, 1961.

————. *Rousseau and Revolution*. New York: Simon & Schuster, 1967.

————. *Interpretations of Life*. New York: Simon & Schuster, 1970.

Dürer, Albrecht. *Diary* (1521). Translated by Udo Middelmann, 1975.

Eden, Murray. "Inadequacies of Neo-Darwinian Evolution As a Scientific Theory." *Mathematical Challenges to the Neo-Darwinian Interpretation of Evolution* (The Wistar Symposium Monograph No. 5, June 1967), pp. 5–12. "Discussion," of same, pp. 12–19.

————. "Heresy in the Halls of Biology—Mathematicians Question Darwin." *Scientific Research,* November 1967, pp. 59–66.

Eicher, D. L. *Geologic Time*. Englewood Cliffs, N.J.: Prentice-Hall, 1968.

Einstein, Albert. "Physics and Reality." *Journal of the Franklin Institute:* 221 (March 1936): 349–382.

Einstein, Alfred. *Mozart, His Character, His Work*. New York: Oxford University Press, 1945.

Eliot, T. S. *The Wasteland and Other Poems*. New York: Harcourt Brace Jovanovich, 1923.

Ellul, Jacques. *The Technological Society*. New York: Knopf, 1964.

Esslin, Martin. *The Theatre of the Absurd*. New York: Doubleday, 1961.

Fichtenau, Heinrich. *The Carolingian Empire*. Atlantic Highlands, N.J.: Humanities, 1957.

Flew, Anthony. "Must Morality Pay?" *The Listener.* 13 October 1966.

Galbraith, John Kenneth and Randhawa, M. S. *The New Industrial State*. Boston: Houghton Mifflin, 1967.

Garin, Eugenio. *Italian Humanism*. Philosophy and Civic Life in the Renaissance. Translated by P. Munz. New York: Harper & Row, 1966.

Gay, Peter, ed. *The Enlightenment*. A Comprehensive Anthology. New York: Simon & Schuster, 1973.

Gaylin, Willard. "Harvesting the Dead." *Harper's Magazine,* September 1974.

Geneva Psalter, 1562.

Gentile, Giovanni. *Leonardo da Vinci*. 1956.

Gibbon, Edward. *The Decline and Fall of the Roman Empire* (1776–1788). 6 vols. New York: Dutton, 1910.

————. *Autobiography*. Oxford University Press.

Gierke, Otto von. *Natural Law and the Theory of Society, 1500–1800*. New York: Cambridge University Press, 1934.

Gombrich, E. H. *The Story of Art*. New York: Oxford University Press, 1966.

Gospel According to the Mark of Silver (12th century).

Gough, Michael. *The Origins of Christian Art*. New York: Praeger, 1973.

Green, E. M. B. *Evangelism in the Early Church*. Grand Rapids: Eerdmans, 1970.

Grout, Donald J. *A History of Western Music*. New York: Norton, 1960.

Guinness, Os. *The Dust of Death*. Downers Grove, Ill.: Inter-Varsity, 1973.

Haeckel, Ernst. *The Riddle of the Universe at the Close of the Nineteenth Century* (1899). Saint Clair Shores, Mich.: Scholarly Press, 1900.

Harris, T. George. "All the World's a Box. An Introduction" (to B. F. Skinner). *Psychology Today* 5:3 (August 1971): 33–35.

Hartt, Frederick. *History of Italian Renaissance Art*. New York: Abrams, 1969.

Headlam, Cecil. *The Story of Chartres*. 1971.

Hegel, George W. F. *The Logic of Hegel* (1812–1816). New York: Oxford University Press, 1892.

Hegel, George W. F. *The Phenomenology of Mind* (1807). Atlantic Highlands, N.J.: Humanities, 1964.

———. *Encyclopaedia of the Philosophical Sciences* (1817).

———. *Lectures on the Philosophy of History* (1822–3). New York: Dover, 1956.

———. *Philosophy of Right* (1821). New York: Oxford University Press, 1942.

Heidegger, Martin. *Being and Time* (1927). New York: Harper & Row, 1962.

———. *What Is Metaphysics?* (1929).

———. *An Introduction to Metaphysics* (1953). New Haven, Conn.: Yale, 1959.

———. *What Is Philosophy?* (1956). Boston: Twayne, 1958.

———. *The Question of Being* (1956). Boston: Twayne, 1958.

———. *Essays in Metaphysics* (1957).

———. *Discourse on Thinking* (1959). New York: Harper & Row, 1966.

Heller, Erich. *The Disinherited Mind.* Chester Springs, Penna.: Dufour, 1953.

Hibbert, Christopher. *Garibaldi and His Enemies.* Boston: Little, Brown, 1966.

Hill, Christopher. *The Century of Revolution, 1603–1714.* New York: Nelson, 1961.

Holmes, Oliver Wendell. *The Common Law* (1881). Boston: Little, Brown, 1964.

Huizinga, Johann. *The Waning of the Middle Ages.* New York: St. Martins, 1924.

———. *Erasmus of Rotterdam* (1924). New York: Doubleday, 1953.

Hutchins, Farley K. *Dietrich Buxtehude* (1955).

Huxley, Aldous. *Brave New World.* New York: Harper & Row, 1932.

———. *The Doors of Perception.* New York: Harper & Row, 1954.

———. *Heaven and Hell.* New York: Harper & Row, 1956.

Huxley, Julian, ed. *The Humanist Frame.* New York: Harper & Row, 1962.

———. *The Human Crisis.* Seattle: University of Washington Press, 1963.

———. *Essays of a Humanist.* New York: Harper & Row, 1964.

Huxley, T. H. *Science and Hebrew Tradition.* Vol. 4 of *Collected Essays* (1902). Westport, Conn.: Greenwood, 1969.

Jaki, Stanley L. *Science and Creation: From Eternal Cycles to an Oscillating Universe.* New York: N. Watson, 1974.

Jaspers, Karl. *Man in the Modern Age.* New York: Doubleday, 1957.

———. *Nietzsche.* Tucson: University of Arizona Press, 1965.

———. *The Origin and Goal of History.* Translated by Michael Bullock. New Haven, Conn.: Yale University Press, 1953.

———. *Philosophical Faith and Revelation.* 1967.

———. *Philosophy.* Translated by E. B. Ashton. 3 vols. Chicago: University of Chicago Press, 1969–1970.

———. *Reason and Existenz.* Translated from German by William Earle. New York: Farrar Straus and Giroux, 1956.

Jones, Alun and Bodmer, Walter F. *Our Future Inheritance: Choice or Chance?* New York: Oxford University Press, 1974.

Kandinsky, Wassily. "About the Question of Form." *The Blue Rider* (1912).

Kant, Immanuel. *Critique of Pure Reason* (1781). New York: Dutton, 1934.

———. *Critique of Practical Reason* (1788). New York: Bobbs, 1956.

———. *Critique of Judgement* (1790). New York: Oxford University Press, 1952.

———. *Prolegomena to Any Future Metaphysics That Will Present Itself As a Science.* New York: Barnes & Noble, 1953.

———. *Religion Within the Limits of Reason Alone.* New York: Harper & Row, 1934.

Katzenellenbogen, Adolf. *The Sculptural Programs of Chartres Cathedral.* Baltimore: Johns Hopkins Press, 1959.

Kaufmann, Walter. *Hegel: Reinterpretation, Texts, and Commentary.* New York: Doubleday, 1965.

Khayyam, Omar. *Rubaiyat of Omar Khayyam.* Translated by Edward Fitzgerald. New York: Doubleday, 1930.

Kierkegaard, Søren. *Either/Or* (1843). Gloucester, Mass.: Peter Smith, 1959.

———. *Fear and Trembling* (1843), and *The Sickness Unto Death* (1849). Princeton, N.J.: Princeton University Press, 1974.

Kierkegaard, Søren. *Philosophical Fragments* (1846). Princeton, N.J.: Princeton University Press, 1974.

———. *Concluding Unscientific Postscript* (1846). Princeton, N.J.: Princeton University Press, 1941.

———. *Purity of Heart* (1847). New York: Harper & Row, 1956.

———. *Christian Discourses,* and *Lilies of the Field,* and *Birds of the Air,* and *Three Discourses at the Communion on Fridays.* New York: Oxford University Press, 1939.

———. *Training in Christianity* (1848). Princeton, N.J.: Princeton University Press, 1944.

Kinsey, Alfred. *Sexual Behavior of the Human Male.* Philadelphia: Saunders, 1948.

———. *Sexual Behavior of the Human Female.* Philadelphia: Saunders, 1953.

Klee, Paul. *Creative Confession* (1920).

Koestler, Arthur. *Darkness at Noon.* New York: Macmillan, 1941.

———. *The Ghost in the Machine.* New York: Macmillan, 1968.

———. "Is Man's Brain an Evolutionary Mistake?" *Horizon* X:2 (Spring 1968): 34–43.

Kristeller, P. O. "Thomism and the Italian Thought of the Renaissance." *Medieval Aspects of Renaissance Learning,* 1974, pp. 27–91.

Kunzle, David. *The History of the Comic Strip: Vol. 1: The Early Comic Strip: Picture Stories & Narrative Strips in the European Broadsheet, ca. 1450–1826.* Berkeley: University of California Press, 1973.

Latourette, Kenneth Scott. *A History of Christianity.* New York: Harper & Row, 1953.

Leach, Edmund. Review in *New York Review of Books,* 3 February 1966, pp. 13, 14.

Lefebvre, Georges. *The French Revolution.* 2 vols. New York: Columbia University Press, 1962–64.

Leff, Gordon. *Medieval Thought: St. Augustine to Ockham.* Santa Fe, N.M.: Gannon, 1958.

Lenin, V. I. and Marx, Karl. *Civil War in France: The Paris Commune* (1917). New York: International Publishing Co., 1968.

Leonardo da Vinci: A Definitive Study. New York: Reynal & Company, 1963.

Lewis, C. S. *That Hideous Strength.* New York: Collier, 1945.

———. *The Discarded Image.* New York: Cambridge University Press, 1964.

Locke, John. *Essay Concerning Human Understanding* (1690). Gloucester, Mass.: Peter Smith, 1973.

Luther, Martin. *Ninety-Five Theses* (1517). Philadelphia: Fortress, 1957.

———. *Luther's Primary Works* (1896).

———. German translation of the Bible (1534).

Lyell, Charles. *Principles of Geology* (1830–33). 3 vols. New York: Hafner Service, 1970.

MacKay, Donald. *The Clockwork Image.* Downers Grove, Ill.: Inter-Varsity, 1974.

Macquarrie, John. "History and the Christ of Faith." *The Listener,* 12 April 1962.

McCurdy, Edward, ed. *Notebooks of Leonardo Da Vinci* (1923). New York: Tudor, 1954.

McManners, John. *The French Revolution and the Church.* New York: Harper & Row, 1969.

McNeill, William H. *A World History.* New York: Oxford University Press, 1971.

Machen, J. Gresham. *Christianity and Culture* (1912). Republished 1969 by L'Abri Fellowship, Huémoz, Switzerland.

Machiavelli, Niccolo. *The Prince* (1513). New York: Penguin, 1961.

———. *The Discourses of Niccolo Machiavelli* (1517). 2 vols. Atlantic Highlands, N.J.: Humanities, 1950.

Machlis, Joseph. *Introduction to Contemporary Music.* New York: Norton, 1961.

Malraux, André. *The Voices of Silence.* New York: Doubleday, 1953.

Malthus, Thomas R. *Population: The First Essay* (1798). Ann Arbor, Mich.: University of Michigan Press, 1959.

Manetti, Antonio di Tuccio. *Vita di Filippo di ser Brunellesco* (15th century).

Manuel, Frank E. *The Prophets of Paris*. Boston: Harvard University Press, 1962.
Marcuse, Herbert. *One Dimensional Man*. Boston: Beacon Press, 1964.
———. *A Critique of Pure Tolerance*. 1969.
Markham, Felix. *Napoleon*. New York: Mentor Books. Imprint New American Library, 1963.
Marx, Karl and Engels, Friedrich. *The Manifesto of the Communist Party* (1848). San Francisco, Calif.: China Books, 1965.
Middelmann, Udo. *Pro-Existence*. Downers Grove, Illinois: Inter-Varsity, 1974.
Moeller, Bernd. *Imperial Cities and the Reformation*. Philadelphia: Fortress, 1972.
Molapoli, Bruno. *Florence*. New York: Holt, Rinehart & Winston, 1972.
Monod, Jacques. *Chance and Necessity*. New York: Knopf, 1971.
Muggeridge, Malcolm. *The Thirties*. 1940.
Muller, Herbert. *The Uses of the Past*. New York: New American Library, 1954.
Needham, Joseph. *The Grand Titration: Science & Society in East and West*. Buffalo, N.Y.: University of Toronto Press, 1970.
Newton, Isaac. *The Mathematical Principles of Natural Philosophy* (1687). 2 vols. 1729 ed. Atlantic Highlands, N.J.: Humanities, 1968.
New Cambridge Modern History. Vol. 2, *The Reformation* (*c. 1520–1559*). New York: Cambridge University Press.
Oppenheimer, J. Robert. "On Science and Culture." *Encounter,* October 1962.
Packer, J. I. *Knowing God*. Downers Grove, Ill.: Inter-Varsity, 1973.
Panikkar, Raymond. *The Unknown Christ of Hinduism*. Atlantic Highlands, N.J.: Humanities, 1968.
Panofsky, Erwin. *Studies in Iconology: Humanistic Themes in the Art of the Renaissance*. Gloucester, Mass.: Peter Smith, 1962.
———. *The Life and Art of Albrecht Dürer*. 2 vols. Princeton, N.J.: Princeton University Press, 1955.
Pevsner, Nikolaus. *An Outline of European Architecture*. New York: Penguin, 1960.
———. *Pioneers of Modern Design: From William Morris to Walter Gropius*. Santa Fe, N.M.: Gannon, 1974.
Plato. *Timaeus* (c. 360–50 B.C.). New York: Dutton.
———. *Plato: Timaeus and Critias*. New York: Penguin, 1972.
Plumb, J. H. *England in the Eighteenth Century*. Santa Fe, N.M.: Gannon, 1950.
Plutarch. *Lives of the Noble Greeks and Romans*. New York: Dell, 1968.
Pocock, J. G. A. "Civic Humanism and Its Role in Anglo-American Thought." *Politics, Language and Time,* 1973, pp. 80–103.
Polanyi, Michael. *Personal Knowledge: Towards a Post-Critical Philosophy*. Chicago: University of Chicago Press, 1958.
Pound, Roscoe. *Jurisprudence*. Vol. 1, St. Paul, Minn.: West Pub., 1959.
Read, Herbert. *The Contrary Experience*. New York: Horizon, 1974.
———. *The Philosophy of Modern Art*. Folcroft, Penna.: Folcroft, 1973.
Ricardo, David. *Principles of Political Economy and Taxation* (1817). New York: Dutton, 1933.
Richardson, Alan. "When Is a Word an Event?" *The Listener,* 3 June 1965.
Rivier, Louis. *Le Peintre Paul Robert* (1930).
Rookmaaker, H. R. *Art and the Public Today* (1968).
———. *Modern Art and the Death of a Culture*. Downers Grove, Ill.: Inter-Varsity, 1970.
———. *Synthetist Art Theories. The Ideas on Art of Gauguin and His Circle* (1959). Republished under the title *Gauguin and Nineteenth Century Art Theory*. Atlantic Highlands, N.J.: Humanities, 1972.
Rousseau, Jean-Jacques. *The Social Contract* (1762). New York: Oxford University Press, 1972.
———. *Politics and the Arts: Letter to M. d'Alembert on the Theatre* (1758). Ithaca, N.Y.: Cornell University Press, 1968.
———. *Emile* (1762). New York: Larousse, 1962.
———. *Confessions* (1766–70). New York: French & European, 1782.
Rutherford, Samuel. *Lex Rex* (1644). (In *The Presbyterian Armoury* 1843.)

Sade, Marquis de. *La Nouvelle Justine* (1791–1797). New York: French & European, 1960.

Sartre, Jean-Paul. *Nausea*. New York: French & European, 1938.

――――. *Existentialisme Est un Humanisme*. New York: French & European, 1947.

Scholes, Percy. *The Oxford Companion to Music* (1938). New York: Oxford University Press, 1970.

Schultz, William L. "The Father's Rights in the Abortion Decision." *Texas Tech Law Review*, VI (Spring, 1975):1075–1094.

Schweitzer, Albert. *The Quest for the Historical Jesus* (1906). New York: Macmillan, 1968.

――――. *J. S. Bach*. New York: Macmillan, 1962.

Senghor, Léopold Ségar. *Selected Poems*. New York: Atheneum, 1964.

――――. *On African Socialism*. New York: Praeger, 1964.

Seznec, Jean. *The Survival of the Pagan Gods*. Princeton, N.J.: Princeton University Press, 1972.

Shute, Nevil. *On the Beach*. New York: Morrow, 1957.

Sire, James W. *The Universe Next Door*. Downers Grove, Ill.: Inter-Varsity, 1976.

Skinner, B. F. *Walden Two* (1948). New York: Macmillan, 1960.

――――. *Science and Human Behavior*. New York: Macmillan, 1953.

――――. *Verbal Behavior*. Englewood Cliffs, N.J.: Prentice-Hall, 1957.

――――. *Beyond Freedom and Dignity*. New York: Knopf, 1971.

Slack, Charles W. *Timothy Leary, the Madness of the Sixties and Me*. New York: Wyden, 1974.

Solzhenitsyn, Alexander. *The Gulag Archipelago* I & II. New York: Harper & Row, 1974, 1975.

――――. *Communism: A Legacy of Terror*. 1975.

Southern, R. W. *The Making of the Middle Ages*. New Haven, Conn.: Yale, 1953.

Spencer, Herbert. *Principles of Biology* (1864–1867). 2 vols.

――――. *Principles of Sociology* (1880–1897). 3 vols. Westport, Conn.: Greenwood, 1974.

――――. *Principles of Ethics* (1892–1893). 2 vols.

Spengler, Oswald. *The Decline of the West* (1918–1922). 2 vols. New York: Knopf, 1945.

Sprigge, Sylvia. *Bernard Berenson: A Biography*. Boston: Houghton Mifflin, 1960.

Strayer, J. R.: Gatzke, H. W.; Harbison, E. H.; Dunbauh, E. *The Mainstream of Civilization*. New York: Harcourt Brace Jovanovich, 1969.

Tarsis, Valeriy. *Ward 7*. New York: Dutton, 1965.

Taylor, Gordon R. *The Biological Time-Bomb*. New York: New American Library, 1969.

Teilhard de Chardin, Pierre. *The Phenomenon of Man*. New York: Harper & Row, 1959.

Tillich, Paul. *The Courage To Be*. New Haven, Conn.: Yale, 1952.

――――. *Dynamics of Faith*. New York: Harper & Row, 1957.

――――. *Systematic Theology* (1951–1963). 3 vols. Chicago: University of Chicago Press.

Toynbee, Arnold. *A Study of History* (1934–1961). 12 vols. New York: McGraw-Hill, 1972.

Trevelyan, G. M. *English Social History* (1946). New York: Barnes & Noble, 1961.

Valla, Lorenzo. *Treatise of Lorenzo Valla on the Donation of Constantine* (1440). Reprint of 1922. New York: Russell & Russell, 1971.

Vasari, Giorgio. *The Lives of the Painters, Sculptors and Architects* (1550). 4 vols. New York: Dutton.

Vesalius, Andreas. *De Humani Corporis Fabrica* (1543).

Virgil. *The Aeneid* (29–19 B.C.). New York: St. Martins Press, 1964.

Voltaire, Francois Marie Arouet de. *Letters Concerning the English Nation* (1733). Buffalo, N.Y.: University of Toronto Press.

Walther, Johann. *Wittenberg Gesangbuch* (1524).

Watson, James D. "Moving Towards the Clonal Man." *The Atlantic* 227:5 (May 1971): 50–53.

Westminster Larger Catechism (1648). 1963.

Whitehead, Alfred North. *Science and the Modern World*. New York: Macmillan, 1926.

Windelband, Wilhelm. *A History of Philosophy* (1898). New York: Harper & Row, 1968.

Witherspoon, Joseph P. "Representative Government, the Federal Judicial and Administrative Bureaucracy, and the Right to Life." *Texas Tech Law Review*, VI (Symposium, 1975):363–384.

Wordsworth, William. "The Tables Turned." *The Complete Poetical Works of William Wordsworth* (1896). Boston: Houghton Mifflin, 1971.

Wycliffe, John. *The New Testament in English According to the Version by J. Wycliffe About A.D. 1380* (1879).